ISBN: 9781313517379

Published by:
HardPress Publishing
8345 NW 66TH ST #2561
MIAMI FL 33166-2626

Email: info@hardpress.net
Web: http://www.hardpress.net

Date Due

MAR 2 7 1961 G P			
NOV 2 2 1967			
	(bdf)	23 233	

Thomas Francis Meagher
(1846)

MEAGHER OF THE SWORD

Speeches of Thomas Francis Meagher in Ireland
1846=1848

His Narrative of Events in Ireland in July, 1848,
Personal Reminiscences of Waterford, Galway,
and his Schooldays

EDITED BY

ARTHUR GRIFFITH

WITH A PREFACE, APPENDICES, INDEX AND
ILLUSTRATIONS

Dublin

M. H. GILL & SON, LTD.

50 UPPER O'CONNELL STREET

1916

PRINTED AND BOUND

BY

M. H. GILL & SON, LTD.
DUBLIN

PREFACE

THE Penal Laws enacted against the Catholics of Ireland in violation of the Treaty of Limerick had some results unforeseen by the English dominion. One was the growth of a wealthy and spirited mercantile class among the members of the penalised religion. Debarred from the liberal professions and employments, and from all part in the conduct of public affairs, industrious and enterprising Catholic townsmen who would neither recant their faith nor forsake their country turned naturally to trade and commerce, and built up a mercantile interest whose spokesmen held a manlier language to the English Oppression of their country and their religion than it had been wont to hear from the spiritless Catholic aristocrats who begged for the right to worship according to their faith as for a favour. This manly class sprang from dire oppression. The destruction of Irish legislative independence and the opening of the English Parliament and patronage to the ambition of Irish Catholics undermined its strong but not established structure. After the passage of the Emancipation Act, a perverted and denationalised social pride in wealthy Catholic circles destined the son to quit the counting-house of his father and assert Catholic equality in the

Four Courts or the English senate. It was held a Catholic triumph when a Catholic mounted the Bench whence he was to sentence to transportation and to death men who essayed to recover the plundered liberties of their country, and True Equality was read in the gazetting of a Catholic Irishman to a commission in an army intended to despoil some hapless people of its lands or its treasures. So the Catholic office-holder and the Catholic office-seeker multiplied, but the Catholic merchant, sturdy and opulent, dwindled and passed away, till a legend grew that modern commerce and industry in Ireland had been the admirable creation and permanent possession of Englishmen and the sons of Englishmen.

Richard O'Gorman, of Dublin, and Thomas Meagher, of Waterford, were two of the last of the great class of Catholic merchants of which Sweetman, Keogh and Byrne were the old types. Thomas Meagher, whose ships carried freights between Waterford and America, married the daughter of another Waterford merchant—Quan— and Thomas Francis Meagher, their eldest son, was born in that city on the 3rd of August, 1823. Regarding Trinity College as anti-Irish and anti-Catholic, his father sent him to Clongowes and Stonyhurst for his education. In the first institution he was bred in ignorance of his country and all that related to it—in the second his preceptors, with some success, laboured to overcome what was termed his " horrible Irish brogue," and succeeded in sending him back to his own country with an Anglo-Irish accent which grated on the ears of his countrymen when he addressed them from the tribune, until the eloquence and native fire of the orator swept the gift of the English school from their jarred consciousness. Meagher returned to Ireland in 1843 with vague plans for a soldier's career in the Austrian army, to which the traditions of the Bradies, Taaffes, Nugents and other Irish families united Irish sympathy ; but he discovered his country, whose history had been debarred in his education, and whose very accent had been pronounced vulgar to him, swaying in a new passion of national vigour. The *Nation* had relit fires of patriotic pride in the people and O'Connell, stimulated by Davis, was sweeping the country with the slogan of " Repeal." Meagher found himself when he found his country. He became the centre around which the young Nationalists of Waterford rallied, and his youthful eloquence sent his fame abroad. This eloquence and enthusiasm carried away O'Connell on his first meeting with Meagher and caused him to exclaim, " Bravo, Young Ireland ! " Afterwards O'Connell was to seek to use " Young Ireland " as an epithet of opprobrium.

In 1844 Meagher came to Dublin with the intention of studying for the Bar. There he met the writers of the *Nation* and became, like each of them, one of the workers in the Repeal movement, in which the real labour of the committees was mainly discharged by Davis and his comrades. His eloquence at the public meetings in Conciliation

Hall quickly made him celebrated in the capital, and any announcement that Meagher would speak crowded the Hall; for his was an eloquence that before was not heard within its walls, where there was no lack of trained and accomplished speakers. Passion and poetry transfigured his words, and he evoked for the first time in many breasts a manly consciousness of national right and dignity. As handsome and chivalrous as he was eloquent, he became something of a popular idol and as eagerly sought after in the social circles of Dublin as his colleague, John Pigot. But he disliked Dublin society for, as he wrote afterwards, "its pretentious aping of English taste, ideas and fashions, for its utter want of all true nobility, all sound love of country, and all generous or elevated sentiment."

In June, 1846, the English Tory Ministry of Sir Robert Peel fell, and the Liberals under Lord John Russell returned to power. O'Connell simultaneously attempted to swing the Repeal movement into support of English Liberalism. The agitation which had been carried on for four years was to be damped down in return for a profuse distribution of patronage through Conciliation Hall, and a promise of remedial measures. Aware of the intrigue, Meagher and the other Young Irelanders vehemently denounced from the platform of Conciliation Hall any discrimination in the attitude of the Repeal movement towards English Whig or Tory, so long as Repeal was denied. The people approved, and the "Tail,"—as the corrupt gang of politicians who fawned on O'Connell and hoped for English Government places, was nick-named—decided that the Young Irelanders must be driven out of Conciliation Hall and represented to the country as Factionists, Revolutionaries, and Infidels. For this purpose resolutions were introduced to which no honest and intelligent man could subscribe and retain his self-respect—resolutions which declared that under no circum-stances was a nation justified in asserting its liberties by force of arms. It was in opposition to these resolutions Meagher delivered the speech that caused him to be afterwards known as Meagher of the Sword. He had carried the audience, at first semi-hostile, towards his side, and the plot against the Young Irelanders was in peril of defeat when O'Connell's son, observing the danger, intervened to declare that either he or Meagher must leave the hall, and thus compelled the secession of the men who had made the Repeal movement a reality.

As the Young Irelanders refused to accept defeat, their opposition to the resolution which assured England that no physical resistance would ever be offered to any measure she took against Ireland or the Irish was represented by the O'Connellite orators and journalists as an attempt to turn the Repeal Association into a revolutionary movement. The leaders of Young Ireland were denounced as infidels secretly conspiring to sub-vert religion, and as traitors in receipt of " French " and " Castle ". gold—devices familiar since the days of the Volunteers in English-controlled Irish politics, and not yet outworn. O'Connell made a special effort to detach Meagher from Young Ireland, for he realised the power of Meagher's eloquence and he was personally attached to the generous and gallant young Irishman. But although Meagher was careless and even weak of will in many matters, he was adamant on questions of national principle.

The Conciliation Hall machine failed to ruin the *Nation* newspaper and erase its writers. A sturdy minority of the people stood firmly by Young Ireland, and when the hurricane of calumny had exhausted itself, and men returned to reflection, a steady stream of recruits flowed towards the maligned Irishmen. The Irish Confederation was founded to receive them, and rally the country against the barter of the National movement to the English Liberal Government. In 1847 a vacancy occurred in the representation of Galway in the English Parliament, and the Confederation decided to send Mitchel, Meagher, and other of its leaders to oppose the Government nominee, Monahan. Conciliation Hall was obliged to affect a virtue which it had decried and follow the example of the Young Irelanders. Monahan was returned by a few votes, to afterwards pack Mitchel's jury and become a judge of what is termed the High Court of Justice in Ireland ; but the battle so well begun against the English nominee and the Irish placehunter reacted on the other constituencies, and the Alliance between the O'Connellites and

Thomas Francis Meagher
(From Professor Gluckmann's daguerreotype)

the English Liberals was in danger of destruction, when the death of Daniel O'Connell plunged the island in grief. The Whigs and corruptionists who controlled Conciliation Hall turned the event to their profit by inventing the story that the Young Irelanders were responsible for O'Connell's death, and fanatical mobs attacked some of the Young Ireland leaders. Physical menace failed, equally with moral intimidation, to deflect the chiefs of the Irish Confederation from their campaign against English Whiggery in Irish National politics, but another event led to divided counsels in the Young Ireland ranks.

This event was the Blight that fell upon the potato crop in Western Europe in the autumn of 1845, and continued to destroy the crop to a lesser or a greater extent for five years. Wurtemburg and other Continental states seriously affected, closed their gates to the export of corn until it was ascertained that the destruction of the potato would not involve famine or hunger to their people. In Ireland, apart from the potato crop, corn and cattle were raised annually on the soil sufficient to provide for a population of some sixteen millions of people. The population of Ireland at the time was under eight and one-half millions. The Young Irelanders demanded that, as in the case of Wurtemburg, the ports should be closed to the export of corn until the people of the country had been succoured. The demand was ignored. A series of Acts was passed, under the guise of relief measures, which accentuated the Famine it

b

was ostensibly designed to alleviate. The farmer who accepted relief was obliged to surrender his lands and himself become a pauper. Hundreds of petty Government offices were created where Famine functionaries waxed fat while the people perished. The corn and cattle of Ireland were annually drafted away to cheaply feed the people of England, and while the sustenance of twelve millions of people was borne out of the Irish harbours, ships laden with food from abroad to succour the producers sailed into these harbours to be discharged under the supervision of the English Government and in some cases to have their charitable cargoes stored to rot, lest the purpose of the benevolent foreigners might be fulfilled and the Irish population be maintained at its dangerous ratio to the population of England.

A Mansion House Committee, composed of all political sections, was formed with Lord Cloncurry as its chairman, which pointed out that the prohibition of the export of the oat crop alone would keep in the country sufficient food to provide for all. The Committee was ignored, but an English Liberal Government sent over the chef of its Reform Club—M. Soyer—to show the starving Irish how to live on a soup containing three ounces of solid food to one quart of water. M. Soyer boiled his soup on a public platform erected above the pit at Arbour Hill in Dublin wherein the bodies of '98 insurgents were rudely buried by their executioners, and he distributed his elixir of Irish life from chained ladles to those who supplicated, while an

English military band discoursed music and the Union Jack waved triumphant above the scene. The Viceregal Court graced the opening of the Government soup-ladles with its presence, and the English newspapers published leading articles for transmission abroad on the general topic of English benevolence and Irish ingratitude, with particular reference to the strenuous exertions England was making to preserve the Irish from the evils of a famine for which Irish improvidence and Celtic laziness were responsible.

At the end of 1847 a Coercion Act, under which it was made felony at the pleasure of the Lord Lieutenant for an Irishman in Ireland to be outside his own house between dusk and morning, was passed through the English Parliament. Mitchel abandoning faith in the Confederation policy of a union of classes—which he held in the circumstances unfeasible, since the landlord class had encouraged the passing of the new Coercion Act—proposed a policy of passive resistance, culminating in armed insurrection and potential revolution. His policy was rejected after debate by 317 votes to 188. The majority of the Young Ireland leaders spoke against the proposal and the speech of Meagher powerfully influenced the vote. Mitchel withdrew from the Confederation and established the *United Irishman*, in which he preached his policy week by week. Meagher, adhering to the Confederation, went to Waterford to contest the Parliamentary representation of the city as an opponent of all English parties and Governments in Ireland. The vacancy was caused by the appointment of O'Connell's son, Daniel, to a Government post, and the O'Connellites nominated as his successor a Kilkenny solicitor named Costello, notorious as a placebeggar. Mitchel, with grim humour, wrote that he was " for Costello," for " Mr. Meagher's return to the British Parliament would do that Parliament too much honour and bring it too much credit. We cannot bear to think of our strongest and most trusted men being, one after another, sent to flatter the pride of our enemies —shorn Samsons making sport for the Philistines or toiling ' at the mill as slaves '—tongues of fire sent down by Providence to kindle a soul within our people employed in pyrotechnic performances for the pleasure of the foreign tyrant. Think of Sheil ! In short we desire to bring that Parliament into contempt in Ireland and to put an end to the ' moral force ' system by the process known as *reductio ad absurdam*. And we have but little fear on the present occasion ; we have confidence in Alderman Delahunty and the organised corruption of Waterford."

Meagher was defeated, and so was Costello, Sir Henry Winston Barron being elected. The French Revolution next startled Ireland and in the wave of enthusiasm for the overthrow of the European despotism erected by the Treaty of Vienna, Mitchel's policy was acclaimed by most of those in the Confederation who had been its opponents. Meagher, O'Brien and Hollywood were despatched to Paris to congratulate the French nation in the name of

Ireland. Lamartine received them courteously but
coldly. He had been threatened by the British
Government with the possible breaking-off of
diplomatic relations if he offered encouragement
to Ireland and he was, of all the French statesmen
of the time, the most susceptible to English
pressure. Ledru-Rollin, Cavaignac and Louis
Napoleon were not unsympathetic. After the
return of the deputation to Dublin, Meagher was
prosecuted for sedition, but owing to an over-
sight, by which the prosecution permitted one
independent citizen to be sworn on the jury, the
Government failed to secure a conviction. An
attack was shortly afterwards essayed on Meagher,
Mitchel and O'Brien while they were attending a
banquet in Limerick, the life of Mitchel being particularly aimed at, but the objective was missed.
At the end of May, Mitchel was arraigned for the
new crime of Treason-Felony, invented to meet
his case, and condemned to penal transportation
for fourteen years. The Dublin Confederates desired to rise in arms, barricade the streets, and
attempt a rescue. They were persuaded by the
other Young Ireland leaders, including Meagher,
not to do so. The reasons advanced were strong
and they were sincerely put forward by men of
undoubted personal courage on whose shoulders
responsibility for the movement rested. In the
light of after years Meagher acknowledged the
advice he gave had not been justified.

Six weeks after the transportation of Mitchel,
Meagher was arrested at his father's house in

Waterford on a second charge of sedition, and brought to Dublin by a troop of cavalry and three companies of infantry. The people of Waterford rose in the streets and barricaded the bridge with the intention of rescuing him from his captors, but he peremptorily forbade them to do so and obliged them to remove the barricades. He was released from custody in Dublin on giving recognisances to appear at the assizes in Limerick, in which county the sedition was charged. On the following Sunday, with Doheny, he addressed a great hosting on Slievenamon, after which he returned to Waterford, whence he came to Dublin again, as he relates in the Personal Narrative published in the present volume, and embarked on his insurgent career. A proposal of Joseph Brenan's involving the beginning of the insurrection in Dublin was rejected and the final scenes took place in Tipperary.

The insurgent leaders made a fatal error when they retreated from Carrick-on-Suir and fell back on rural districts where there were neither organisation, armament, nor knowledge of their identity among the people. The last hope was quenched by O'Brien's refusal at the Council of War held in Ballingarry on the 28th of July to permit the necessary supplies for his followers to be commandeered and to offer farms rent-free, in the event of victory to all who joined the insurgent standard. Meagher, M'Manus, O'Donoghue, Dillon, O'Mahony, Doheny, Stephens, James Cantwell,[1] Devin Reilly,

---

[1] A Dublin Confederate leader and hotel proprietor. He died in 1875.

Cavanagh,[1] Wright,[2] Cunningham[3] and Leyne,[4] took part in the council, and on its conclusion Meagher, Doheny, Leyne, Stephens, and some others, left to attempt to rally and organise forces at Slievenamon and in the Comeraghs with which to threaten the garrison of Clonmel. The affair at Ballingarry, however, the next day disarranged their plans and after a fortnight's wanderings in Tipperary, Meagher, Leyne and O'Donoghue were arrested at Rathgannon, near Thurles, and brought to Dublin where they were confined in Kilmainham Jail with O'Brien and, subsequently, with M'Manus, until the opening, in October, of a special Commission at Clonmel, presided over by Chief Justices Blackburne and Doherty. Four well-packed juries convicted O'Brien, M'Manus, O'Donoghue, and Meagher of high treason, and they were sentenced to be hanged, drawn and quartered.[5]

[1] Afterwards an officer in the American army. He was slain in the American Civil War.

[2] Afterwards a successful New York lawyer.

[3] Afterwards well known as an American journalist.

[4] Maurice Leyne, whose mother was a daughter of Daniel O'Connell, was the only member of the O'Connell family who identified himself with Young Ireland. Owing to the failure of a Crown witness to identify him, the Government abandoned the prosecution against him. He afterwards joined Gavan Duffy on the staff of the revived *Nation*, and died prematurely in 1854.

[5] One Catholic, a Unionist, was permitted on Meagher's Jury. The jurors were: Jas. Willington of Castle Willington; Augustus Hartford of Willington Lodge; Samuel Ryan of Anna Villa; Thos. Lyndsley of Lindville; Benjamin Hawkshaw, Falleen; Benjamin Hawkshaw, Knockane; Edward Chadwick, Ballinard; Richard Kennedy, Knockballymaher; Richard Mason, Clonkenny; Richard Hamersley, Bansha House; Thomas Heirden, Summerhill; and Nicholas Greene, Knockanaspie.

However, General Sir Charles Napier had in his possession a letter dated June 25, 1832, sent from the Home Office in London at the direction of some of the men who constituted the government of England in 1848, nominating him to take command of the Birmingham section of an English insurrection planned by the English Liberals in that year. He was subpoenaed to produce it at the trials in Clonmel, but the Judges refused to permit it to be received. Thereupon it was published in the press and its publication made the carrying out of the death-sentence impossible to Lord John Russell and his Government colleagues who had planned ten years before to commit High Treason against the Constitution of their own country. The sentences were changed to transportation for life, and Meagher, in January, 1852, succeeded in escaping to America, where he was received with enthusiasm, and where the remainder of his eventful life was spent. In turn orator, journalist, lawyer, explorer, and soldier, he raised the celebrated Irish Brigade which under his gallant leadership in the American Civil War enhanced the military reputation of Ireland. "Meagher," wrote the Confederate Commander, General Lee, " though not equal to Cleburne in military genius, rivalled him in bravery and in the affection of his soldiers. The gallant stand which his bold brigade made on the heights of Fredericksburg is well known. Never were men so brave. They ennobled their race by their splendid gallantry on that desperate occasion."

In founding the brigade Meagher had hope of

returning at its head to Ireland, for the relations between the Northern States and England were strained and on the arrest of the Confederate envoys, Mason and Slidell, when sailing under the British flag, by a Federal cruiser, he wrote exultantly to his Brigade that war with England was imminent and that the Irish-American soldiers would be the first chosen to land in Ireland. But war did not ensue, and his bright hope of returning to Ireland at the head of an Army of Deliverance was quenched.

At the conclusion of the war Meagher was appointed Secretary and subsequently Acting-Governor of Montana. In that position he incurred the hostility of the professional politicians who lost some of their profits by his upright administration. Threats were muttered against him. One July evening he arrived at Fort Benton on official duty and went aboard a moored river steamer to rest for the night. A few hours later a cry was heard and Meagher disappeared down the river. His death was generally attributed to accident. A few years ago a man named Miller confessed to having murdered him for hire, but subsequently withdrew his confession. Whether accident or an assassin's hand ended the life of Thomas Francis Meagher is not likely to be ever ascertained.

Meagher has appealed to the popular imagination in Ireland more warmly than any other Irish patriot of the nineteenth century except Robert Emmet. Chivalrous, eloquent, generous, ardent and handsome he inspired personal affection and public trust.   In the Young Ireland movement he was not of the greatest men.   In strength of intellect and character he did not stand on the plane with men such as Davis and Mitchel.   But he was the most picturesque and gallant figure of Young Ireland and he stands above all his colleagues, and indeed above all Irishmen of his century as the National Orator.   In the speeches he delivered in Ireland from 1846 to 1848 he will live for ever. They are the authentic and eloquent voice of Irish Nationalism.   Save Emmet's Speech from the Dock no modern oratory has rung so true to the Irish Nation as the oratory of Meagher.   The Young Ireland movement had its philosophers, its poets, its statesmen, but without Meagher it would have been incomplete.   In him it gave to Ireland the National Tribune.   It gave to Ireland, too, in Thomas Francis Meagher a knightly exemplar for young Irishmen, one who never forgot or forsook the cause of his native land, or doubted its ultimate victory.   "God speed the Irish Nation to liberty and power," was the last prayer written by " Meagher of the Sword."

ARTHUR GRIFFITH.

CONTENTS

ILLUSTRATIONS

SPEECHES ON IRELAND
1846-1848

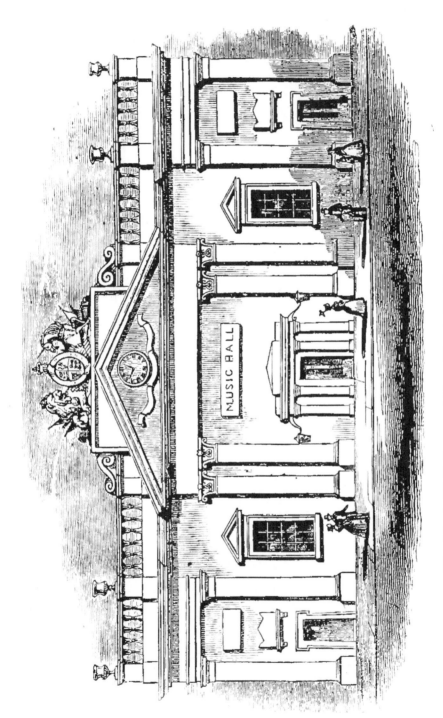

The Music Hall, Lower Abbey Street, Dublin, 1848

On the Union

SPEECH IN CONCILIATION HALL, FEBRUARY 16TH, 1846

Sir, we have pledged ourselves never to accept the Union—to accept the Union upon no terms—nor any modification of the Union. It ill becomes a country like ours—a country with an ancient fame—a country that gave light to Europe whilst Europe's oldest State of this day was yet an infant in civilisation and in arms —a country that has written down great names upon the brightest page of European literature—a country that has sent orators into the senate whose eloquence, to the latest day, will inspire free sentiments, and dictate bold acts—a country that has sent soldiers into the field whose courage and whose honour it will ever be our duty to imitate—a country whose sculptors rank high in Rome, and whose painters have won for Irish genius a proud pre-eminence even in the capital of the stranger—a country whose musicians may be said to stand this day in glorious rivalship with those of Italy, and whose poets have had their melodies re-echoed from the most polished courts of Europe to the loneliest dwellings in the deep forests beyond the Mississippi—it ill becomes a country so distinguished and respectable to serve as the subaltern of England, qualified as she is to take up an eminent position, and stand erect in the face of Europe. It is hers to command, for she possesses the materials of manly power and stately opulence. Education is abroad, and her people are being tutored in the arts and virtues of an enlightened manhood. They are being taught how to enjoy, and how to preserve, the beatitude of freedom. A spirit of brotherhood is alive, and breathing through the land. Old antipathies are losing ground—traditional distinctions of sect and party are being now effaced. Irrespective of descent or creed, we begin at last to appreciate the abilities and virtues of all our fellow-countrymen. We now look into history with the generous pride of the nationalist, not with the cramped prejudice of the partisan. We do homage to Irish valour, whether it conquers on the walls of Derry or capitulates with honour before the ramparts of Limerick ; and, sir, we award the laurel to Irish genius, whether it has lit its flame within the walls of old Trinity or drawn its inspiration from the sanctuary of Saint Omer's. Acting in this spirit, we shall repair the errors and reverse the mean condition of the past. If not, we perpetuate the evil that has for so many years consigned this country to the calamities of war and the infirmities of vassalage. " We must tolerate each other," said Henry Grattan, the inspired preacher of Irish nationality—he whose eloquence, as Moore has described it, was the very music of Freedom—" We must tolerate each other, or we must tolerate the common enemy." After years of social disorder, years of detestable recrimination, between factions, and provinces, and creeds, we are on the march to freedom. A nation, organised and disciplined, instructed and inspired, under the guidance of wise spirits, and in the dawning light of a glorious future, makes head against a powerful supremacy. On the march let us sustain a firm, a gallant, and a courteous bearing. Let us avoid all offence to those who pass us by ; and, by rude affronts, let us not drive still further from our ranks those who at present decline to join. If aspersed, we must not stop to retaliate. With proud hearts let us look forward to the event that will refute all calumnies—that will vindicate our motives and recompense our labours. An honourable forbearance towards those who censure us, a generous respect for those who differ from us, will do much to diminish the difficulties that impede our progress. Let us cherish, and, upon every occasion, manifest an anxiety for the preservation of the rights of all our fellow-countrymen—their rights as citizens—their municipal rights—the privileges which their rank in society has given them—the position which their wealth has purchased or their education has conferred—and we will in time, and before long, efface the impression that we seek for Repeal with a view to crush those rights, to erect a Church-ascendancy, to injure property, and create a slave-class. But, sir, whilst we thus act towards those who dissent from the principles we profess, let us not forget the duties we owe each other. The goodwill it becomes us to evince towards our opponents, the same should we cultivate amongst ourselves. Above all, let us cherish, and in its full integrity maintain, the right of free discussion. With his views identified with ours upon the one great question, let us not accuse of treason to the national cause the associate who may deem this measure advisable or that measure inexpedient. Upon subordinate questions—questions of detail—there must naturally arise in this assembly a difference of opinion. If views adverse to the majority be entertained, we should solicit their exposition, and meet them by honest argument. If the majority rule, let the minority be heard. Toleration of opinion will generate confidence amongst all classes, and lay the sure basis of national independence. But, sir, whilst we thus endeavour wisely to conciliate, let us not, to the strongest foe, nor in the most tempting emergency, weakly capitulate.

A decisive attitude—an unequivocal tone—language that cannot be construed by the English press into the renunciation or the postponement of our claim—these should be the characteristics of this assembly at the present crisis, if we desire to convince the opponents of our freedom that our sentiments are sincere and our vow irrevocable. Let earnest truth, stern fidelity to principle, love for all who bear the name of Irishmen, sustain, ennoble, and immortalise this cause. Thus shall we reverse the dark fortunes of the Irish race, and call forth here a new nation from the ruins of the old. Thus shall a parliament moulded from the soil, racy of the soil, pregnant with the sympathies and glowing with the genius of the soil, be here raised up. Thus shall an honourable kingdom be enabled to fulfil the great ends that a bounteous Providence hath assigned her—which ends have been signified to her in the resources of her soil and the abilities of her sons.

English Liberal Government in Ireland

SPEECH IN CONCILIATION HALL, JUNE 15TH, 1846, UPON THE ACCESSION OF THE WHIGS TO OFFICE.

We are told, sir, by the London papers, that the days of the Conservative ministry are numbered. The seals of office, it is said, will soon be held by a Whig Premier, and with the change of power, it is surmised, that a change of policy with regard to Ireland will take place. Whether that surmise be true or false, I know not ; but this I know, that whatever statesmen rule the empire, whatever policy prevails, the principles of this Association are immutable, and, amid the clash and shiftings of the imperial factions, will remain unshaken. Sir, I state this boldly ; for the suspicion is abroad that the national cause will be sacrificed to the Whigs, and that the people, who are now striding on to freedom, will be purchased back into factious vassalage. The Whigs, themselves, calculate upon your apostacy—the Conservatives predict it. They cannot believe that you are in earnest—at least it seems difficult to convince them of your truth. On the hustings you must dispel their incredulity, read them an honest lesson, and vindicate your characters. On their return to power, the Whigs, I trust, shall find, that in their absence, you have become a reformed people—that you have abjured the errors of faction, and have been instructed in the truths of patriotism. They shall find, I trust, that a new era has here commenced—that you have been roused to a sense of your inherent power, and, with the conviction that you possess an ability equal to the sustainment of a bold position, you have vowed never more to act the Sepoy for English faction.   To their reproach, sir, it must be said, that the people of this country have been too long the credulous menials of English Liberalism—dedicating to foreign partisanship those fine energies which should have been exclusively reserved for the duties of Irish citizenship.   Till now you have had no faith in the faculties of your country.   You implored from reform clubs in London that which a free senate in your old capital could alone confer.   Upon the hustings your tone was English, not Irish.   You stood by the promises of Russell—you foreswore the principles of Grattan.   You shouted for municipal reform—you forgot your manufactures.   You cried out for free trade—having no very important exchange of commodities to promote.   You petitioned for a supply of franchises, that Irish Radicalism might grow strong, when you should have demanded back those rights which would have made the Irish nation great.   The aristocrat of Bedford marshalled you against the plebeian of Tamworth, when, lifting up a distinct flag, you should have marched and struck against them both, Sir, it was full time that this should cease, and that the spirit of the country should manifest itself in an independent policy.   Let me not be told that the Whigs were our benefactors, and deserve our gratitude. They were, indeed, the benefactors of " moderate " Catholics and " liberal " Protestants, but the Catholic democracy and the Protestant aristocracy were alike neglected and insulted by them.   What memorial, may I ask, have they left behind them that claims our respect, and would win us to their ranks ?   It is true their appointments were, for the most part, judicious. There were honourable men elevated to the bench during their administration—honorable men, I grant you—but men " whose overtopping eminence," as our illustrious friend, Thomas Davis, has written, " was such as made their acceptance of a judgeship no promotion." And I believe, sir, there are few, if any, instances on record of partisan prejudices mingling with the dispensation of justice whilst they held office. Upon this question, however, I will not dwell, for it is a debatable question in this country, and, if discussed, might revive the antipathies of party. But I look beyond the Queen's Bench, beyond the court of petty sessions, beyond the police barrack, beyond the glebe house, and I demand, what was the condition of the people, what was the condition of the country, during the reign of the late Whig government? Your commerce, did that thrive? —your manufactures, were they encouraged?—your fisheries, were they protected?—your waste lands— they are 2,000,000 acres—were they reclaimed? How fared the Irish artisan—how fared the Irish peasant? The one pined, as he yet pines, in your beggared cities —the other starved, as he yet starves, upon your fruitful soil. Catholic barristers, who made reform speeches at Morpeth dinners, and quoted the Earl Grey and the *Edinburgh Review*, at anti-Tory demonstrations—these gentlemen came in for silk gowns, and other genteel perquisites; but you—you, the sons of toil, " the men of horny hand and melting heart "— you, the thousands, knew no change, Poorlaw commissioners were appointed—they were Englishmen and Scotchmen, for the most part. They came in for large salaries, and grew opulent upon their mission of charity. In this case, the indigence of Lazarus was the very making of Dives. The poorhouses were built, and were

soon stocked with vermined rags, and broken hearts—
with orphaned childhood, fevered manhood, and
desolate old age. Whilst these coarse specimens of
the Tudor Gothic were being thus filled, your Custom-
house was drained ; ahd now it stands upon your silent
quay, like one of those noble merchant houses that
crumble to the shores of the Adriatic, telling us that—

> " Venice lost and won,
> Her thirteen-hundred years of freedom done,
> Sinks, like a sea-weed, into whence she rose."

Sir, I have been told that the Marquis of Normanby
was a true nobleman. I have been told that he was
a man of enlightened views and generous impulses—
that he was just, benevolent, and chivalrous. Were we
English, and were Ireland the predominant power, I
might, perhaps, desire no other viceroy. We being
Irish—this land being Ireland—I demand an Irish
viceroy for the Irish court. The Geraldines have an
older title to the Castle than the House of Phipps.
Associated with the name of Normanby, I know there
are many brilliant reminiscences. Beauty and Fashion,
deputy-lieutenants who propose Whig candidates at
county elections, a swarm of expectant barristers,
perhaps a solicitor or two—men of " moderate " politics
and " enlightened " tendencies—would vote him back
again. In his time there were gala days at the Castle
—many a gay carnival—many a dazzling dance in St.
Patrick's Hall. But were there bright eyes, and happy
hearts, and busy hands in the tenements of the Liberty ?
Society—the perfumed society of your squires !—was
happy in those days, and loved the amiable Whig
government, and would, no doubt, in gratitude for the
viceregal balls at which it flounced and whirled, vote
for Whig candidates to-morrow. But, sir, the society

that is not exempted from the primeval curse—the society that wears out strong sinews to earn the privilege of bread—the society that knows no day of rest, no day of joy, but God's own holiday—that day on which He bids the toiler go forth and soothe his sorrows amid the glories of His creation—that day on which many a worn hand may wreathe a garland of flowers that has been weaving a crown of thorns the live-long week—the society that decks out fashion, that rears up the mansions of the rich, and by which alone, if there was danger on the coast to-morrow, this land could be furnished with a stalwart guard for its defence—this, the elder, the stronger, the nobler society, has no such memories—no such incentives to sub-serviency. Roused from the slumber into which the insidious eloquence and plausible philosophy of liberalism had lulled them, the people have started up ; and now, for the first time, see before them a country of which they had not dreamt, and a new destiny revealing itself to them, like the sun from behind their old hills, and that destiny expanding into glory, as it mounts the heaven, and settles high above the Island. No, sir, the people of Ireland can never more be duped into subserviency by assurances of sympathy, and promises of redress. We have become incredulous of party—we distrust, despise, denounce it. We recognise, at last, the truth of a maxim uttered many years ago by Swift, that " party is the madness of the many for the gain of the few ; " and we have learned to regard a Whig government in Ireland as little else than a state relief committee for political mendicants, most of whom are political impostors. Nor do we forget the Ebrington manifesto. Sir, that was a coarse insult to the manhood of the country, and the manhood of the country must resent it—resent it by being honest, for

honesty deals sweeping vengeance on the Whigs. You
recollect that attempt of theirs to purchase up, in the
market of the Castle, the fresh strength, the glowing
genius, the bold enthusiasm of the country. They did
not address themselves to the old men of Ireland—to
those whose faltering footsteps were waking the echoes
of the grave, and who, in a few years, at most, would
be laid to rest among their fathers. No, they addressed
the youth of Ireland, knowing well that the youth of
a country are the trustees of her prosperity—the
prætorians of her freedom. To them they held out the
golden chalice of the Treasury corruptionists, that so
the young, free soul of Ireland might drink, and having
drunk, sink down for ever, a diseased and pensioned
slave. " Young men," said they, " a long life is before
you—the luxuries of office—the privileges of place.
To taste the former, to acquire the latter, you must
qualify by recreancy, and befit yourselves by servitude.
Renounce, then, the manly duties, reject the pure
honours of honest citizenship—cease to be the unpaid
servants of your country—become the hirelings of
party. You are young Irishmen, and have read the
history of your country. Disclaim, then, the doctrines
of Grattan, the integrity of Flood ; accept the maxims,
emulate the perfidies of Castlereagh and Fitzgibbon.
You are scholars, and have read the history of Greece
and Rome. From the story of Sparta learn nothing
but the obedience of the Helots. From the pictured
page of Livy learn, if you like, the ambition of the
Cæsars, but shun the stern incorruptibility of the
Gracchii. Thus will you climb to power, gain access
to the viceregal table, and be invited to masquerades
at Windsor. Thus, if your ambition be parliamentary,
will you qualify for Melbourne Port, or some other
convenient Whig borough ; and when, at length,

removed from that country whose wretchedness would have been to you a constant pang, and whose politics would have been an incessant drain upon your resources, and when mingling in the lordly society of London, or sitting on the Treasury bench beside your patrician benefactors, oh! you will bless the Government that patronised servility, and thank your God that you have had a country to sell." But, sir, it is said that a great change has taken place in English politics, and that the Whigs have been converted to the cause of Ireland. A very recent conversion, it must be admitted, if it has occurred, for I hold in my hand the letter addressed by Viscount Melbourne to the secretary of the Association a few weeks since. It is well to read it now :—

" South Street,
February 24th, 1846.

" Sir,—I beg leave to acknowledge your letter of the 20th *inst.,* and to inform you, in reply, that it is my decided opinion that the measure now before the House of Lords, which has for its object the more effectual prevention and the more certain discovery of the frightful crimes which prevail in many parts of Ireland, has clearly been delayed too long, and cannot now be pressed with too much celerity.

" I remain, sir, your faithful and obedient servant,

" MELBOURNE.

" To the Secretary of the
Loyal National Repeal Association, Ireland."

Forget those sentiments if you can—forgive them if you like—breathing, as they do, a spirit of the most dogged despotism, and then believe that the rumoured conversion of the Whigs is sincere. Believe it, and forget that, in the House of Commons, Lord John

Russell and his colleagues voted for the first reading of
the Coercion Bill—voted against the liberty of Ireland,
to comply with " the usual custom of the house."
Believe it, and forget, that this time last year their
most eloquent confederate announced from his seat in
parliament that the price of your independence should
be a civil war. But, sir, I have to apologise. After
all, this is not the tone in which I should address a
people who have vowed, before man and God, to raise
up a nation here in these western waters, and to make
that nation as free as the freest that now bears a flag
upon the sea, and guards a senate upon the land. It
was not to recede and apostatise that you advanced so
far, and believe in a new fate. It was not for this that
you evoked the memories of a great event—that you
looked back to the church of Dungannon, and embraced
the principles, though you could not unsheathe the
swords of the patriot soldiers of '82. It was not for
this that you gathered in thousands upon the hill of
Tara, and hailed your leader upon the Rath of Mullaghmast, as the Romans did Rienzi in the Palace of the
Capitol. There you swore that Ireland should be called
once more a " free nation "—that she should have a
senate to protect—a commerce to enrich her. After
this, associate with the Whigs ; lend them your voices
—" your most sweet voices ; " let your demands
dwindle down to their powers of concession ; unite
with them in their oppression of the Orangemen, who
are your brothers ; give over your notions about self-
government—those notions are very absurd ; go back
to Precursorship—it's just the thing—it's very genteel ;
don't say a word about Irish artists and the encouragement of Irish genius ; back the poor law commissioners,
and sustain the new police ; be practical—that is, be
partisan ; be sensible—that is, cease to be honest ; be

rational—that is, conceive a very poor opinion of your country; fall as Athens fell, whose soul

> " No foreign foe could quell,
> Till from itself it fell—
> Till self-abasement paved the way
> To villain bonds and despot sway."

Thus will your country win the eloquent sympathies of Whig orators, and, " when the times improve," the kind consideration of Whig statesmen; but, mind you, America will indict her as a swindler, and France placard her as a coward. As I said before, I should not pursue this strain, knowing, as I do, your determination, knowing that you would repel the man who, in this Hall, would vote a compromise, and beat down the traitor, whoever he might be. I would not have done so but the report was abroad that our demands would moderate with the advent of the Whigs, and that the spirit of this Association would be affected by the transition of patronage from one English faction to another. Our future acts, I have no doubt, will teach our opponents the error of this report, and prove to them that we are in earnest, that we mean what we say, and that out of this contest we will not back, come what may. The next elections will prove to them that we have gone into this struggle with a firm purpose to fight it out to the last, and make a good end of it, with the help of God. The cry upon the hustings must be " Repeal," and nothing else. The members of this Association, the people of Ireland, are pledged to nothing else; and from those hustings, I trust, there will be heard many an honest shout of " Down with the Whigs—down with corruption." Let the people look out, select their representatives in time, and be assured they are true men. They have been deceived before. At former elections men have not hesitated to take pledges which they had no intention to redeem—men who, even in the English Commons have been the eloquent advocates of that measure which they now do not blush to designate a " splendid phantom." Beware of Whig candidates. Accept no man in whose integrity you do not place full reliance, and whose heart, you may have reason to suspect, is not thoroughly in the cause he professes to uphold. Demand from those gentlemen who solicit your votes the most explicit declaration—plain, straightforward, conclusive declarations. Vote for no man who is not an enrolled member of this Association, and who will not pledge himself to you to work here in this Hall, and vote hereafter in the English Commons, for the unconditional Repeal of the Legislative Union. I know, sir, that to pursue this line of conduct manfully, a sacrifice of personal interest—more than all, a sacrifice of private feeling—may be required from some of us. But the cause is worthy of the most severe sacrifice which men could undergo. I tell you candidly, if my father was in parliament, and had up to this period refused to join this Association, were he at the next election to present himself to his constituency and ask their votes again, I would be the first to vote against him. It is better that the hearts of a few should be pained, than that the great heart of the nation should be broken. Hereafter, for whatever we may endure— and as yet we have suffered nothing—we shall receive an ample recompense. For myself, and for those with whom I most associate, I can answer to the country. If we, who have been suspected for our honesty, and censured for our zeal—we, who will love the country, though the country may not love us—if we be not called away in the morning of our life, like our illustrious friend, Thomas Davis, our prophet and our guide—he whose integrity we shall ever strive to emulate though his labours we may not equal—he whom it is but just to number amongst those of whom a glorious poet has written—

" That as soon
As they had touched the earth with native flame,
Fled back like eagles to their living noon—"

If we be not called away like as he has been—if it be our fate to live and witness the triumph, toiling for which he died, then shall we receive our recompense —a free, young nation will look upon us in her glory, and bid us be glad of heart amongst her free sons— and when, at length, our time hath come, we shall sleep not in the Desert, but in the Promised Land.

Irish Youth and English Whiggery

SPEECH IN CONCILIATION HALL, JUNE 22nd, 1846.

Sir, I do not apologise to the meeting for taking part in the discussion that has arisen. The observations I consider it my duty to make will be few, for my friends who preceded me have left me little to say. The principles they maintain, the opinions they hold, have been defended by them with courage and ability. I have embraced those principles—I profess those opinions. The defence which my friends have made is my defence. That it was no weak defence your applause sufficiently attests. That it was called for, no one will deny who heard the speech that was delivered by Mr. Fitzpatrick[1] at the commencement of our proceedings this day. That gentleman reproached us with "the elaborate preparation of our speeches," and he did so in a speech that was evidently prepared. If it is a fault to speak with premeditation—if it is a fault so to train our thoughts and frame our language that we may appear before this assembly in a manner worthy of its character ; if this be censurable, then is Mr. Fitzpatrick not exempt from blame. In uttering these taunts he impairs his own title to forensic fame. He preaches against a practice in which, for the last few days, he must have been most sedulously engaged. He is a scholar, I

[1] Leader of the attack upon the Young Irelanders. Afterwards rewarded by the English Government with a Colonial Law-Officership.

16

A Meeting in the Music Hall

believe, and in this instance will not consider the quotation inappropriate :—

" Clodius accusat mœchus."

Sir, this gentleman, inspired, no doubt, with the zeal of a true patriot, rose to denounce past differences and he gave effect to his denunciation by provoking new dissensions. He was not present at the last battle—he had no opportunity of evincing his courage or of testing his skill—therefore, for his own especial benefit, he should get up a fresh one to-day. He repudiates disunion, but the result is discord. He preaches peace, and preaches it so forcibly as to provoke a war. The attack has been begun—we have been struck, but from our position we will not flinch. The imputations with which we have been insulted, the charges with which we have been aggrieved, we shall meet, and boldly meet. That we suspect the integrity of our leader, we deny. That we have assailed him, let the people decide. You have our assurance that, in denouncing the Whigs, we designed no attack upon the leader of this Association. Accept that assurance, or reject it as you may find reason to do. If you believe us to be men of truth, accept it. If you believe us to be false, reject the assurance, and denounce our acts. But we have been told that in denouncing the Whigs, we insulted the people. In warning the people against the Whigs, we are told that we implied a corrupt tendency in the people. Sir, we remembered what the Whigs had done in other times, and were prompted by the recollection to warn those whom they deceived before. If to warn be to insult, then do we plead guilty, and we await the penalty. Did I consider the defence of the Whigs that has been made here this day of such a nature as to induce you to look

upon them with more favorable eyes than you did a
few days since, I should not hesitate to restate my
opinions upon the policy of that party. But I know
your truth, and feel assured that the most eloquent
advocate they could purchase would fail to effect a
compromise of the national question—fail to induce
your acceptance of the most " liberal measure " they
can concede as an equivalent for the independence you
are ambitious to restore. Perhaps this sentiment
ought not to have escaped me. We are young men,
" juvenile orators," and should not venture to speak
on your behalf. Mr. O'Connell, in his letter, alludes
to our youth—Mr. Fitzpatrick reproves it. If youth
be a fault, it is a fault we cannot help. Each day
corrects it, however, and that is a consoling reflection.
If it be an intrusion on our parts to come to this Hall,
to aid your efforts and to propagate your principles, I
can only say it is an intrusion which your applause
has sanctioned. For myself, I think it right to say,
that when I came to Dublin this winter I did not
expect that I should have had the honour of sustaining
so conspicuous a part as I believe I have done in your
councils. It was not my intention to have assumed
this part. It was forced upon me, and, to the entreaty
of my friends, I was induced to yield. Believe me,
whatever a young man may gain by successful displays
in public, he incurs much by these displays that pains
and depresses him. If he wins the panegyric of some
he is sure to excite the envy of others. He is pained
by suspicions, secret rumours, direct attacks. His
motives are impugned, his acts condemned ; these are
the penalties attached to youth. More than this, if
he suffers from the malice of his foes, he must submit
to the sarcasm of his elder friends. In replying to the
charges that have been made against us, we feel that

we labour under a serious disadvantage. Youth is a season of promise more than of retrospect. We cannot rest upon the memory of past services—we cannot appeal to your gratitude. Upon our principles alone we take our stand—in your patriotism we place our trust. Mr. Fitzpatrick congratulates himself upon the " five millions " that back him, and regrets that we can only muster " five." An error in his political arithmetic, no doubt. The " five millions " are not against the five—perhaps it is not too much to say the " five millions " are with the " five." One thing I know, that those who are familiar with us are aware that we do not speak in public what we do not speak in private—that between our public and our private sentiments there is no discrepancy—that we do not sneer in private at the men whom we eulogise in public. We do not make Repeal a jest, for we have made it a vow. As we have acted, thus we shall continue to act. You may exclude us from this Hall. I say you may exclude us from this Hall, but you will not separate us from the country. Your applause did not call forth our love of country—your denunciation will not repress it. Exclusion from this Hall will not affect our sentiments, our principles, our resolves. On the contrary, there are many things in a popular agitation that tend rather to enervate than strengthen sentiments of a generous nature. There are many things in the depths of a political society that repel, offend, disgust. Removed from these, our hearts are pure, and our minds are free. Beyond these walls we have many incentives to love our country, and to serve her well. Her lofty mountains, her old ruins, full of a glorious history—her old music—the memories of her soldiers, her statesmen, and her poets—these you cannot deprive us of. So long as we possess these, so long shall Ireland inspire our love and claim our service. Nor can I believe that you will forget our names. Least of all will you forget the men who gave to you a new literature. You will not forget the men who have given to you those songs that have cheered the heart of the old man and have kindled into fire the thoughts of youth—those songs which the peasant may teach the echo on the mountain, and which may yet be heard upon a field of triumph. This, sir, is certain, we shall leave this Hall as we entered it—the unpaid servants of our country. We shall leave it with our honour unimpaired, though our influence may be crushed—we shall leave it asserting the right of free opinion, and our determination to defend it— and if, hereafter, you regret the step you may have taken against us, and once more require our aid, though you may have acted towards us as the citizens of Rome once did towards Coriolanus of Corioli, we will not imitate his recreant revenge—we will not go over to the Volsci—but return to your ranks, and fight beneath the flag from which you drove us.

The O'Connell-Whig Alliance

SPEECH IN CONCILIATION HALL, JULY 13TH, 1846.

I beg leave, my Lord Mayor, to say a few words upon the report that has been brought up from the committee by Mr. O'Connell, relative to the Dungarvan election. Mr. O'Connell has stated that the report was unanimously adopted. I wish to explain what occurred in the committee. I spoke against the resolution that was adopted—I urged a contest. It is true that when the question was put from the chair I did not express my dissent. That was a mistake I assure you. I did not assent to that report—I could not do so in conscience. No candidate appeared, that is true—no candidate was put forward, I believe. That fact, I conceive, was the only one that justified the decision that was made by the committee—it is the only one that can justify the Association in giving its sanction to that report. My lord, I sincerely regret that no effort was made to procure a candidate, and that a different course was not advised by the committee. I regret exceedingly that the battle for Repeal was not fought upon the hustings of Dungarvan, against all odds, and in the teeth of every risk. The influence of the Duke of Devonshire has been alluded to. If the fear of ducal influence, my lord, is to deter us from the assertion of our rights, farewell, then, say I, to public honour, to public virtue, to public liberty in Ireland. If in the Cavendishes there lies a stronger spell than in the banner of Repeal, our cause, in truth, is hopeless. Had we won the battle, the result is obvious. A new impulse would have been given to the country, and a spirit have been evoked that might have prompted the less resolute constituencies of the country to the firm assertion of the national principle. Had we sustained a defeat, even then, my lord, we would have gained not a few advantages. In the first place, we would have convinced the opponents of Repeal that we were thoroughly in earnest, and have rescued the Association from the aspersions of its enemies. This done, the ground on which we stand would have been strengthened by a more implicit belief in our sincerity. In the next place, a defeat might have proved a serviceable lesson to the Repealers of Dungarvan, teaching them the nature and extent of their resources, and how far those resources should be improved, so that a second defeat might be impossible. Above all, my lord, a contest in Dungarvan, however it might have eventuated, would have taught the Whigs that the heart of Ireland was bent upon Repeal, and that, even in the most adverse circumstances, it would not permit the promises of a party to obviate the principles of a people. A contest would have taught the Whigs that we are here organised not to serve them, but to emancipate ourselves. It would have taught them that we look beyond the boons, the sympathies, the appointments which an English political school may acquire the temporary power to distribute, and that we aspire to the wealth, the influence, the independence which an Irish parliament sitting in this the Irish capital, composed exclusively of Irish citizens, and wholly exempt from English control, would have the permanent ability to confer. My lord, I fear that the election of Richard Sheil, unopposed, as it has been, will cast a stain upon the records of this Association. That is my opinion, and by that opinion I will abide. If another exception be made—if another constituency be exempted from the Repeal test, then I frankly tell you, I must say that a gross injustice has been done in the cases of Cork and Cashel to Serjeant Murphy and to Serjeant Stock. The constituencies of those places made great sacrifices to assert the national principle. Serjeant Stack was a man of sound ability and stern integrity. Against him there was never uttered a complaint by his constituents. Serjeant Murphy was a scholar, a gentleman, and a patriot. He was an ornament to the Irish representative body ; and, my lord, I know not whether the electors of Cork conferred a greater honour upon Serjeant Murphy by selecting him as their representative, than Serjeant Murphy conferred upon the electors of Cork by representing them. In making these remarks, my lord, I trust I shall not be misconceived. I do not urge a factious resistance to the Whigs. I do not say that we should not sanction the measures they propose for the amelioration of the country. On the contrary, I say that we are bound to sanction those measures, and to aid in their promotion. But what I mean to convey is this, that we ought not, and on principle we cannot, manifest more favour towards the Whigs now that they are in office, than during the late administration we felt it our duty to manifest towards the Conservatives. During the late administration we gave our support to the Conservatives when they brought forward measures that were deemed beneficial to the interests and the institutions of this country. The Irish members voted with them on the Maynooth grant—voted with them on the corn question. On these occasions your conduct was wise, but it was not partisan. Act, then, towards the Whigs precisely as you have acted towards the Conservatives. Thus, my lord, will this Association sustain its independent character; and whilst it acquires a few benefits, it will not compromise a great principle. Then, my lord, it seems to me that, in giving our support to the Whigs whenever we may be called upon to give that support, we should be most careful lest we narrow the basis of this Association. What, may I ask, is the nature of that basis? It is broad and comprehensive—as broad and comprehensive as the island, the national liberties of which it is our ambition to erect upon it. It was made thus so that all sects and parties in the country might here confederate, linked together in one common sentiment for the achievement of one great comprehensive object. It was not limited to Whig dimensions —it was not limited to Conservative dimensions—it was not limited to Protestant dimensions—it was not limited to Catholic dimensions—it was made broad and comprehensive, as I said before, so that every Irish citizen might come here, no matter what his politics might be—no matter what his theology might be—no matter what his lineage might be—and win back for Ireland the right of self-government—a right, my lord, that is common to every party, and which, if justly exercised, will serve every interest in the state. If we do not act towards the Whigs precisely as we have acted towards the Conservatives—if we do not preserve a strict impartiality between both parties— if we do not maintain an independent position—if, on the contrary, we permit this Association to assume a Whig aspect, and be guided by a Whig spirit, then we narrow the basis on which we now stand; we shall exclude the Irish Conservatives—we may exclude the Irish Radicals. The Manchester League has been frequently referred to in this Hall. It is a guiding model, as it is an inspiring hope. That great confederacy was organised for one purpose, and one purpose only ; it was based upon one broad principle ; it was the auxiliary of no party ; it included men of all parties, I believe. I recollect a speech delivered by Mr. Cobden, at a meeting in Gloucester, previous to the meeting of parliament. In that speech the great champion of Free Trade observed that in the League thousands were associated, having but one common sentiment to combine them—that, for instance, his friend, Mr. Bright, and he differed upon a number of questions—perhaps upon no other question but the corn laws did their opinions coincide. Such was the basis of the Manchester League, now a great historic memory—such do I conceive the basis of this Association to be—such would I have it to remain. Besides, my lord, it appears to me that, if the Whig government is sincere in the professions it has made, and if, as it has been asserted, it can command a great legislative power, the good measures which have been promised by them will be carried without our special aid, I trust. The measures of the present minister will be passed, I hope, without any wavering on his part—without any compromise on ours. The concession of privileges that have been long withheld—the enactment of laws that have been long denied, will not, I hope, produce in Ireland the result the Whigs predict. It is true, my lord, that some men may desert from the national ranks, take place, abandon Repeal, and violate the national vow. It is the curse of society that from principles the most sacred there have ever been apostates. I consider that Repeal is not an open question—I conceive that any Repealer taking office under the present government would be an apostate from the cause. My lord, for this cause I have no fear, I trust in the growing spirit of the country—in the thoughtful and truthful spirit of a new mind. I will conclude now by referring to an observation made by the honourable member for Kilkenny[1]—namely, that any person not concurring in the repudiation of physical force should cease to be a member of the Association. I agree that no other means should be adopted in the Association but moral means and peaceful means ; but, my lord, whilst I am prepared to co-operate with you and the other members of the Association in carrying out the present policy— and I will do so until that policy either succeed, or that you determine that it is futile—I say if you determine that it is futile and that Repeal cannot be carried by such means, then I am prepared to adopt another policy—a policy no less honourable though it may be more perilous—a policy which I cannot disclaim as inefficient or immoral, for great names have sanctioned its adoption, and noble events have attested its efficiency.

[This speech was continually interrupted by O'Connell and his supporters].

[1] John O'Connell.

The Sword

THE SECESSION SPEECH ON THE "PEACE RESOLU-
TIONS" AND THE EXCLUSION OF THE "NATION"
NEWSPAPER FROM THE REPEAL ASSOCIATION,
JULY 26TH, 1846.

My Lord Mayor, I will commence as Mr. Mitchel
concluded, by an allusion to the Whigs. I fully concur
with my friend that the "most comprehensive measures" which the Whig minister may propose, will
fail to lift this country up to that position which she
has the right to occupy, and the power to maintain.
A Whig minister, I admit, may improve the province—
he will not restore the nation. Franchises, "equal
laws," tenant compensation bills, "liberal appointments," in a word, "full justice" (as they say) may
ameliorate—they will not exalt. They may meet the
necessities—they will not call forth the abilities of the
country. The errors of the past may be repaired—the
hopes of the future will not be fulfilled. With a vote
in one pocket, a lease in the other, and "full justice"
before him at the Petty Sessions, in the shape of a
"restored magistrate," the humblest peasant may be
told that he is free ; but, my lord, he will not have the
character of a freeman—his spirit to dare, his energy
to act. From the stateliest mansion, down to the poorest
cottage in the land, the inactivity, the meanness, the
debasement which provincialism engenders will be
perceptible. These are not the crude sentiments of

27

youth, though the mere commercial politician, who has deduced his ideas of self-government from the table of imports and exports, may satirise them as such. Age has uttered them, my lord, and the experience of eighty years has preached them to the people. A few weeks since, and there stood up in the Court of Queen's Bench an old and venerable man,[1] to teach the country the great lessons he had learned in his youth beneath the portico of the Irish Senate House, and which, during a long life, he had treasured in his heart as the costliest legacy which a true citizen could bequeath the land that gave him birth. What said this aged orator? " National independence does not necessarily lead to national virtue and happiness ; but reason and experience demonstrate that public spirit and general happiness are looked for in vain under the withering influence of provincial subjection. The very consciousness of being dependant on another power for advancement in the scale of national being weighs down the spirit of a people, manacles the efforts of genius, depresses the energies of virtue, blunts the sense of common glory and common good, and produces an insulated selfishness of character, the surest mark of debasement in the individual, and mortality in the State." My lord, it was once said by an eminent citizen of Rome, the elder Pliny, that " we owe our youth and manhood to our country, but we owe our declining age to ourselves." This may have been the maxim of the Roman—it is not the maxim of the Irish patriot. One might have thought that the anxieties, the labours, the vicissitudes of a long career had dimmed the fire which burned in the heart of the illustrious old man whose words I have cited ; but now, almost from the shadow of death, he comes forth

---

[1] Robert Holmes.

with the vigour of youth and the authority of age, to serve the country, in the defence of which he once bore arms, by an example, my lord, that must shame the coward, rouse the sluggard, and stimulate the bold. These sentiments have sunk deep into the public mind. They are recited as the national creed. Whilst those sentiments inspire the people, I have no fear for the national cause—I do not dread the venal influence of the Whigs (here much interruption occurred, which being suppressed Mr. Meagher proceeded). I am glad that gentlemen have thought proper to interrupt me, for it gives me an opportunity of stating, that it is my determination to say every word I think fit—the more especially as I conceive that the issue, which the honourable member for Kilkenny so painfully anticipates, is at hand, and that, perhaps, this is the last time I may have the honour of meeting you in this Hall, and expressing to you the opinions which I hold, and to which I shall ever firmly adhere. I was speaking of the true sentiments which should animate the people. Inspired by such sentiments, the people of this country will look beyond the mere redress of existing wrongs, and strive for the attainment of future power. A good government may, indeed, redress the grievances of an injured people ; but a strong people alone can build up a great nation. To be strong a people must be self-reliant, self-ruled, self-sustained. The dependency of one people upon another, even for the benefits of legislation, is the deepest source of national weakness. By an unnatural law it exempts a people from their first duties—their first responsibilities. When you exempt a people from these duties, from these responsibilities, you generate in them a distrust in their own powers—thus you enervate, if you do not utterly destroy, that bold spirit which a sense of these responsibilities is sure to inspire, and which the exercise of these duties never fails to invigorate. Where this spirit does not actuate, the country may be tranquil—it will not be prosperous. It may exist—it will not thrive. It may hold together—it will not advance. Peace it may enjoy, for peace and serfdom are compatible. But, my lord, it will neither accumulate wealth nor win a character. It will neither benefit mankind by the enterprise of its merchants, nor instruct mankind by the examples of its statesmen. I make these observations, for it is the custom of some moderate politicians to say, that when the Whigs have accomplished the " pacification " of the country, there will be little or no necessity for Repeal. My lord, there is something else, there is everything else, to be done when the work of " pacification " has been accomplished —and here I will observe, that the prosperity of a country is, perhaps, the sole guarantee for its tranquillity, and that the more universal the prosperity, the more permanent will be the repose. But the Whigs will enrich as well as pacify ! Grant it, my lord. Then do I conceive that the necessity for Repeal will augment. Great interests demand great safeguards, and the prosperity of a nation requires the protection of a national senate. Hereafter a national senate may require the protection of a national army. So much for the prosperity with which we are threatened ; and which, it is said by gentlemen on the opposite shore of the Irish Sea, will crush this Association, and bury the enthusiasts, who clamour for Irish nationality in a sepulchre of gold. And yet, I must say, that this prediction is feebly sustained by the ministerial programme that has lately appeared. On the evening of the 16th, the Whig premier, in answer to a question that was put to him by the member for Finsbury, Mr.

Duncombe, is reported to have made this consolatory announcement : " We consider that the social grievances of Ireland are those which are most prominent—and to which it is most likely to be in our power to afford, not a complete and immediate remedy, but some remedy, some kind of improvement, so that some kind of hope may be entertained that some ten or twelve years hence the country will, by the measures we undertake, be in a far better state with respect to the frightful destitution and misery which now prevails in that country. We have that practical object in view." After that most consolatory announcement, my lord, let those who have the patience of Job and the poverty of Lazarus, continue in good faith " to wait on Providence and the Whigs "—continue to entertain " some kind of hope " that if not " a complete and immediate remedy," at least " some remedy," " some improvement," will place this country in " a far better state " than it is at present, " some ten or twelve years hence." After that, let those who prefer the periodical boons of a Whig government to that which would be the abiding blessing of an Irish parliament—let those who deny to Ireland what they assert for Poland—let those who would inflict, as Henry Grattan said, an eternal disability upon this country, to which Providence has assigned the largest facilities for power—let those who would ratify the " base swap," as Mr. Sheil once stigmatized the Act of Union, and who would stamp perfection upon that deed of perfidy—let those

> " Plod on in sluggish misery,
> Rotting from sire to son, from age to age,
> Proud of their trampled nature."

But we, my lord, who are assembled in this Hall, and in whose hearts the Union has not bred the slave's disease—we have not been imperialised—we are here to undo that work, which, forty-six years ago, dishonoured the ancient peerage, and subjugated the people of our country. My lord, to assist the people of Ireland to undo that work I came to this Hall. I came here to repeal the Act of Union—I came here for nothing else. Upon every other question I feel myself at perfect liberty to differ from each and every one of you. Upon questions of finance ; questions of a religious character ; questions of an educational character ; questions of municipal policy ; questions that may arise from the proceedings of the legislature : upon all these questions I feel myself at perfect liberty to differ from each and every one of you. Yet more, my lord, I maintain that it is my right to express my opinion upon each of these questions, if necessary. The right of free opinion I have here upheld : in the exercise of that right I have differed, sometimes, from the leader of this Association, and would do so again. That right I will not abandon ; I will maintain it to the last. In doing so, let me not be told that I seek to undermine the influence of the leader of this Association, and am insensible to his services. My lord, I will uphold his just influence, and I am grateful for his services. This is the first time I have spoken in these terms of that illustrious Irishman, in this Hall. I did not do so before—I felt it was unnecessary. I hate unnecessary praise : I scorn to receive it—I scorn to bestow it. No, my lord, I am not ungrateful to the man who struck the fetters off my arms, whilst I was yet a child ; and by whose influence my father—the first Catholic who did so for two hundred years—sat, for the last two years, in the civic chair of an ancient city. But, my lord, the same God who gave to that great man the power to strike down an odious ascendancy in this country, and enabled him to institute, in this land, the glorious law of religious equality—the same God gave to me a mind that is my own—a mind that has not been mortgaged to the opinions of any man or any set of men ; a mind that I was to use, and not surrender. My lord, in the exercise of that right, which I have here endeavoured to uphold—a right which this Association should preserve inviolate, if it desires not to become a despotism—in the exercise of that right I have differed from Mr. O'Connell on previous occasions, and differ from him now. I do not agree with him in the opinion he entertains of my friend, Charles Gavan Duffy—that man whom I am proud indeed to call my friend, though he is a " convicted conspirator," and suffered for you in Richmond Prison. I do not think he is a " maligner " ; I do not think he has lost, or deserves to lose, the public favour. I have no more connection with the *Nation* than I have with the *Times*. I, therefore, feel no delicacy in appearing here this day in defence of its principles, with which I avow myself identified. My lord, it is to me a source of true delight and honest pride to speak this day in defence of that great journal. I do not fear to assume the position. Exalted as it be, it is easy to maintain it. The character of that journal is above reproach ; and the ability that sustains it has won a European fame. The genius of which it is the offspring, the truth of which it is the oracle, have been recognised, my lord, by friends and foes. I care not how it may be assailed ; I care not howsoever great may be the talent, howsoever high may be the position of those who now consider it their duty to impeach its writings : I do think that it has won too splendid a reputation to lose the influence it has acquired. The people, whose enthusiasm has been kindled by the impetuous fire of its verse, and whose sentiments have been ennobled by the earnest purity of its teaching, will not ratify the censure that has been pronounced upon it in this Hall. Truth will have its day of triumph, as well as its day of trial ; and I do believe that the fearless patriotism which, in those pages, has braved the prejudices of the day, to enunciate new truths, will triumph in the end. My lord, such do I believe to be the character, such do I anticipate will be the fate of the principles that are now impeached. This brings me to what may be called the " question of the day." Before I enter upon that question, however, I will allude to one observation which fell from the honourable member for Kilkenny, and which may be said to refer to those who have expressed an opinion that has been construed into a declaration of war. The honourable gentleman said, in reference, I presume, to those who dissented from the resolutions of Monday, that those who were loudest in their declaration of war, were usually the most backward in acting up to those declarations. My lord, I do not find fault with the honourable gentleman for giving expression to a very ordinary saying ; but this I will say, that I did not volunteer the opinion he condemns : to the declaration of that opinion I was forced. You left me no alternative—I should compromise my opinion, or avow it. To be honest I avowed it. I did not do so to brag, as they say. We have had too much of that " bragging " in Ireland—I would be the last to imitate the custom. Well, I dissented from those " peace resolutions," as they are called. Why so ? In the first place, my lord, I conceive there was not the least necessity for them. No member of this Association advised it. No member of this Association, I believe, would be so infatuate as to do so. In the existing circumstances of the country an incitement to arms would be senseless, and, therefore, wicked. To talk, now-a-days, of repealing the Act of Union by the force of arms, would be to rhapsodise. If the attempt were made, it would be a decided failure. There might be riot in the street —there would be no revolution in the country. Our esteemed under-secretary, Mr. Crean, will more effectively promote the cause of Repeal by registering votes in Green Street, than registering fire-arms in the Head-Police Office. Conciliation Hall on Burgh Quay is more impregnable than a rebel camp on Vinegar Hill ; and the hustings at Dundalk will be more successfully stormed than the magazine in the park. The registry club, the reading-room, the hustings, these are the only positions in the country we can occupy. Voters' certificates, books, reports, these are the only weapons we can employ. Therefore, my lord, I do advocate the peaceful policy of this Association. It is the only policy we can adopt. If that policy be pursued with truth, with courage, with fixed determination of purpose, I firmly believe it will succeed. But, my lord, I dissented from the resolutions before us, for other reasons. I stated the first—now I come to the second. I dissented from them, for I felt that, by assenting to them, I should have pledged myself to the unqualified repudiation of physical force in all countries, at all times, and in every circumstance. This I could not do ; for, my lord, I do not abhor the use of arms in the vindication of national rights. There are times when arms will alone suffice, and when political ameliorations call for a drop of blood, and many thousand drops of blood. Opinion, I admit, will operate against opinion. But, as the honourable member for Kilkenny observed, force must be used against force. The soldier is proof against an argument, but he is not proof against a

bullet. The man that will listen to reason, let him be
reasoned with ; but it is the weaponed arm of the
patriot that can alone avail against battalioned despotism. Then, my lord, I do not disclaim the use of arms
as immoral, nor do I believe it is the truth to say,
that the God of heaven withholds his sanction from the
use of arms. From that night in which, in the valley
of Bethulia, He nerved the arm of the Jewish girl to
smite the drunken tyrant in his tent, down to the hour
in which He blessed the insurgent chivalry of the
Belgian priests, His Almighty hand hath ever been
stretched forth from His throne of light, to consecrate
the flag of freedom—to bless the patriot sword. Be
it for the defence, or be it for the assertion of a nation's
liberty, I look upon the sword as a sacred weapon.
And if, my lord, it has sometimes reddened the shroud
of the oppressor—like the anointed rod of the high
priest, it has, as often, blossomed into flowers to deck
the freeman's brow. Abhor the sword ? Stigmatise
the sword ? No, my lord, for in the passes of the
Tyrol it cut to pieces the banner of the Bavarian, and
through those cragged passes cut a path to fame for
the peasant insurrectionist of Innsbruck. Abhor the
sword ? Stigmatise the sword ? No, my lord, for
at its blow, and in the quivering of its crimson light
a giant nation sprang up from the waters of the
Atlantic, and by its redeeming magic the fettered
colony became a daring, free Republic. Abhor the
sword ? Stigmatise the sword ? No, my lord, for it
swept the Dutch marauders out of the fine old towns
of Belgium—swept them back to their phlegmatic
swamps, and knocked their flag and sceptre, their
laws and bayonets, into the sluggish waters of the
Scheldt. My lord, I learned that it was the right of
a nation to govern itself—not in this Hall, but upon

the ramparts of Antwerp. This, the first article of a
nation's creed, I learned upon those ramparts, where
freedom was justly estimated, and where the possession
of the precious gift was purchased by the effusion of
generous blood. My lord, I honour the Belgians, I
admire the Belgians, I love the Belgians for their
enthusiasm, their courage, their success, and I, for
one, will not stigmatise, for I do not abhor, the means
by which they obtained a Citizen King, a Chamber of
Deputies. [Here John O'Connell interposed to prevent
Meagher being further heard, and the Young Irelanders
in a body quitted Conciliation Hall for ever].

Ireland and America

Speech at the Banquet to the Officers of the American Relief Ships, 1846.

Mr. Chairman and Gentlemen,—I almost hesitate to thank you for the high honour you have conferred upon me, in requesting me to speak to the health of the Ladies of America, for in doing so, you have imposed upon me a very serious task. This I sincerely feel. . . . . In this assembly, every political school has its teachers —every creed has its adherents—and I may safely say, that this banquet is the tribute of United Ireland to the representative of American benevolence. Being such, I am at once reminded of the dinner which took place after the battle of Saratoga, at which Gates and Burgoyne—the rival soldiers—sat together. Strange scene ! Ireland, the beaten and the bankrupt, entertains America, the victorious and the prosperous ! Stranger still ! The flag of the Victor decorates this hall— decorates our harbour—not, indeed, in triumph, but in sympathy—not to commemorate the defeat, but to predict the resurrection, of a fallen people ! One thing is certain—we are sincere upon this occasion. There is truth in this compliment. For the first time in her career, Ireland has reason to be grateful to a foreign power. Foreign power, sir ! Why should I designate that country a " foreign power," which has proved itself our sister country ? England, they sometimes say, is our sister country. We deny the relationship— we discard it. We claim America as our sister, and claiming her as such, we have assembled here this night. Should a stranger, viewing this brilliant scene, inquire of me, why it is that, amid the desolation of this day—whilst famine is in the land—whilst the hearse-plumes darken the summer scenery of the island—whilst death sows his harvest, and the earth teems not with the seeds of life, but with the seeds of corruption—should he inquire of me, why it is, that, amid this desolation, we hold high festival, hang out our banners, and thus carouse—I should reply, ' Sir, the citizens of Dublin have met to pay a compliment to a plain citizen of America, which they would not pay—' no, not for all the gold in Venice '—to the minister of England." Pursuing his inquiries, should he ask, why is this ? I should reply, " Sir, there is a country lying beneath that crimson canopy on which we gaze in these bright evenings—a country exulting in a vigorous and victorious youth—a country with which we are incorporated by no Union Act—a country from which we are separated, not by a little channel, but by a mighty ocean—and this distant country, finding that our island, after an affiliation for centuries with the most opulent kingdom on earth, has been plunged into the deepest excesses of destitution and disease—and believing that those fine ships which, a few years since, were the avenging angels of freedom, and guarded its domain with a sword of fire, might be entrusted with a kindlier mission, and be the messengers of life as they had been the messengers of death—guided not by the principles of political economy, but impelled by the holiest passions of humanity—this young nation has come to our rescue, and thus we behold the eagle— which, by the banks of the Delaware, scared away the spoiler from its offspring—we behold this eagle speeding across the wave, to chase from the shores of Old Dunleary the vulture of the Famine." Sir, it is not that this is an assembly in which all religious sects and political schools associate—it is not that this is a festive occasion in which we forget our differences, and mingle our sympathies for a common country—it is not for these reasons that this assembly is so pleasing to me. I do not urge my opinions upon any one. I speak them freely, it is true, but I trust without offence. But I tell you, gentlemen, this assembly is pleasing to me, because it is instructive. Sir, in the presence of the American citizens, we are reminded by what means a nation may cease to be poor, and how it may become great. In the presence of the American citizens, we are taught, that a nation achieving its liberty acquires the power that enables it to be a benefactor to the distressed communities of the earth. If the right of taxation had not been legally disputed in the village of Lexington—if the Stamp Act had not been constitutionally repealed on the plains of Saratoga—America would not now possess the wealth out of which she relieves the indigence of Ireland. The toast, moreover, to which you have invited me to speak, dictates a noble lesson to this country. The ladies of America refused to wear English manufacture. The ladies of America refused to drink the tea that came taxed from England. If you honour these illustrious ladies, imitate their virtue, and be their rivals in heroic citizenship. If their example be imitated here, I think the day will come when the Irish flag will be hailed in the port of Boston. But if, in the vicissitudes to which all nations are exposed, danger should fall upon the great Republic, and if the choice be made to us to desert or befriend the land of Washington and Franklin, I, for one, will prefer to be grateful to the Samaritan, rather than be loyal to the Levite.

The O'Connellites

Sir, it is a righteous duty to instruct the slave, but it is a proud privilege to address the freeman. That privilege I now enjoy, I avail myself of it to vindicate my character, that I may hereafter be of service to my country. With that view my friends have come here to-night, and I trust not in vain. Here, in this splendid hall, on the first anniversary of the Richmond imprisonment, did we assemble, clad in the uniform of the Irish nation ; and here, before the civic representatives of our chief cities, and the patriot members of the legislature, did we vow that we would never desist from seeking a Repeal of the Legislative Union by all peaceable, moral and constitutional means, until a parliament was restored to Ireland. That is the vow of the Rotunda. Public men have charged us with the violation of that vow. We have met here to answer the charge. Weak, indeed, would be our efforts to serve this land, if suspicion rested on those efforts, and if the people whom we ambition to emancipate, we tutored to distrust us. Slanders unanswered become destructive. The silence of the slandered gives them force and currency, and in time they are accepted as truths because they have not been denounced as falsehoods. Submit to the slander and you fall—meet it boldly, beat it back with a strong hand and you save your character and preserve your influence. Anxious for the confidence of the country, that we may be able to act efficiently with the country—for where there is no trust there will be no co-operation—we state our opinions distinctly that the country, thinking for itself, may judge us rightly. For my part I consider myself exceedingly fortunate in being thus permitted to resume my interrupted speech. I hope we are not going to have a similar interruption here to that in Conciliation Hall. Some say I have much to answer for. The guilt of the physical force debate has been exclusively attached to me. Mr. Lawless, for instance, at a meeting of his constituents, shortly after his election, censured me for having introduced it. What are the facts ? On the 13th of July the " peace resolutions " were moved by Mr. O'Connell. The same day the report on the Dungarvan Election was brought up. I spoke to that report—I did not speak to the resolutions. I merely stated that as they embodied an abstract principle of which I could not approve, I was compelled to dissent from them. They were then put from the chair and carried. The following Monday there was not the slightest controversy upon the question of the " forces." The meeting passed over quietly. I made a few observations, I recollect, to the effect that although there were some letters read that day which were most offensive to me personally, and to those with whom I had been identified, I would prove my anxiety for the cause by not replying to them as they deserved, and join my friend Mr. Mitchel in his earnest prayer that all dissensions in that Hall should from thenceforth cease. Mr. O'Neill cordially concurred in those sentiments and stated he was convinced that no member of the Association intended to advocate the insane principle of physical force. On the 23rd July, Mr. John O'Connell arrives from London for the express purpose as stated on the following Monday, the 27th, of bringing the matter to an issue. Mark this. The question that was decided by the Association on the 13th is re-opened by Mr. John O'Connell on the 27th, for the express purpose of drawing a " marked distinction between Young and Old Ireland." Sir, that line has been too deeply drawn and this meeting attests the fatal success of those who felt it to be their duty to divide. Mr. John O'Connell entered fully into the question of the " forces " and provoked discussion, if he did not invite it. To justify his abhorrence of the sword as an agent of political amelioration he cited the social disorders of America, of France, of Belgium, the liberties of which countries had been won by the sword. I fully concurred in his condemnation of the sword, as an instrument unfitted to achieve the independence of Ireland. I stated this distinctly. But, recollecting that it had been destructive of despotism in other lands, I refused to join him in the sweeping condemnation he had made, and was proceeding to justify my dissent—passionately, I will admit, for who can recount the triumphs of liberty and not speak in the language of passion ?—when Mr. John O'Connell declared that my sentiments imperilled the Association and that either he or I should leave that Hall. Mr. Smith O'Brien protested against this interruption as an attempt to check the legitimate expression of an opinion to which he stated, I was not merely invited, but compelled. Mr. John O'Connell persisted, usurped the authority of the Chairman, declared that my language was seditious and insisted on my not being heard. We had no alternative but to leave the Hall. We left it—left it in the possession of those who had invoked the spirit of freedom but to assail it, who had provoked a discusssion but to violate the first principle of discussion, who had driven us to the avowal of our opinions but to misrepresent and abuse those opinions. We left the Hall, sir, convinced that independent men would not any longer be permitted to remain there, and trusting to the intelligence of the country for the vindication of our conduct. We thought, too, that the Association would in time re verse the policy which, still continuing, has now arrayed against it the intellect and the integrity of the country. With this hope we refrained from the condemnation of that policy. The *Nation*, speaking for the seceders, adopted the language rather of conciliation than rebuke. Week after week we anxiously waited in silence for the adjustment of those differences which had shattered the national assembly and thrown it in fragments at the feet of the Whig Minister. This wise adjustment we were led to expect from the speech delivered by Mr. John O'Connell after we had been compelled to leave the Hall: " It is no source of joy to me that we have witnessed this departure. There cannot be a feeling of triumph—there cannot be a single pleasurable feeling in my heart at witnessing the loss to the Association of such a man as Smith O'Brien, at witnessing the departure of those excellent men from amongst us. This is not a time to speak, it is a time to weep. Let us then retire from this Hall to mourn over the loss we have sustained. Let us not think of meeting till Monday next when I hope Mr. O'Connell will be here to repair the breach that has inevitably occurred." Mr. O'Connell arrives in town during the week and on Monday, October 5th, instead of endeavouring to " repair the breach," from his place in Conciliation Hall he arraigns us as traitors to Repeal. We are denounced as revolutionists and charged with having opposed the peace policy of the Association. How is this charge sustained ? It is sustained by the language of Mr. O'Gorman, who stated, on the 13th of July in the presence of Mr. O'Connell, that " in order that there should be no misconception on the subject so far as he (Mr. O'Gorman) was concerned he would at once say that he was not at all an advocate for the use of physical force. As a member of the Association he was bound by its laws and regulations. One of these was, that its object was not to be attained by the use of physical force but by moral means alone." Is the charge sustained by the language of Mr. Mitchel who stated on the same day in the presence of Mr. O'Connell that " this is a legally organised and constitutional society seeking to attain its objects, as all the world knows, by peaceable means, and none other. Constitutional agitation is the very basis of it, and nobody who contemplates any other mode of bringing about the independence of the country has any right to come here or to consider himself a fit member of our Association. I believe, sir, the national legislative independence of Ireland can be won by these peaceful means if honestly, boldly and steadily carried out, and with these convictions I should certainly feel it my duty, if I knew any member who, either in this Hall or out of it, either by speaking or writing, should attempt to incite the people to arms or violence as a method of obtaining their liberty, while this Association lasts, to report that member to the committee and move his expulsion." Is the charge sustained by the language of Mr. Barry, who stated on the 7th June, " that it was perfectly plain to all that it was the determination of the Association to work out its object by means of moral force and that alone ? " Is the charge sustained by the language which I used on the 28th of July when I distinctly stated that " I do advocate the peaceful policy of the Association ; it is the only policy we can and should adopt. If that policy be pursued with truth, with courage, with stern determination of purpose, I do firmly believe that it will succeed." Sir, over and over again we pledge ourselves to the peace policy of the Association and are ready to do so again if necessary. But it is in vain. We are opposed to a Whig alliance. We demand that the Association should pursue the same policy under the Whig as it did under the Conservative administration. We insist upon Repeal and not upon " eleven measures," and are therefore denounced as revolutionists. Sir, it is my sincere conviction and I believe it is the growing conviction of the country, that the leaders of the Association had determined upon driving us from Conciliation Hall, and that, had we assented to the " peace resolutions," others would have been introduced to which we could not with commonsense subscribe. For instance, they might have brought in a resolution declaring it contrary to " faith and morals " to visit the Sultan and rank apostacy to smoke a chibouc. And if in opposing this resolution I had ventured to glance at the minarets of St. Sophia or the legends of the Koran, I would surely have been voted a renegade from the faith of my fathers, since for having alluded to the passes of the Tyrol and the ramparts of Antwerp I have been arraigned as a rebel. Depend upon it, if we had not been proclaimed as insurrectionists, we would have been anathematised as Mussulmen. If the object were not to drive us from the Hall I can see no other object in bringing forward those resolutions. It became necessary, they say, to restate the fundamental rules of the Association. If this were so, why not restate them as they were originally framed ? Had this been done there could have been no dissent. But an abstract principle is introduced to which we cannot conscientiously subscribe, and then confounding the new principle with the old rule, they charge us with a violation of the fundamental rule of the Association. Observe then, how the wise decrees of the Repeal Committee swell the ranks of the revolutionists. Mr. M'Gee writes to Mr. Ray for his card, states that he fully concurs in the principles and policy of moral force and will say nothing about physical force, as he dislikes meddling with abstract principles. Mr. Ray forthwith addresses Mr. M'Gee, " that it appears that he is not and cannot be a member of the Repeal Association." Mr. Haughton whose sympathies are with us, for I believe they are ever with the cause of truth, of justice, and of freedom, totally dissents from the opinions of Young Ireland upon the abstract of physical force, but disapproves of the mode adopted to repress those opinions. He has been since convicted of Young Irelandism, and " by order of the committee " enrolled in the category of revolution. Three Repeal wardens of Cappoquin write to Mr. Ray on the 12th of November stating that having abandoned all hope of a reconciliation, " in consequence of the language used by Mr. O'Connell towards Smith O'Brien," they beg to resign all connection with the Association. Mr. Ray replies to these gentlemen and intimates to them the loyal delight of the Association at parting with men who unquestionably contemplate a resort to arms. " Masters, I charge you," says Dogberry to the Watchmen—" I charge you in the prince's name, accuse these men." " This man said, sir, that John Don, the prince's brother, was a villain." " Prince John a villain ! why, this is flat perjury, to call a prince's brother a villain." " I'm for freedom of discussion," says Mr. Shea Lawlor ; " This is physical force ! " exclaims the committee. " I'm for the publication of the accounts," intimates Mr.

Martin ; " You oppose the peace policy," rejoins Mr.
Ray. " I protest against placehunting," writes Mr.
Brady from Cork ; "Sir, you contemplate a resort to
arms," rejoins the Secretary from Dublin. " We can't
get on without a good cry," hints Mr. Taper to Mr. Tad-
pole. For a dissolution without a cry, as Mr. D'Israeli
observes in the " Taper Philosophy," " was the world
without a sun." Sir, I trust I shall be excused for thus
trifling with the " peace resolutions " and the subsequent
decrees of the Association. But it is as difficult, after
all, to treat these topics seriously as to describe the
characters of a farce with sublimity, and yet there is
true reason to be serious. Through a fatal policy the
most powerful confederacy that ever yet was organised
to win a nation's freedom is broken up, its treasury
exhausted, its influence blasted. Look to the national
movement. Where is the disciplined nerve, the earnest
integrity, the rapid enthusiasm of '43. Look back to
that year—your sight is dazzled with the flame—survey
the present, and you shiver before the cloud. What
did we then behold ? a zeal that was almost precipitate
—a pride of country that almost swelled into presumption. What do we now deplore ? a " peace
policy " that degenerates into indolence, a tameness
that verges on debasement. Whence this relapse,
whence this fall ? It dates from the Hustings of
Dungarvan. Where shall it cease ? Here. So say
we all of us here in the Rotunda—a spot ennobled
by the convention of 1783, sanctified by the vow of
1845. Sir, we impeach the present policy of the
Association, and we impeach it not because we have
become seceders, but because we continue to be Repealers. In doing so we are accused of ingratitude
to an old and illustrious benefactor. The accusation
is a slander. The Catholic Emancipator has secured

Clonmel Gaol,
Oct. 24th 1848

My dear Sir,
I feel sincere pleasure in forwarding you the accompanying paragraphs, and in expressing my own, I have to assure you of the grateful sentiments of my two companions, for the deep sympathy you have manifested for our fate.

Believe me,
My dear Sir,
Your faithful friend
Thomas Francis Meagher

A Letter from Meagher

our gratitude. The Leader of the Repeal Association has forfeited our allegiance. This is just, I say. Gratitude to a benefactor should never degenerate into subserviency, and it is servitude and the worst of servitudes to co-operate when convictions do not coincide. Catholic Emancipation was indeed too dearly purchased if the forfeiture of free opinion was the price. The confederates of the great emancipator we were proud to be—his vassals, never. We ambition to work for our country, but we shall not work for it in chains. The nobility of the cause suffers from the debasement of the advocate. And though he, who was once our leader, may arraign us for treachery to the country and use his influence to make that country our assailant, he shall still command our respect, while the country shall have our love—

> Men and brothers ! we loved this land
> > For its beauty, but more for its grief ;
> We offered the homage of heart and of hand
> > To it and its chosen chief.
> We offered our hearts with their fiery heat,
> > Our hands with their youthful glow ;
> But never to slavishly lie at his feet
> > Or be spurned from your ranks as a foe.

Sir, great emergencies demand severe sacrifices, and the laws of nations, not to say the injunctions of leaders, have been disobeyed when they stood in the way of liberty. Be it yours to imitate the example of one whom the historian has immortalised and the true patriot most reveres. Two thousand years since, Pelopidas and Epaminondas stood accused for disobedience of the public orders. Pelopidas with craven soul, bowed before his accusers, confessed his guilt and hardly obtained forgiveness. Epaminondas—how

4

brilliant, how inspiring is the contrast—exulting in
the act for which he was arraigned, confronted his
accusers and declared he was ready to meet his death
if on his monument would be inscribed—" He wasted
Laconia, the territory of the enemy—he united the
Arcadians—restored liberty to Greece—and did so
against his country's will." Which of these two men
shall be your model. I should not inquire. I do not
fear that a spirit of servile sycophancy will win you to
the imitation of the former, for I know that a spirit
of heroic honesty will prompt you to the emulation of
the latter. Demanding the independence of your
country you will act the part of independent men—
insisting upon her freedom you will preserve your own.
In this spirit, sir, we impeach the present policy of the
Association and we impeach it because it conflicts with
the policy of '43. We impeach that policy because
it assails the liberty of the press and violates the first
principles of discussion. We impeach that policy
because it affiliates the Repeal Association to an English
faction, and forms an alliance that must vitiate the
energies of the former. The Association encourages
its members to become the stipendiaries of the minister,
and we oppose a license that tends to give strength
to the minister, and produces weakness in the people.
The servant of the minister will cease to be the confederate of the people. The hand that has once clutched
the gold of the Treasury will never again be clenched
against the usurpations of the minister. The glare of
the Castle ball-room blinds men to the sins of the
executive. The tongue that has lisped compliments
at the viceregal table will be slow to utter condemnation
from the tribune of Conciliation Hall. Why, I ask,
is not the minister denounced? The people starve,
and the career of the minister in this country is tracked

by peasants' graves. He patronises the pampered merchant of his own splendid country—he heeds not the famished beggar of the bankrupt land. The ships of the rich London citizen, like winged demons, bear away on each swelling tide the food of the island, as if Death had chartered them to drive his ghastly trade, and yet the minister is not denounced. Is this the minister with whom we are called upon to coalesce—is this the minister in whose pay it is honourable for the Irish Nationalist to serve? Forbid it, Heaven! Better, far better, be the poorest artisan that earns his bread by honest drudgery, than the wealthiest subordinate of such a minister. Sir, this old system must come down. Claiming public liberty, we must cultivate public virtue, and it shall be so. A new generation begins to act in Ireland—a generation pledged against all English alliances, a generation pledged to make this island a free nation and pledged to do so in the most clear, straightforward, righteous way. The events of the day invite us to proceed. Nations that had for centuries lost their freedom are breaking through their fetters, and we behold them resuming with youthful vigour their old positions. Italy! Italy awakes to a new destiny and from her sculptured sepulchre Europe hails her dazzling resurrection. The bayonet of the Austrian will no longer intimidate where once the sceptre of the Cæsars swayed. In the Church of Saint John Lateran, a wiser and a holier Rienzi has appeared, and the Roman citizen blesses the new Tribune as he goes forth from the Vatican to regenerate and free. On the summit of the Aventine the Temple of Liberty shall again be reared—the laurel shall replace the ivy on the fragments of the Forum, and whilst the scholar rears his genius beneath the shadow of its ancient glories, the future statesmen of this our island will learn from the mitred ruler the purest lessons of liberality—the wisest measures of reform. Sir, Italy has ceased to be the mere guard-house of the Austrian trooper—Ireland must cease to be the fee-farm of the English jobber. " To God and man we made oath, that we would never cease to strive until an Irish nation stood supreme upon this island." These are the solemn words of one whose noble heart is mouldering beneath the shroud in the cemetery of Mount Jerome, but the cold vault has not imprisoned his passionate spirit, nor shall the glorious mission which he preached to the young men of Ireland be unfulfilled by us. His genius breathes and burns beyond the grave, and as it inspires the present so shall it illuminate the future, Like him through good report and ill, we will work on to win the freedom and exalt the character of our country ; , and though that country may be taught to curse us for a day—though slander be awhile the penalty which our integrity may incur, and though the aged hand that ought to beckon us to advance may strive to beat us back, we shall still press on—faithful, come what may, to the vow we plighted in this Hall. Death alone shall crush us—despotism, be it foreign or domestic, shall not.

Union with England

Speech in the Rotunda at the Opening of the
Irish Confederation, January 13th, 1847.

Sir, there was a levee at the Castle this morning.
Gentlemen went there to pay their respects to the
representative of royalty: we have met here, this
night, to testify our allegiance to liberty. I will not
inquire which is the more honourable act ; but I think
the latter more useful. Where a court resides a parliament should sit. A court, without a senate, can do
little for the public good ; it may do much for the
public harm. The court of the province may distribute
favours, and teach a propriety of demeanour. The
senate of the free nation distributes blessings, and inspires the community with virtue. Little did the poet
hero of Missolonghi, when he passionately rebuked the
homage that was paid a sceptred profligate in this
city, twenty-five years since—little did he imagine
that at this day his words would be so disastrously
fulfilled—

> " The Castle still stands, tho' the senate's no more,
>   And the Famine that dwells on her freedomless crags
> Is extending its steps to her desolate shore."

Sir, the Castle has been preserved, whilst the senate
has been destroyed, and the blood and poison in which
it was destroyed have given birth to a hideous famine.
When the English minister introduced the Act of
Union into the English Commons, he did not venture

53

to justify his scheme upon the inability of a domestic parliament to legislate beneficially for Ireland. The prosperity of the nation—to which Lord Clare, Mr. Plunket, Mr. Grattan, and several other members bore testimony in the Irish Commons, and to which Mr. Sheridan and Mr. Burdett bore testimony in the English Commons—this prosperity was so obvious, and so distinctly traceable to the efficient legislation of the Irish parliament, that some other argument, besides that of incapacity, should be urged for its destruction. The minister admitted the good that had been done—admitted the commerce that had thriven, the arts that had flourished, the eminent position that had been attained by the country, with the wise assistance of her parliament. He did not charge that parliament with incapacity, for the evidences of capacity met him in the face. He did not charge that parliament with the corruption of its last moments, for his was the hand that planted death where once the sword of the volunteer had infused vitality. He did not charge that parliament with those grievous defects which impaired its character, but which, we must assert, were rather the defects of the age than the defects of the institution. No ; he advanced a more serious charge, and appealed from the virtue to the avarice of the people. The Irish parliament was arraigned for standing between the people of Ireland and the blessings of English connection. " You have prospered," said the minister, " under a native parliament. Accept a foreign parliament, and your prosperity will amaze. Incorporate the countries, and you incorporate their interests. Participate in the imperial labours, and you participate in the imperial profits. Recognise London as your chief city, and your nobility will be identified with the proudest patricians in Europe. Consolidate the exchequers, and in the periods of distress which, through the dispensations of heaven, await all nations, you will experience the munificence of the empire. Consolidate the exchequers, and you will revel in the treasures of the colonies. Consolidate the exchequers, and you will feast with us upon the spoils of India. You now stand alone. You require a guardian. The ambition of France will drive her bayonets against your shore, and the Island will be gazetted as the property of the stranger. Unite with us, and you may defy the Corsican —unite with us, and you may defy the world—unite with us, and as we ascend to a height on which the Roman soldier never trod, from which the Spanish merchant never gazed, you will accompany us in our flight, and the states that will bend in recognition of our power, will admire your wisdom, and be dazzled with your wealth." Sir, in what year, since the enactment of the Union, will the disciples of William Pitt find the fulfilment of that promise? In 1801, when the English parliament visited this country with an Insurrection Act? In 1803, when that parliament imposed a martial law? In 1807, when the Insurrection Act of 1801 is renewed, continuing in force until 1810? In 1814, when, for a third time, the Insurrection Act of 1801 is renewed, and inflicted up to 1824? In 1836, when the Lord High Chancellor of England spurns you as aliens in language, in religion, and in blood? In 1839, when you claimed equal franchises with the people of England, and are denied them by the Whig Secretary for Ireland? In 1843, when a minister of the crown declares that concession has reached its limits, and an assassin proclamation proscribes your right of petition? In 1846, when the Coercion Bill is levelled against your liberties, and the

Arms' Act is re-introduced by the Whigs? Tell me—is it fulfilled in 1847, when the Treasury confiscates the Island, and famine piles upon it a pyramid of coffins? A lie! exclaims the broken manufacturer. A lie! protests the swindled landlord. A lie! a lie! shrieks the skeleton from the putrid hovels of Skibbereen. "Depend upon it," said Mr. Bushe, speaking of the Act of Union, in the Irish Commons—"depend upon it, a day of reckoning will come—posterity will overhaul this transaction." Sir, the day of reckoning has come—posterity overhauls the base transaction! The right which national pride had not the virtue to dictate—the right which national enterprise had not the spirit to demand—a national calamity has now the fortunate terror to enforce. Heretofore, the right of self-government was claimed as an instrument to ameliorate; now it is claimed as an instrument to save. Heretofore, it was claimed that the people might be gifted with the franchise; now it is claimed that the people may have the privilege of bread. We demand from England this right. We demand the restoration of our parliament, and we demand it, not as a remote, but as an immediate measure. It is the only true measure of relief. The pestilence came from heaven, but the inability of the country to mitigate that pestilence we ascribe to the avarice of man. England, in her lust of empire, has deprived us of those large means, that social wealth, that manufacturing capital, which would have enabled our country to meet the necessities of this dark crisis. The Union, as you have been often told, has wrought the ruin of your trade, your manufactures, your arts. It has sanctioned if it has not compelled, absenteeism. It has beggared the mechanic. It now starves the peasant. It has destroyed your home market. It has taken from you the power to devote the resources of the country to the wants of the people. You have no control over these resources. They are forbidden fruit. You dare not touch them. If this be not so, why is your export trade so flourishing, whilst your import trade expires? If this be not so, how comes it that the absentee crams his coffer, whilst the sexton fills the churchyard? If this be not so, how comes it that your city quays are thronged, whilst the village street is desolate? If this be not so, how comes it that whilst the merchant ship bears away the harvest from your shore, the parish bier conveys the reaper to his grave? Sir, England has bound this Island hand and foot. The Island is her slave. She robs the Island of its food, for it has not the power to guard it. If the Island does not break its fetters England will write its epitaph. Listen to a few facts. I hold in my hand a statement of Irish exports from the 1st of August to the 1st of January. From this statement you will perceive that England seizes on our food, whilst death seizes on our people: Total export of provisions from the ports of Waterford, Cork, Limerick, and Belfast, from 1st August, 1846, to the 1st January, 1847: Pork, barrels, 37,123; bacon, flitches, 222,608; butter, firkins, 388,455; hams, hhds., 1,971; beef, tierces, 2,555; wheat, barrels, 48,526; oats, barrels, 443,232; barley, barrels, 12,029; oatmeal, cwts., 7,210; flour, cwts., 144,185; pigs, 44,659; cows, 9,007; sheep, 10,288. Yet, this is what the English economist would designate the prosperity of Ireland. From this table Lord Monteagle would expatiate upon the benefits of English connection. From this table Mr. Montgomery Martin would prove, with the keenest precision, the advantages to Ireland of the legislative Union. From this table Mr. Macaulay —who threatened us with a civil war in the name of the Whigs, and was answered by the honourable member for Limerick, as a man who threatened despotism should be always answered—from this table Mr. Macaulay would surely conclude that Irish prosperity was a sound reality—that Irish famine was a factious metaphor. But, sir, I shall dwell no longer upon this dismal theme. For a moment let us forget the famine —" if it be possible, let this bitter cup pass away." It is difficult, indeed, to close our eyes to the horror. Go where you will, and you must face it. Go to the church —in the pulpit it stands beside the priest, and recounts to him its havoc. Go to the social board, and there it sits, and chills the current of the soul. Amid the radiant scenery of my native South its shadow falls and scares you from the mountain and the glen. But you have vowed to win the freedom of your country, and you must wail no more. The voice of Ireland has been too sad. Had it been more stern, it would have been obeyed long since. For the future we must not supplicate, but demand—we must not entreat, but enforce. We must insist upon the right of this country to govern itself, with the firmness which the importance of the right demands, and which the power of our opponent necessitates. Urge that right on higher grounds than those on which it has been hitherto implored. Demand it, not merely to redress wrongs, but to acquire power. Demand it as the right which a nation must possess if it ambitions fortune, and aspires to station. Deprived of this right, the nation is destitute of self-reliance. Destitute of this great virtue, the nation has no inward strength, no inherent influence. Through the bounty of the ruling state it may exist ; but a nation thus sustained, is sustained by a hand from without, not by a soul from within. Should it derive prosperity from this source, the nation,

I maintain, is yet more enslaved. It loses all faith in its own faculties, and is soothed and pampered into debasement. The spirit of the freeman no longer acts —the gratitude of the slave destroys it. Sustained by the bounty—participating in the civic rights of the predominant country, it may become a useful appendage to that country—waste its blood for the supremacy of a Union Flag—gild an Imperial Senate with its purchased genius—be visited by the Sovereign, be flattered by the minister, be eulogised in the journals of the empire ; but, sir, such a country will have no true prosperity—will occupy no high position—will exhibit no fine virtues—will accomplish no great acts ; it may fatten in its fetters—it will write no name in history. " To depend upon the honour of another country, is to depend upon her will ; and to depend upon the will of another country, is the definition of slavery." This was the doctrine of Henry Grattan—let it be our motto. Union with England, for no purpose—union with England, for no price—union with England, on no terms ! Let them extend the franchise—reclaim the waste lands—promote the coast fisheries—improve their drainage acts—ay, let them vote their millions to check the starvation with which we charge them—the Union Act must be repealed. No foreign hand can bestow the prosperity which a national soul has the power to create. No gift can compensate a nation for its liberty. This was the sentiment of Mr. Foster, who declared that if England could give up all her revenue, and all her trade to Ireland, he would not barter for them the free constitution of his country. This was the sentiment of Mr. Plunket when he denounced the Union as a barter of liberty for money, and pronounced the nation that would enter into such a traffic, for any advantage whatsoever, to be criminal and besotted.

This was the sentiment of Mr. O'Connell, in 1800, when, speaking for the Catholics, he declared, that if emancipation was offered for their consent to the measure, they would reject it with prompt indignation—that if the alternative were offered them, of the Union, or the re-enactment of the penal code in all its pristine horrors, they would prefer the latter, without hesitation, as the lesser and more sufferable evil. Sir, we must act in the spirit of these sentiments. We must rescue the country from the control of every English minister. It was our boast, in 1843, that Ireland was the difficulty of Sir Robert Peel. Let us be just in 1847, and make it the difficulty of Lord John Russell. It is time for us to prefer the freedom of our country to the patronage of the crown. I firmly believe that Ireland has suffered more from the subserviency of her sons than from the dictation of her foes. " Liberal appointments " have pleased us too much. Amongst us, the Tapers and the Tadpoles have been too numerous a class— the patriots who believe that the country will be saved if they receive from £600 to £1,200 a year. Give me a resident nobility, a resident gentry, an industrious population. Give me a commerce to enrich the country, and a navy to protect that commerce. Give me a national flag, to inspire the country with a proper pride, and a national militia to defend that flag. Give me, for my country, these great faculties, these great attributes, and I care not who wears the ermine in the Queen's Bench—I care not who officiates in the Castle-yard—I care not who adjudicates in the Police Office— I care not who the high sheriff of the county may be— I care not who the beadle of the parish may be. If there be social evils in the country, there will be a national legislature to correct them ; and even if that legislature has not the power to correct those evils, the blessings which it is sure to confer will more than counteract them. The resolution I propose will pledge us to an absolute independence of all English parties, and exclude from the Irish Confederation any member of the council who will accept or solicit an office of emolument under any government not pledged to Repeal. It gives me sincere delight to move this resolution. I know you will adopt it—I am confident you will act up to it boldly. Public men have said that the cause of Repeal is strengthened by Repealers taking places. I maintain that the cause is weakened. The system decimates the ranks. In 1843 where were the Repealers who assumed the official garb after the movement of 1834 ? Repealers, occupying office, may not abandon their opinions, but they withdraw their services. You cannot serve the minister who is pledged to maintain the Union, and serve the people who are pledged to repeal it. Will a report on the financial grievances, inflicted by the Union, accompany a Treasury minute from London ? Will a Repeal pamphlet issue from the Board of Works ? The Trojans fought the Greeks, through the streets of Troy, in Grecian armour. Will the Repealers fight the Whigs, upon the hustings, with Whig favours in their pockets ? Recollect the Union was carried by Irishmen receiving English gold. Depend upon it, the same system will not accelerate its repeal. Sir, we must have an end of this place-begging. The task we have assumed is a serious one. To accomplish it well, our energies must have full play. The trappings of the Treasury will restrict them more than the shackles of the prison. State liveries usually encumber men, and detain them at the Castle gates. Not a doubt of it, sir, we shall work the freer when we wear no royal harness. To the accomplishment of this great task we earnestly invite

all ranks and parties in the country. It is not the
cause of Radicalism. It is not the cause of Sectarian-
ism. It is the cause of Ireland—a noble cause! a
cause in which the Irish peer should feel as deeply
interested as the Irish peasant—in which the Irish
Protestant should associate with the Irish Catholic—in
which the Irish Conservative should co-operate with the
Irish Radical. Sir, I will not appeal to the Irish
peer, for I am not his equal. Yet I will tell him, that
to act as the hereditary peer of this ancient kingdom
would be a more honourable distinction than to serve
as an elected peer in the parliament of that country
which has usurped his ancestral right. In England,
where there resides the proudest nobility in the world
—a nobility that would not yield to the Contarini of
Venice, to the Colonna of Rome, to the Montmorenci
of France—the Irish peer is a powerless subordinate.
In Ireland, his native land, he would have no superior
in rank ; if he had virtue and ability, he would have
no superior in power. I will not appeal to the Irish
landlord, for I have no land, yet I will tell him, that
he has too long sacrificed the interests of Ireland,
little knowing that by so doing he sacrificed his own,
and that now, to save his property, he must save the
country—to save the country he must assert her
freedom. But, sir, I will appeal to the Irish Protestant who stands aloof, for I am his brother. Let
not the altar stand between us and our freedom. Let
not the history of the past be the prophecy of the
future. Even in that history his eye will glance on
brighter chapters than those which record the defence
of Derry, or the triumph of Aughrim. On the 4th day
of November, 1779, the Protestant Volunteers of this
city and county met in College Green and piled their
arms round the statue of King William. They met

round the statue of that king whom the Irish Protestant has been vainly taught to worship, and the Irish Catholic wantonly to execrate—they met round that statue, not to revive the factions of the Boyne— not that the waters of that river should sweep away again the shattered banner of the Catholic—but that those waters might float for ever the commerce of a free nation. Protestant citizens! cultivate the fine virtues of that period; embrace the faith of which Molyneux was the bold apostle; renounce the supremacy of England; abjure the errors of provincialism. Let not the dread of Catholic ascendancy deter you. If such an ascendancy were preached, here is one hand at least that would be clenched against it. Yes, here are four thousand arms to give it battle. And now I will appeal to the young men of Ireland—for I am one of that proscribed class. A noble mission is open to them—let them accept it with enthusiasm, and fulfil it with integrity. If they do so, the independence of the nation will be restored, and they themselves shall win a righteous fame. A free nation will vote them to her senate in their maturer years, and when they die, upon their tombs will be inscribed that nation's gratitude. Let not the sneers of those in whose hearts no generous impulse throbs, in whose minds no lofty purpose dwells, deter them from the task. Men who have grown selfish amid the insincerities of society, who have grown harsh from the buffets of the world, will bid them mind their business—their profession. Sir, our country is our dearest object—to win its freedom is our first duty. It is not the decree of heaven, I believe, that the sympathies of the young heart, the abilities with which most young minds are gifted, should be narrowed to the trade we follow, the profession we pursue. These sympathies are too large, these abilities too strong, to be narrowed to the purposes of a sordid egotism. These sympathies, these abilities, were so conferred that they might embrace the Island, and be the ramparts of its liberty. To us the God of heaven has thus been good, not that we should " crawl from the cradle to the grave," doing nothing for mankind, but that we should so act as to leave a memory behind us for the good to bless, and the free to glorify. Sir, were I to rely upon the effect which my words might have, I should indeed despair. Youth, which brings with it an energy to act, seldom confers authority ; and if the appeals which its enthusiasm dictates sometimes have the fortune to move, it more frequently happens that the rashness, of which it is susceptible, has the effect to deter. But the revolution of opinion, which now shakes society in Ireland, gives me true hope. " I believe that Ireland will soon be called upon to govern herself," said Mr. Delmege in the Music Hall. " Ireland shall govern herself "—so insists this meeting. Sir,[1] you who are the descendant of an Irish king—go to the English Commons, and tell the English Commons what you have seen this night—tell the English Commons, that in this Hall—a spot sacred to the people of Ireland, for here, in 1783, the Convention sat, with a mitred reformer at its head—sacred to them, for here, in 1845, their civic chiefs made solemn oath that the independence of this country should be restored—sacred to them, for here, in 1847, has been established the sanctuary of free opinion ; tell the English Commons, sir, that here four thousand citizens assembled on this night to decide the destiny of the Union. Tell the English Commons, that these citizens decide that the destiny of the Union shall be the destruction of the Union. Should the minister ask you why is this, tell the minister that the

[1] Smith O'Brien.

Patrick O'Donohoe, Vice President of the Club
Sixth day after sentence of death

Clonmel Gaol 29ᵗʰ Octr 48.

Terence Bellew McManus

On a Sunday morning in a
cold chill cell ——————

Thomas Francis Meagher
Member of the
" Cherokee Council of Fire "

Clonmel Gaol,
Oct. 29ᵗʰ 1848.

Autographs of the State Prisoners in Clonmel Gaol

Union sentences the country to ruin, and that the country will not submit to the sentence. Should the minister assure you, that, for the future, there shall be a fair Union, and not a false Union—" a real Union, and not a parchment Union "—tell the minister that we shall have no Union, be it for better or for worse. Tell the minister, sir, that a new race of men now act in Ireland—men who will neither starve as the victims, nor serve as the vassals of the British Empire. Have I spoken your sentiments—have I announced your determination truly? Yes, the spirit that nerved the Red Hand of Ulster—the spirit that made the walls of Limerick impregnable, and forced the conquerors of the Boyne to negotiate by the waters of the Shannon —the spirit that dictated the letters of Swift and the instructions of Lucas—the spirit that summoned the armed missionaries of freedom to the altar of Dungannon, and gave to Charlemont the dignity which his accomplishments would never have attained—the spirit that touched with fire the tongue of Grattan, and endowed his words with the magic of his sword—the spirit that sanctified the scaffold of the Geraldine, and bade the lyre of Moore vibrate through the world— the spirit that called forth the genius of Davis from the cloisters of Old Trinity, and which consecrates his grave—the spirit that at this day, in the city of the Pontiff, unfurls the flag of Sarsfield, and animates the Irish sculptor as he bids the marble speak the passion of the Irish Tribune—the spirit which defied at Mallow, and vowed at Mullaghmast—this spirit which the bayonet could not drive back—which the bribe could not satiate—which misfortune could not quell—is moving vividly through the land. The ruins that ennoble, the scenes that beautify, the memories that illuminate, the music that inspires our native land,

5

have preserved it pure amid the vicious factions of the past, and the venal bargains of later years. The visitation that now storms upon the land has stung into generous activity. Did public virtue cease to animate, the Senate House which, even in its desecrated state, lends an Italian glory to this metropolis, would forbid it to expire. The temple is there—the creed has been announced—the priests will enter and officiate. It shall be so. The spirit of Nationality, rooted in our hearts, is as immovable as the altar of the Druid, pillared in our soil.

Whiggery and Famine

SPEECH AT THE GALWAY ELECTION, FEB. 12th, 1847.

Gentlemen, I have come here to protest against the government of England, for which government you have been solicited to vote this day. The struggle begun this morning upon the hustings of your old town, is not a struggle between two men—it is a struggle between two countries. On the one side—the side of the Whig candidate—hangs the red banner, beneath which your senate has been sacked, your commerce has been wrecked, your nobility have been dishonoured, your peasantry have been starved. On the other side —the side of the Repeal candidate—floats the green flag, for which the artillery of 1782 won a legitimate respect—beneath which your senate sat, your commerce thrived, your nobility were honoured, your peasants prospered. Until the last three years that flag has been deserted by us. With the tameness of slaves we submitted to its proscription. We saw it torn from our merchant ships, and whilst we lacked the ability to guard it upon the seas, we had not the virtue to guard it upon the hustings. Everywhere the supremacy of the red flag was recognised by us— recognised by us, whether it was borne by the military or the political agent of England. What difference, I will ask, did it make that it was sometimes decorated with the insignia of the Whigs? Decorated with the blue ribbon of the Pitt or the buff ribbon of the Fox school, it was still the same cursed testimony of foreign mastership—still the same crimson scroll on which our

67

incapacity for business was set forth, and the terms of
our base apprenticeship were engrossed. Year after
year were we content to be the sutlers of English
faction—content to echo back the cant and clamour of
English Radicalism. At one time blessing a Reform
Bill, as if it gave us political power ; at another time
rushing after the glittering equipage of a Whig viceroy,
as if his smiles were productive of manufactures, and
his liberal appointments had been the precursors of
national institutions. All this time we forgot, that,
for the nation to exist, the nation should have its arts,
its fisheries, its manufactures, its commerce ; and that
a franchise bill, corporate reform acts, liberal appointments, and so forth, are of very little importance com-
pared to bread for the million. Doubtless, there were
some excellent innovations at the Castle about this
time, for St. Patrick's Hall was no longer shut to the
Catholic barrister. The ermine, too, had ceased to
be the sacred monopoly of Protestantism. The Catholic
and Protestant became equally entitled to it, and,
with the police uniform, it was made common to both.
The hall of the Four Courts rang with the praises of
Normanby, and the statue of Justice which decorates
that hall was pronounced by the best judges to be the
very image of Russell. Public dinners were frequently
held, and the people of Ireland were congratulated on
the tranquillity of the country, and the promotion of
able demagogues to power. The people heard the
toasts that were shouted at those dinners—heard the
selfish canticles of faction—heard that the salvation of
Ireland was identical with the liberal disposal of silk
gowns—heard that the elevation of Ireland would be
accomplished by the elevation of noisy democrats to
office—the people heard these things, and believed that
their freedom was at hand. They believed so, for they

had not as yet looked well into the country, and saw what was really wanting there. But 1843 came, and a voice from Tara bade the people organise for liberty. On the site of the Irish monarchy, the spell of a factious vassalage was broken—provincialism was abjured— nationality was vowed. In that year, you, the citizens of Galway, pledged yourselves to devote every effort to the attainment of Irish independence. You organised —and in your foremost rank shone the coronet of the Ffrenches, with the mitre of St. Jarlath's. You con- tributed to the exchequer of the movement ; your merchants opened their coffers ; your artisans—and I see many of them here to-night—coined the sweat of their brows into gold, and offered it up as the ransom of our liberties. Then came the 30th of May, 1845, and you sent your Town Commissioners to the Rotunda, where the chiefs of the national movement received the homage of the people. That was no false homage—it was sincere—for the men who offered it aspired to freedom. On that day your representatives pledged themselves on your behalf—now mark the words !— that corruption should not seduce, nor deceit cajole, nor intimidation deter you from seeking the attainment of a national legislature. Gentlemen, the time has come to redeem that vow. This struggle will test your truth, your purity, your heroism. Your honour is at stake—your integrity is in question—your character is on trial. Vows can be easily made. Expediency may advise them—enthusiasm may dictate them. The difficulty and the virtue is to fulfil them. When that vow was made, did you not hear the jeering prophecy, that it would eventuate in a solemn false- hood ? Did you not hear it said that you had neither the intention nor the integrity to redeem that vow— that you might threaten, but dare not strike ? It was

said so in London—it was said so in Chesham Place—
it was said so in Dublin : let me tell you it is so written
in the predictions of the Castle. Will you vilely verify
the anticipations of Chesham Place—will you basely
authenticate the predictions of the Castle ? Re-
nounced by Cashel—threatened in Wexford—supplanted
in Dundalk—routed from Mayo—What ! shall the
refugees of Whiggery find in Galway a spot where, at
last, the gold of the Cabinet will contaminate the virtue
of the people ? I ask you, what will be the result of
this election ? Shall Galway be a slave market ?
Shall this ancient Irish town be degraded into an English
borough ?—and will you, its citizens, sacrifice your
principles and your name, embrace provincialism, and
henceforth exult in the title of West Britons ? I
should apologise for thus addressing you—or rather,
you should bid me cease, and indignantly assert that,
come what may, no Whig official shall ever testify
your recreancy in the Senate House of England. Why
should it be otherwise ? Since 1845, your opinions,
surely, have not changed ? If so, what has changed
them ? The famine ? The prompt benevolence of
the English government ? The generosity of the
English Commons ? What imperial proselytiser has
seduced you from the cause, in the defence of which,
in 1843, you would have passionately bled ? The
prompt benevolence of the English government ?
How has this been manifested ? In the timely suspension of the navigation laws ? In the establishment of
corn depots ? In the prohibition of the export of
Irish produce ? By the summoning of parliament in
November ? Bear this in mind—whilst the peasants
have perished, without leaving a coin to purchase a
winding sheet, the merchants have bought their purple
and fine linen with their famine prices, for the English

market should be protected—thus, the English economists have ruled it. In the blasted field, beneath the
putrid crop, the merchant has sunk a shaft and found
a gold mine, for the English minister would not in-
convenience the trade of Liverpool and London. And
is it the servant of this minister whom you will support?
If you prefer a bribe to freedom—if you prefer to be
the Swiss guard of a foreign minister, rather than be
the National guard of a free kingdom, vote for him, and
be dishonest and debased. Vote for the Whig candidate,
and vote for provincialism. Vote for the Whig candidate, and vote for alien laws. Vote for the Whig
candidate, and vote for a civil war before Repeal—for
that is the Whig alternative. Vote for the Whig candidate, and vote for economy and starvation. Vote for
him—vote for him—and then cringe back to your homes,
and there thank God that you have had a country to
sell! Have you nerved your souls for this crime?
Beware of it! I will not tell you that the eyes of the
nation—the eyes of Europe are upon you. That is
the cant of every hustings. But this I tell you, there
are a few men yet breathing in Skibbereen, and their
death-glance is upon you. Vote for the Whig candidate, and their last shriek will proclaim that you have
voted for the pensioned misers who refused them
bread. There is a place, too, called Schull, in the county
Cork, the churchyard of which place—as a tenant told
his landlord the other day—is the only red field in the
wide, wide county. There are eyes, wild with the
agonies of hunger, looking out from that fell spot upon
you, and if you vote against your native land, the
burning tongue of the starving peasant will froth its
curse upon you, and upon your children. Gentlemen,
I have now done, and I fear not for you, nor for the
country. I believe there is in Galway the virtue to

preserve the honour of its citizens—the virtue to assert the liberty of the country. What, though it cost you even serious sacrifices—what though you gain nothing, at this moment, by your honest votes, save the blessing of a tranquil conscience and a proud heart —still be true to the faith and glory of Henry Grattan. Fling aside—trample under foot—the bribes and promises of Russell. Be true to the principles of 1782 —be true to the resolutions of 1843—be true to the vow of 1845—and with pure hands, with hands un-stained by the glittering poison of the English Treasury, amid the graves and desolation of 1847, lay the foundations of a future nation.

Irish Slaves and English Corruption

SPEECH DELIVERED AT THE GALWAY ELECTION,
FEBRUARY 14TH, 1847.

Gentlemen, you saw the men who voted for the Whig candidate on Saturday. Did they advance to the hustings like men who felt they had a country, and were conscious that their votes would be recorded for her liberty? No, they went there like slaves—insensible to the dictates of patriotism—insensible to its thrilling invocations for redress. The troops, under the armed guardianship of which they were driven to utter sentence against the independence of their country, proclaimed the cause for which their venal franchise was compelled. Did not the proud escort that attended the tenants of Lord Clanricarde to the courthouse proclaim that to the supremacy of England those venal tenants sacrificed their souls? The troops that were arrayed against your right to petition upon the field of Clontarf were fit companions indeed for the slaves who were herded together to vote against your right to legislate. Those men might as well have voted in manacles. But if their hands were free, their souls were fettered; and if they wore not the garb of convicts, they exhibited all the debasement of criminals. Yet these men had illustrious models of depravity—models selected from the brightest page of Irish history, as some Whig orator would designate the narrative of the Union. They had Fitzgibbon—they had Castlereagh—the titled miscreants who pur-

73

chased English coronets by the destruction of the Irish Senate. Castlereagh purchased something else—an English grave. This, at least, was a privilege to Ireland—to be exempt from the contamination of the dust which, when breathing, had drenched our Senate with corruption and our land with blood. Let England still claim such treasures, and let no Irish traitor— no tenant of Clanricarde—rot beneath the soil in which the bones of Swift, of Tone, and Davis, have been laid to rest. Turn from this soiled and revolting picture, and contemplate the reverse. You saw the men who voted for the Repeal candidate. Did they register their votes under the sabres of hussars ? No ; they voted for their country, and, were, therefore, under no obligation to the liveried champions of the English flag. They went up to the hustings like honest citizens, and were protected, not by the musket of the soldier, but by the arm of the God of Hosts. Their souls were as untrammelled as their limbs, and, recording their votes, they were distinguished for the manliness which men who love freedom can alone exhibit. They voted like men who knew well that the scheme of the Whigs is to soothe this country into degradation, and they looked like men who scorned to be soothed for that purpose—scorned the vile scheme that would prostrate this country by patronage—scorned the vile scheme that would perpetuate the Union by making it prolific in small boons. Men of Galway, to the hustings on the morrow, in the same gallant spirit. Show no mercy to these Whigs ! Swamp them before the sun sets, and let the night fall upon the broken flag-staff and baffled cohorts of the English Minister ! Let the Minister hear of his defeat on Wednesday morning, and curse the virtue that had no price. There must be no jubilee in Chesham Place at the expense of Irish liberty. There must be no delegate from Galway authorised to sustain the dictation of the English Commons—authorised to sustain the dictation that has been assumed to coerce, to enslave, to starve this country. What will the Commons say when the Solicitor-General for Ireland takes his seat on the Treasury Bench as the Whig member for this borough ? Will they say that the threat uttered by the Paymaster of the Forces has forced you to capitulate ? No ; I do not think they will charge you with cowardice, but I am sure they will arraign you for corruption. They will say that venality has accomplished what battalions could not achieve, and that the money-bags of the Mint can do more for the English interest in Ireland than all the batteries of Woolwich. And, let me tell you, these money-bags have been flung across the Channel into Galway. Trust me, the Whig Government will fight this battle to the last farthing. This I sincerely believe—this I deliberately avow. I am justified in this belief, for it is notorious that the favourite weapon of the Whig Government is corruption. It is the boast of these Whigs that they alone can govern Ireland—that they can mesmerise the Irish beggars ! Prove to them that this boast is a falsehood—prove to them that you will not be governed by them, and that Ireland shall be their difficulty and their scourge. What claims have these Whigs upon us ? None save what corruption constitutes. Their liberal appointments ? How do these appointments serve the country ? How much wealth flows into Ireland by the member for Dungarvan [1] being Master of the Mint ? Recollect this, the Whigs voted twenty millions to emancipate the Africans—they refuse to sanction a loan of sixteen millions to employ the Irish. Vote for their nominee,

[1] Richard Lalor Sheil.

and you will vote against the noble proposition of the Protectionist leader. And has it come to this that you will vote for non-employment—for starvation—for deaths by the minute, and inquests by the hour. Will you vote for this Government of economists—this Government of misers—this Government of grave-diggers? Before you do so, read the advertisement on the walls of the Treasury—" Funerals supplied to all parts of the country." That is the true way to tranquillise the country! That is the true way to hush the tumult of sedition! That is the true way to incorporate the countries, and make the Union binding! If we do not beat those Whigs out of Galway—if we do not fight them for every inch of Irish ground—if we do not drive them across the Channel—they will starve this country into a wilderness, and, at the opening of the next session, they will bid their royal mistress congratulate her assembled Parliament upon the success-ful government and the peace of Ireland. And they insist, too, that the executive of this wilderness shall be a chief of police, a poor-law commissioner, and a commissary-general. Will you submit to this? Do you prefer a soup-kitchen to a custom house? Do you prefer graveyards to corn-fields? Do you prefer the Board of Works to a national senate? Do you prefer the insolent rule of Scotch and English officials to the beneficent legislation of Irish Peers and Irish Commoners? Heaven forbid that the blight which putrified your food should infect your souls! Heaven forbid that the famine should tame you into debase-ment, and that the spirit which has triumphed over the prison and the scaffold should surrender to the corruptionist at last! I asked you, a moment since, how much wealth flows into Ireland by the member for Dungarvan being Master of the Mint? I must tell you this : there is a little stream of it always dropping through the Castle Yard ; but sometimes there are extraordinary spring-tides—just about election times—and then that tide swells and deepens, and rises so high, and rushes so rapidly, that it frequently sweeps away the votes of the people—sweeps away their placards—sweeps away their banners—sweeps away their committee rooms—and, in the end, throws up a Whig official upon the white shore of England. Beware of this spring-tide ; it is sweeping through Galway this moment—through lane and street. Its glittering waters intoxicate and debase. The wretches who drink them fall into the current and are whirled away—the drenched and battered spoils of England. And is this the end of all you have vowed and done ? And has it come to this, that after the defiances, the resolutions, the organisation of 1843, England shall plant her foot upon the neck of Ireland and exclaim : " Behold my bribed and drunken slave ! " I do not exaggerate. The battle of Ireland is being fought in Galway. If the Whigs take Galway—Ireland falls. Shall Ireland fall ? Incur defeat and you shall have her bitter curse. Win the battle and you shall have her proud blessing. Your virtue and your victory will fire the coward and regenerate the venal—your example will be followed—the Whigs will be driven from Wexford, from Waterford, from Mallow, from Dungarvan ; their bribes will be trampled in the dust, their strongest citadels be stormed ; the integrity of the people shall prevail against the venality of the faction, the Union Act shall share the fate of the Penal Code, and mankind shall hail the birth, the career, the glory of an Irish nation.

National Politics

SPEECH IN THE MUSIC HALL, APRIL 7TH, 1847, AT
THE THIRD MEETING OF THE IRISH CONFEDERATION.

The proceedings of this night, sir, will, no doubt, incur the censure of those gentlemen who maintain that politics have nothing to do with the state of the country. It will be said by them, that it is heartless to talk about Repeal when the people require relief. It will be said by them, that the doctrines of nationality should not be preached whilst the nation is on its knees, begging for its bread. Sir, these gentlemen would adjourn the question of Irish independence, to criticise the " boil and bubble " of a French cook. They would turn their backs upon the old parliament house, in College Green, to dive into the mysteries of the soup kitchen at Kingsbridge. Yet, sir, I agree with these gentlemen to a certain extent. Party politics have nothing to do with the state of the country. " Who is in, and who is out—who has this, and who has that ? "—these questions have nothing to do with the state of the country. But national politics have everything to do with the state of the country, and these we shall guard and propagate. Gentlemen who tell us to postpone the question of Repeal, whilst the famine is on the wing, dictate a course that would perpetuate the disease and beggary of the land. They advise a step that would make the Union Act, in truth, " a final settlement." They recommend a policy that would violate our vow, disband our forces, and let in the enemy. Once down, England would keep us down.

78

Sir, there must be no pause, no adjournment, no truce. Repeal is now a question, not so much of political power, as of actual physical existence. Self-government has become a question of self-preservation. A national parliament is the only efficient relief committee that can be organized—the only one that can have the wisdom to devise, and the power to carry out, any measures calculated to save the life and improve the prospects of this country. The famine has already done enough for England. It shall not do more. It shall not do its worst—it shall not force us to capitulate. What has the famine done for England? The famine has been her best recruiting sergeant—it has purchased thousands into her brilliant and licentious legions. The famine has been her best miner—it has discovered gold mines for her merchants in bankrupt cities and de-populated villages. The famine has been her best swordsman—it has cut down thousands of her peasant foes. But there is one spot where this powerful agent of English lust must halt—one spot where it shall purchase no recruits—one spot where it shall plant no cypress and rear no trophy—one spot where it shall cease to do the business and the butchery of England. It shall halt—it shall be powerless and paralysed—where the Confederation sits. What say they in England now? What says the *Times*, the eloquent and mighty organ of English opinion? " Ireland is now at the mercy of England. For the first time in the course of centuries England may rule Ireland, and treat her as a thoroughly conquered country." Ay, Ireland is now at the mercy of England! Ireland is now a thoroughly conquered country! England has won her crowning victory! The war of centuries is at a close! The archers of Strongbow have failed—the Ironsides of Cromwell have failed—

the spies and yeomen of Castlereagh have failed—
the patronage and proscriptions of Ebrington have
failed—the proclamations and state prosecutions of
De Grey have failed—the procrastinations and economy
of Russell have triumphed! Let a thanksgiving be
preached from the pulpit of St. Paul's—let the Lords
and Commons of England vote their gratitude to the
victorious economist—let the guns of London Tower
proclaim the triumph which has cost, in past years,
coffers of gold and torrents of blood, and in this year
a wholesale system of starvation to achieve. England!
your gallant impetuous enemy is dead—your " great
difficulty " is at an end. Ireland, or rather the remains
of Ireland, are yours at last. Your red ensign flies—
not from the Rath of Mullaghmast, where you played
the cut-throat—not from Limerick wall, where you
played the perjurer—not from the senate-house, where
you played the swindler—not from the custom-house,
where you played the robber—but it flies from her
thousand graveyards, where the titled niggards of your
cabinet have won the battle which your soldiers could
not terminate. Celebrate your victory! Bid your
Scourge steamer, from the western coast, convey
some memorial of your conquest, and, in the hall
where the flags and cannons you have captured from
a world of foes are grouped together, let a shroud,
stripped from some privileged corpse—for few have
them now—be for its proper price displayed. Stop
not here! Change your war-crest. America has her
eagle—let England have her vulture! What emblem
more fit for the rapacious power, whose statesmanship
depopulates, and whose commerce is gorged with
famine prices? That is her proper signal. It will
commemorate a greater victory than that of Agincourt,
than that of Blenheim, than that of Moodkee. It will

commemorate the victories of Schull, of Skibbereen, of
Bantry. But, sir, this is a false alarm. Whatever the
monarch journalist of Europe may say, Ireland, thank
God! is not down yet. She is on her knees ; but
her withered hand is clenched against the giant, and
she has yet the power to strike. Last year, from the
Carpathian heights, we heard the shout of the Polish
insurrectionist—" There is hope for Poland whilst in
Poland there is a life to lose." Sir, there is hope for
Ireland whilst in Ireland there is a life to lose. True
it is, thousands upon thousands of our people have
been swept down, but thousands upon thousands
still survive, and the fate of the dead should quicken
the purpose of the living. The stakes are too high for
us to give up the game, until the last card has been
played—too high for us to fling ourselves in despair
upon the coffins of our starved and swindled partners.
A peasant population, generous and heroic, is at stake.
A mechanic population, intelligent and upright, is at
stake. These great classes—that form the very nerve
and marrow of a nation—without which a nation cannot
be saved—without which there is, in fact, no nation to
be saved—without which a professional class is so much
parchment and powdered horsehair—and a nobility a
mere glittering spectre—these great primary classes
are at stake. Shall these, too, be the spoils of England ? Has she not won enough already ; has she
not pocketed enough of your money ? And what
she has got, is she not determined to keep ? You
have seen a letter from Mr. Grogan, a few weeks
since, to the Lord Mayor. It appears that England
will ship off the Irish beggars from Liverpool ; she
will not ship off the Irish absentees from London.
And, tell me, has she not eaten enough of your food,
and has she not broken down enough of your manufac-

6

tures, and has she not buried enough of your people? Recount for a moment, a few of your losses. The cotton manufacture of Dublin, which employed 14,000 operatives, has been destroyed. The 3,400 silk-looms of the Liberty have been destroyed. The stuff and serge manufacture, which employed 1,491 operatives, has been destroyed. The calico-looms of Balbriggan have been destroyed. The flannel manufacture of Rathdrum has been destroyed. The blanket manufacture of Kilkenny has been destroyed. The camlet trade of Bandon, which produced £100,000 a year, has been destroyed. The worsted and stuff manufactures of Waterford have been destroyed. The rateen and frieze manufactures of Carrick-on-Suir have been destroyed. One business, alone, survives! One business, alone, thrives, and flourishes, and dreads no bankruptcy! That fortunate business—which the Union Act has not struck down, but which the Union Act has stood by—which the absentee drain has not slackened, but has stimulated—which the drainage acts and navigation laws of the Imperial Senate have not deadened, but invigorated—that favoured, and privileged, and patronised business, is the Irish coffin-maker's. He, alone, of our thousand tradesmen and mechanics, has benefitted by the Union—he, alone, is safe from the general insolvency—he, alone, has reason to be grateful to the Imperial Senate—he, alone, is justified in voting, at the next election, for the accomplices of the Whig minister of England. Sir, the fate which the prophet of the Lamentations announced, three thousand years ago, to the people of Israel, has come to pass this year in this island of faith, of genius, and of sorrow: "And I will bring a nation upon you from far—an ancient nation—a nation of mighty men, whose quiver is like to an open sepulchre;

and they shall eat up thine harvest and thy bread, which thy sons and daughters should eat ; and thy vines and fig trees ; and they shall eat up thy flocks and thy herds, which thy sons and daughters should eat ; and they shall impoverish thy fenced cities, wherein thou trusted." Yet, sir, out of this tribulation and this woe, there is a path to a brighter fate and a happier land. The God of Israel and of Ireland never yet sent a scourge, that He did not send the means whereby its evils might be alleviated. The same voice that bid the fiery serpents to the desert, ordained that an image should be erected there for the chastised to look to, and be saved ; and the same tongue that uttered the prophecy I have recited to you, promised that " the city should be built up—that the vines should grow again upon the mountains of Samaria— that the song should be heard once more from the height of Zion—and they who were in captivity and mourning should sing again with gladness, and shout among the chief of the nations." Sir, out of our captivity and mourning we shall surely go forth, if we truly love this land, and act with the courage which true love inspires. We must have nothing to do with these whining counsellors who bid us sound a truce, retire from the field, visit the sick, and bury the dead. The minister has committed too many crimes against this country to have an hour's repose. In this very hall, a few days since, an honest and an able fellow-citizen of yours, Mr. Fitzgibbon, distinctly proved, in a speech of great argumentative power, and great statistical research, that the present desperate condition of the country was to be ascribed, not to the ignorance, not to the negligence, not to the mistake of the minister, but to a downright and deliberate compact of his with the mercantile interest of England, by which the lives of the Irish people were mercilessly surrendered to the cupidity of the British merchants. Sir, I know not when, or where the scourge inflicted by this minister will cease to devastate. Those whom the famine has spared are flying to the emigrant ships, and rushing, panic-struck, from the land where England has lodged the foundations of her despotism in the graves of the people. I hold in my hands returns of the number of emigrants from the ports of Dublin, Waterford, Limerick, and Cork, for the present season. Now, it appears from these returns, that, although the season has only just somewhat commenced—that, although, in fact, one month only of the emigration season has expired—the number of emigrants from the above-mentioned ports is nearly treble the number that left during the entire season in '46. Again, I must observe that these returns are imperfect—the emigrants that have sailed from Liverpool, and other English ports, not being included in them. And the worst of it all is, that it is not the mere bone and sinew we are losing in this way, but the only current capital of the country. Yet, sir, it is almost selfish to deplore this emigration. Why should we grudge our generous and heroic peasantry a better home, in a new country? Why should we grudge them their emancipation from English rule? Why should we grudge them their life, their bread, their liberty? The sun, each evening as he passes over the graves of their fallen brothers, beckons them to follow him, in his golden track, across the waves, to a land of freedom. Let them go! For a while, at least, let them leave this island, where England has planted her own beggars, in the shape of chief secretaries, and poor-law commissioners, and archbishops. Let them go to the land where English law was flung to the four winds—where a young stripling of a colony sprang up, and dashed an old and sturdy empire to the earth. There they will be safe from English law, and, therefore, safe from beggary, from starvation, and from pestilence. But, sir, we have vowed to remain here, and meet whatever fate is coming. And now, that thousands have rotted into the earth which gave them birth— and now, that thousands are flying from our shores, that they may not tempt the scourge to strike them —we are bound to work the harder—to do double duty—that, at least, the remnant of an old and honourable nation may be saved. Sir, we must adopt a policy suited to these times. We have now to struggle, not merely against adverse opinions, but against death itself. The desperate condition of the country demands a bold and decisive policy. From this hour, sir, let us have done with the English parliament—on this very night, sir, let us resolve to close our accounts with that parliament. Send no more petitions across the Channel. For fifty years you have petitioned, and the result has been 500,000 deaths. Henceforth, be that parliament accursed! Spurn it as a fraud, a nullity, a usurpation. Spurn it as such on the authority of Saurin, who declared that the Union Act was not obligatory on conscience; that, in the abstract, resistance to it was a duty; and the exhibition of that resistance a mere question of prudence. Spurn it as such on the authority of Plunket, who declared the incompetency of parliament to pass the Act of Union —declared that if such an act should pass it would be a nullity, and no man in Ireland would be bound to obey it. Spurn it as such, on the authority of Grattan, who declared that the competency of parliament to pass the Act of Union, was the competency of delinquency, the competency of abdication, the competency of treason! Confederates of Dublin! you know that this Imperial Parliament is a fraud, a nullity, a usurpation. You know it is worse than all this. You know that it is a curse—a penalty—a plague. You are knaves if you do not speak your conviction—you are cowards if you do not act as your conviction bids you act. If you adopt petitions send them to the Queen. She has a right to wear an Irish crown. We shall assert that right. She has a right to summon her Irish Parliament to sit in this city, and, spite of the disloyal and defrauding minister—spite of the disloyal and defrauding Commons, who would suspend the royal functions—we shall boldly and loyally assert that right. The Irish crown must no longer be a cipher. The Irish sceptre, and the Irish flag, must cease to be mere figures of speech—they must become empowered and recognised realities. The members of your Council have determined, by a recent resolution, to support at the hustings no candidate for representative honours who will not pledge himself to an absolute independence of all English parties—who will not pledge himself, against taking or soliciting, for himself or others, any office of emolument under any English government whatsoever. Some gentlemen may say, this is going too far. I contend it does not go half far enough ; and I am delighted to find you agree with me in the opinion. The fact is, we must go much farther. At our next meeting—I am speaking my own sentiments very frankly to you, and, of course, no one is responsible for them but myself—at our next meeting, I think it would be most advisable for us to adopt a resolution to this effect : That the members of the Irish Confederation shall support, at the hustings, no candidates for representative honours who will not pledge themselves to stay at home, and deliberate in this city and in no place else, upon the best means to save this king-dom. One circumstance, at least, is favourable to our policy, and assures us of success—the power of the Whigs is at an end in Ireland. No man now dare stand up, in an assembly of Irish citizens, to recommend the " paternal Whigs " to the filial confidence of the Irish people. The country, thank God, is done with them for ever. Their patronage will no longer save them with the people. Their jail deliveries will no longer save them with the people. Nothing, sir, will save them with the Irish people. They may have their command nights at the theatre and they may bow, and kiss hands, to an enchanted dress circle, and a gazing pit—they may dine at the Mansion House—take wine, all round, with the Sword Bearer, the Water Bailiff, the City Marshal, the Town Councillors and Aldermen of the Reformed Corporation, and drink the " Prosperity of Old Ireland " to the tune of " Rule, Britannia, Rule ! "—on the same day that the new docks at Birkenhead are opened by Lord Morpeth, they may graciously open, on the Irish side of the Channel, a Grand Metropolitan Head Soup-Kitchen—they may furnish a select party of the blind, the crippled, and the dumb of the Mendicity, with a " guard of honour," during their experimental repast—they may embellish the beggary of the nation with all the elegance of the Castle, and all the pageantry of the barrack—they may make a most glittering display of our most sickening degradation, and the bugles of their garrison may summon the fashion of the squares, and the aristocracy of the clubs, to the coronation of Irish pauperism, and the final consummation of the Union —nought will avail them. Their fate is decided—there is a sentence written against them, in the blood of the people, upon the walls of their council chamber, and many other inquests, besides that of Galway, have found them guilty of the wilful murder of the people. And now that we are done with these Whigs— now that we fully understand what their " comprehensive measures " mean—what their " ameliorations " mean—what their " political economy " leads to—what their " reductions of 20 per cent." accomplish—now that we are fully convinced that they are the most complimentary and the most conscienceless—the most promising and the most prevaricating—the most patronising, and the most perfidious—the most paternal, and the most murderous—of our English enemies— now that we have broken, from henceforth and for ever, from all English parties—now that we shall pest them no longer with our petitions, nor rack them with our prayers—now that we hold their Commons, as far as we are concerned, to be a fraud, a nullity, and a usurpation—now that we scout it as a penalty, and loathe it as a plague—now, indeed, that, in our souls, we firmly and passionately believe, that

" Our hope, our strength, is in ourselves alone,"

let us look, with all the anxiety and earnestness which a last struggle should inspire, into our own country, and see what power we have there to save its life and win its freedom. Let us see if we cannot give a few practical answers to a few of Bishop Berkeley's queries. Let us see, in fact, if we cannot devise some mode by which the quiver of this mighty foe, that has come upon us, shall cease to be like an open sepulchre; by which this nation shall keep to itself the harvest, and the bread, and the flocks, and the herds, which her sons and daughters should eat, and by which our fenced cities shall not be impoverished. Sir, I desire to have this done, not by the isolated power of one

great section, but by the aggregate power of all sections
of the Irish community. I desire that the Irish nation
should act, not in divisions, but in one solid square. I
am one of the people, but I am no democrat. I am for
an equality of civil rights—but I am no republican.
I am for vesting the responsibilities and the duties of
government in three estates. I think that, in a free
state, an aristocracy is a wise—an ennobling institution.
Like all human institutions, it has its evil suscepti-
bilities ; and the history of aristocracy, like all other
histories, has its chapters of crime and folly. But I
can conceive no state complete without it. It is the
graceful and pictured architrave of the great temple,
sacred to law and freedom, of which the people are the
enduring foundations and the sustaining pillars. Whilst
the peasant tills the land, in which the law should
recognise his right of proprietorship, as it is in France,
as it is in Prussia—whilst the mechanic plies his craft,
from which the law should keep aloof the crushing
influences of foreign competition, as it is in Germany,
as it is in Belgium—whilst the merchant supplies the
deficiencies of the soil with the superfluities of other
lands, and drives a princely trade beneath the auspices
of a native flag—whilst the priest protects the purity
of the altar, and the scholar vindicates the reputation
of the schools—let the noble—residing amongst those
who enrich his inheritance by their toil, or contribute
to his luxury by their skill—be the patron of those
pursuits in which the purer genius of a nation lives—
pursuits which chasten and expand a nation's soul—
which lift it to what is high, and prompt it to what is
daring—which infuse the spirit of immortality into the
very ruins of a nation, and which, even when the
labours of a nation are at a close—when its commercial
energies are dead—when its mechanic faculties have

ceased to act, bids it live—as Athens lives, as Florence lives, as Venice lives—in the lessons of the historian, and the raptures of the poet. Thus, sir, with each of the several classes of the community fulfilling its distinct mission, and, in a separate sphere, contributing to the peace, and wealth, and vigour of the entire state, do I desire this island to advance in a righteous and an eminent career—sustained by its inherent strength—governed by its native wisdom—ennobled by its native genius—thankful for its sustenance to no foreign sympathiser—thankful for its security to no foreign soldier—a model, rather than a warning, a blessing, rather than a burden, to the nations that surround her—no longer exciting their pity by the spectacle of its infirmities, but commanding their respect by the exhibition of its powers. But, sir, a time comes when the people can wait no longer for the aristocracy. There is a time when the titles of the nobility must give way to the charter of the people. There is a time when the established laws of the land forfeit their sanctity and become a curse. The time when these titles of the nobility must give way— when these " established laws of the land " must cease to act—is when a nation's life is quivering on its lip. Standing in this assembly of the people, I, who have sprung from the people ; I, who have no honours to boast of, save those honours which the people have conferred upon my father ; I, who never sat at the table of a lord, and am as thoroughly indifferent to the compliments of the order as I am thoroughly anxious for their co-operation in this struggle ; standing in this assembly of the people, in the name of the people, I now make this last appeal to the aristocracy of Ireland. I do so, that in our day of triumph, we may lead no fellow-countryman in chains, nor scout him as an alien from our ranks. There is not an hour—no, not an instant to be lost. Every grave that opens to receive a victim of English rule, widens and deepens the chasm that has, for years, divided the two great classes of the country. Sir, it is useless to argue it—the people, without the aristocracy, when driven to the last extremity, have the power to win their freedom. One thing, at least, is certain—the people will not consent to live another year in a wilderness and a graveyard. I alone do not say so. The bold historian of the crimes and victories of Cromwell has said so. Lords and Commons of Ireland ! hear his words, and be instructed by them—" And when the general result has come to the length of perennial, wholesale starvation, argument, extenuation, logic, pity, and patience on that subject may be as considered as drawing to a close. All just men, of what outward colour so ever in politics or otherwise, will say—' This cannot last. Heaven disowns it—Earth is against it. Ireland will be burnt into one black, unpeopled field of ashes rather than this should last.' "

Placehunting

Speech Delivered in the Music Hall, July 7th, 1847, Against the Solicitation and Acceptance of Places, Salaries, etc., from the English Government.

I have the honour, sir, to second the resolution proposed by Mr. O'Gorman. The advice to which it refers, and which this meeting is called upon to sanction, has been censured. I am prepared to defend it ; and, I trust, this meeting will have reason to declare that it is wise, expedient, just. Reviewing the political movements that have taken place in Ireland for some years past, it seems to me, sir, that in this country those principles of public virtue have been systematically decried which give to a people their truest dignity and their surest strength. At different times, in other countries, when the people found it necessary to recover or augment their rights, we have seen the finest attributes of the heart and mind called forth, and society present the most brilliant instances of morality and heroism which mankind could furnish. In such countries the progress of liberty has been the progress of virtue. Thus has the history of freedom become the second gospel of humanity—an inspiration to those who suffer—an instruction to those who struggle. True it is, there have been faults, there have been errors, there have been crimes in the revolutions to which I now advert, which fling a shadow across the epitaph of many an honoured grave. But, high above these errors and these crimes, ascends the genius and the virtue of these revolutions—pure, brilliant, and imperishable. Let us consult the star. If we read not the destiny of our country in its glory, in its purity we read the virtues that qualify for freedom, and ennoble the citizen even in his chains. We read that truth, generosity, self-sacrifice, have been the virtues of the true patriot, and the strongest weapons of his success. It has not been so in Ireland for many years. Truth has been frittered away by expediency— generosity has been supplanted by selfishness—self-sacrifice has been lampooned as an ancient folly, which, in these less classic, but more philosophic times, it would be downright lunacy to imitate. But what is the character of our cause ? It is wise, generous, and heroic. Wise, for the necessities and interests of our country·dictate it. Generous, for it includes the rights of all—the rights of the democracy, the priesthood, the nobility. Heroic, for it inspires the loftiest ambition— suggesting schemes the boldest that the courage of a nation could attempt—the grandest that the ability of a nation could accomplish. The genius of Ireland has been its apostle—the chivalry of Ireland has been its champion. Triumphant in the brightest period of our history—encircled with the dazzling memories of an Irish senate, an Irish commerce, an Irish army—it is the noblest cause, sir, in which an Irish citizen could have the ambition to serve, or the heroism to suffer. Forty-seven years have passed by since that cause was sold for place and pension, and in the very hall where Henry Grattan impeached the corruption of the minister, and the perfidy of the placeman, we hear this day the clank of gold, which bids us still remember the base bargain that was ratified within its walls. Let it clank and glitter still ! It will be a warning to the people.

It will remind them of the vice that led to vassalage, and which—still prevailing, still greedy, still rapacious—degrades the character of the country, effeminates its power, and repels its liberty. Not by the perpetuation of this vice, but by its utter extinction, will the national cause—the cause of Swift, of Charlemont, and of Grattan—advance and triumph. This doctrine, we are told, is exceedingly erroneous. To Repeal the Union, it is essential that Repealers should take places—that is the correct doctrine! To give the minister a decisive stroke, it is expedient to equip the patriot hand with gold! Strenuously oppose the minister, you must, first of all, beg of the minister, then be his very humble servant, and, if possible, conclude with being his much obliged servant! The financial statement between the two countries cannot be properly made out until some Repeal accountant has had a friendly intercourse with the Treasury, and a propitious acquaintance with the Mint! Absenteeism has been enormously increased by the Union, and, therefore, it is that our peaceful Repealer procures a colonial appointment, and, exemplifying in his person all the evils of the system, administers British law, beyond the seas, upon strictly Repeal principles! Impoverished by the Union—beggared by the Union—driven to the last extremity of destitution by the Union—it is advisable that we should prove all this to the minister and the parliament with our pockets full of salaries, and our family circumstances in full bloom! Denouncing the rapacity of England, we are to share her spoils. Impeaching the minister, we are to become his hirelings. Claiming independence, shouting for independence, foaming for independence, we are to crawl, betimes, to the Castle, and there crave the luxuries and the shackles of the slave. Thus we are told to act! Thus we are implored to agitate! This is the great, peaceful, moral, and constitutional doctrine! This, the true way to make us the noblest people on the face of the globe, and restore Ireland to her place amongst the nations of the earth! Mean, venal, and destructive doctrine! teaching the tongue to cool and compliment, that has burned and denounced. Mean, venal, and destructive doctrine! teaching the people, on their march to freedom, to kneel and dance before the golden idol in the desert. Mean, venal, and destructive doctrine! teaching whining, teaching flattery, teaching falsehood. Scout it, spurn it, fling it back to the Castle from whence it came—there let it lie amongst the treasured instructions of tyranny, and the precious revelations of treason! Sir, we oppose Mr. John O'Connell because he is the advocate of this system. We oppose him, because he has positively declared that he will solicit places from the English government for his friends. We oppose him, because we conscientiously believe that he sustains a system which enervates the national strength, and therefore imperils the national cause. This we sincerely believe, and experience justifies the belief. Look back to the year 1833—note the conspicuous Repealers of that year. Mark down those amongst them who took Place after the memorable debate in April, '34. Run through the newspapers of the last ten or thirteen years, and tell me, in what political position do you detect these priceless patriots? In the chair of Conciliation Hall—in the committee box—in the reserved seats for strangers—on Tara, with the gallant peasantry of Kildare and Meath—on the Green of Donnybrook, with the bannered and battalioned trades of Dublin—in the Rotunda, on the 30th of May, 1845, where citizenship received the honours of monarchy, and was invested with more than its legitimate authority ? Why, sir, you might as well inquire if these gentlemen had left a card in the moon, or had been at a pic-nic in the bowels of Vesuvius. The porter outside the Chief Secretary's in the Upper Castle Yard, will tell you where they have been. The butlers in the Viceregal Lodge will tell you where they have been. The policeman on the beat at Chesham Place will tell you where they have been. The coiners in the Mint will tell you where they have been. The clerks of the Board of Trade may let you know something concerning their mercantile anxieties. I hold in my hand a book, entitled " The Voice of the Nation." I beg leave to read the following extract from it : " When the last agony of the Whigs was approaching, great was the desire to conciliate and make friends. . . . Notice had been taken at the Castle of the immense number of applications pressing in from those who, throughout various localities in Ireland, had been ' leaders of the people ' in former agitations. These applications were carefully registered and noted ; and when the list was found to contain the names of a large majority of such persons, the ' declaration ' was made as a proclamation and warning to them, and made with only too shameful success. Nearly all those leaders were silenced. They did, indeed,

' Fall down,
And foul corruption triumphed over them ! '

Corruption, that other arm of England, whenever she seeks to strike down the rising liberties of Ireland ! Force, when we give her the excuse for using it ! Corruption, when she cannot provoke us to give her that excuse ! " Who wrote this ? A jealous and embittered Conservative ? A vehement and vicious re-

William Smith O'Brien

volutionist? A discarded Orangeman? A flippant and sarcastic infidel? A Chartist Repealer, gentlemen? No—it was the honourable member for Kilkenny—he who, in the very death-chamber of his father, snatches at the vacant crown, and strives to balance in his little hand the massive sceptre which the colossal king alone could wield! Out of his own mouth do we condemn the apologist of place-begging. We arm ourselves with its written sentence against corruption, and with that sentence we give him battle on the hustings. Sir, we have seen the result of this system in the first agitation for Repeal, and, whatever it may cost, we shall oppose it in the second. Sanction this system, and you set the seeds of venality in that body, which, to be formidable, must be exempt from all impurities. Sanction this system, and you entice men to the national lists, who, but for the golden apples scattered along the course, would never join you in the race to freedom. Thus it is that gentlemen will appear upon the hustings as Repeal candidates, who do not in truth ambition the independence of the country, but avail themselves of the cry to extort from the minister a compensation for their presumed apostacy. Lamartine, in his history of the Girondists, has said of Danton that " he merely threatened the court to make the court desirous of buying him—that he only opened his mouth to have it stuffed with gold." Sir, there have been, there are, and there will be, hundreds of Repealers to whom this description will precisely apply, and, if we do not utterly break up the system that produces them, we will propagate the contaminating race, until the whole manhood of the country has become diseased and powerless. And, sir, with God's good blessing, whilst we have nerve and voice, we will urge this war against corruption, and the people will back us, I am confident.

7

They must be heartily sick of the system that has exacted so many sacrifices from them, whilst it has contributed exclusively to the benefit of their leaders. Cork has done its duty in this respect. The citizens of the southern capital have met, and they declare that this venality shall cease. I trust sincerely, that the example will be followed, and that the pledge, which was exacted in Cork, will be exacted in Limerick, in Mayo, in Dundalk, in Kilkenny, in Dungarvan, in every borough, and in every county, where a Repeal candidate presents himself. As to Waterford, my father is one of the Repeal candidates for that city. Now, proud as I would be to see my father represent his native city—proud as I would be to share with him the fatigue and the vexation of the contest—proud as I would be to see him triumph over the ministerialist who at present represents that city—proud as I would be to stand by him on the hustings when the people hailed him as the successful opponent of an insolent imperialism—proud as, I know, I would then feel, with the thought that I had done my utmost to level the Whig power at the feet of my fellow-citizen—yet I do sincerely tell you that if he does not subscribe to the pledge of the Confederation—though I know he hates Whiggery from his heart—though I know that he would scorn to ask the slightest favour of any faction—yet I will feel bound in conscience not to vote for him. But, sir, we are told, that soliciting places for others is quite a different thing from the representative soliciting place or pension for himself. I admit there is a difference. In my mind, however, the difference consists in the latter being the more injurious and discreditable case. For, in the former case, the representative gets his place, or whatever else it may be, and we are sure to have done with him. Like the great Athenian, he is seized with an excessive hoarseness the moment he grasps the cup of Herpalus, and, owing to the bandage round his neck, cannot possibly harangue against the Macedonian! But, in the former case, the representative remains amongst us—day after day multiplying his obligations to the government by a series of golden links—day after day stimulating amongst the people a gross appetite for the dregs and droppings of a foreign court, when he should expand their ambition, and bid them seek in the prosperity of their country, and in that alone, the purest and most unfailing source of private happiness. Sir, once for all, we must have an end of this money-making in the public forum. The pursuit of liberty must cease to be a traffic. Let it resume amongst us its ancient glory—let it be with us a passionate heroism. Fear not dissension. Dissension is good where truth is to be saved. Repeal does not triumph, I contend, where the repeal principles of Conciliation Hall prevail. Repeal does not incur defeat where these principles are swamped by Whiggery or Conservatism. In the former case it is Whiggery, masked and muffled, that succeeds—in the latter it is Whiggery, masked and muffled, that is beaten. Disdaining, then, the calumnies of the public writer, and the invectives of the public orator; however bitter society may sneer; however coarsely a section of the multitude may curse; assert this righteous principle. Rescue the cause of Ireland from the profanation of those who beg, and the control of those who bribe. Ennoble the strife for liberty, and be it here, as it has been in other countries, a gallant sacrifice—not a vulgar game. Conform to one precept of the English parliament—depend upon your own resources. Demanding independence, be thoroughly independent. Be as independent of this Russell, the English minister,

as of Metternich of Vienna, or Guizot of Paris.   Cherish
in its full integrity this fine virtue, without which there
will be no true liberty amongst you, whatever be your
institutions.   Bereft of it, the heart of the nation will
be cold, and cramped, and sordid.   Bereft of it, the
arts will have no enduring impulse, and commerce
no invigorating soul.   Bereft of it, society degenerates,
and the mean, the frivolous, and the vicious triumph.
The idler, the miser, and the coward, may laugh at
these sentiments.   The worms of the Castle, I know,
would eat them from the hearts of the young, the
generous, and the gifted.   The old champions of
faction—in whose withered souls all that is pure and
generous in our nature has rotted out—may drive their
poisoned pens, and ply their tainted tongues, in their
profane crusade against them.   Then, too, may come
the dull philosopher of the age to rebuke our folly,
our want of sense, our indiscretion ; and proclaim that
patriotism, a wild and glittering passion, has died out
—that it could not coincide with civilization, the
steam-engine, and free trade.   It is false !   The virtue
that gave to Paganism its dazzling lustre—to barbarism
its redeeming trait—to Christianity its heroic form,
is not dead.   It still lives to preserve, to console, to
sanctify humanity.   It has its altar in every clime—
its worship and festivities.   On the heathered hills
of Scotland, the sword of Wallace is yet a bright
tradition.   The genius of France, in the brilliant
literature of the day, pays its enthusiastic homage
to the piety and heroism of the young maid of Orleans.
In her new senate hall, England bids her sculptor
place, among the effigies of her greatest sons, the
images of her Hampden and her Russell.   In the gay
and graceful capital of Belgium, the daring hand of
Geefs has reared a monument, full of glorious meaning,

to the three hundred martyrs of the revolution. By the soft, blue waters of Lake Lucerne stands the chapel of William Tell. On the anniversary of his revolt and victory, across those waters, as they glitter in the July sun, skim the light boats of the allied cantons. From the prows hang the banners of the republic, and as they near the sacred spot, the daughters of Lucerne chant the hymns of their old, poetic land. Then bursts forth the glad *Te Deum*, and heaven hears again the voice of that wild chivalry of the mountains which, five centuries since, pierced the white eagle of Vienna, and flung it bleeding on the rocks of Uri. At Innsbruck, in the black side of the old cathedral, the peasant of the Tyrol kneels before the statue of Andreas Hofer. In the defiles and valleys of the Tyrol, who forgets the day on which he fell within the walls of Mantua? It is a festive day all through his quiet, noble land. In that old cathedral his inspiring memory is recalled amid the pageantries of the altar—his image appears in every house—his victories and virtues are proclaimed in the songs of the people—and when the sun goes down, a chain of fires—in the deep, red light of which the eagle spreads his wings and holds his giddy revelry—proclaim the glory of the chief, whose blood has made his native land a sainted spot in Europe. Sir, shall we not join in this glorious worship, and here in this Island—anointed by the blood of many a good and gallant man—shall we not have the faith, the duties, the festivities of patriotism? You discard the weapons of these heroic men—do not discard their virtues. Elevate the national character, and serve the national cause with generous hearts and stainless hands. You have pledged yourselves to strive in this Confederation for the independence of your country, within the limits of the Constitution. Keep within the Constitution, but do not compromise the virtue of the state. Confront corruption wherever it appears—scourge it from the hustings—scourge it from the public forum—and whilst proceeding with the noble task to which you have vowed your lives and fortunes, let this proud thought enrapture and invigorate your hearts, that in seeking the independence of your country you have preserved its virtue from the seductions of a powerful minister and the infidelity of bad citizens.

The Citizen and the Mob

JULY 15TH, 1847.

[The Confederation, defying the threats of the O'Connellite mob in Dublin, continued to hold its usual public meetings, after t e cry was raised that " the Young Irelanders had killed O'Connell." On the night of July 15th, Meagher presided at a public meeting of the Confederation in the Music Hall, Abbey Street, which was surrounded by a furious rabble. After the conclusion of the meeting, Meagher, Mitchel, O'Gorman and the other Young Ireland leaders were attacked in Abbey Street and O'Connell Street by the mob, one member of which attempted to stab Meagher. The Confederates, thereafter organised a body of 400 of their members, chiefly skilled artisans and clerks, who acted as a bodyguard for the Young Ireland leaders on their way to and from the public meetings of the Confederation and in a few weeks the attempt to suppress freedom of speech in Dublin was sternly ended.]

Gentlemen, I sincerely thank you for the honour you have now conferred upon me. At any time I would esteem it an enviable privilege to occupy the chair of the Irish Confederation. On the present occasion I consider it a very eminent distinction. We have met here this night for a special reason. We have met here this night to maintain the privileges of the Citizen against the despotism of the Mob. The right to meet in public council we are prepared to vindicate in defiance of every threat—in the teeth of every peril. That right we would not surrender to the minister though he came to demand it commissioned by the Parliament and backed by the army. Neither shall we surrender it to the rabble, though they come to extort it with their blows and steep it in our blood. This time last year the secession took place. Since then we have stood erect in spite of the most vicious enmity.

Misrepresentations were tried and they have failed.
Indictments for high treason were tried and they have
failed. Charges of infidelity were tried and they have
done us very little harm. Charges of intriguing with
the Castle were placarded about the town, and they
have served to amuse the public, to sell a paper—and
that is all. In private as in public the venal tongue
for the last twelve months has been busy at its task
of defamation. Every effort that malice could suggest,
that depravity could patronise, that penury could be
bribed to perfect, has been made to crush us beneath
the feet of the people amongst whom we had dared to
preach the true principles of freedom. Upheld by a
sense of right, strengthened by the sympathies of the
upright and intelligent portion of the community, we
battled through the winter and maintained the position
we thought it our duty to assume. But malice had not
done its utmost, it appears. There was yet another
arrow in the quiver, and that should take the lives of
those whom falsehood and invective had not struck
down. Gentlemen, the attempt has been made to put
us down by brute force—it was made on the last night
of meeting, and because it was made we are here this
night. Let the coarse enemies of Conciliation Hall
renew the attempt. Against them, to the death, we
shall maintain the right of Citizens to meet, wherever
and whenever they think best, to consult upon the
public interests. No power shall deprive us of that
right whilst we have life to worship and to guard it.
The sceptre shall not deprive us of that right—neither
shall the bludgeon. But this is what we had just
reason to expect. It has been the fate of many better
men who have preceded us, and thus it will be to the
end of time. The career of truth is through a crowd of
perils, and freedom is not so much the gift of fortune

as it is the reward of suffering. Nerved by these attacks, proceed as you have begun. Confederates of Dublin, remember the proud title that has been conferred upon you. When you came forth in November last, two thousand strong, to make war against a policy that had debauched and diseased the political power of your country, you were styled the pioneers of Irish freedom. The intelligence of the country hailed you as such, the virtue of the country blessed you as such, the enthusiasm of the country worshipped you as such. Sustain the title and keep the van. Depend upon it, the nation will in time fall in, and the march to the old Senate house will be made along the road which it will have been your heroic achievement to have opened. It is quite true that your enrolled associates are few. Do not conceal it—avow it manfully—your organised forces are not numerous. But each day brings a new conscript to your ranks, for the principles of the Confederation are becoming the principles of the country. You were the first to pronounce against place-begging. From this hall went forth the decree that the representatives of the people should not beg from the Government of England ; that in doing so the representatives of the people impaired the character, diseased the strength, imperilled the liberty of Ireland ; therefore that the representatives who become the beggars of the minister would be guilty against the country and should be declared its enemies. The provinces ratify the decree. Cork affirms that it is wise, virtuous, and essential. Limerick affirms that it is wise, virtuous, and essential. Galway affirms that it is wise, virtuous, and essential. Everywhere the people have hailed this decree—have read, have studied and have sanctioned it. Thus it is, that whilst you have not as yet acquired the power to emancipate the country, you have inspired the virtue that prevents it from being sold. You have saved the country from being for the second time the renegade sutler of the Whig faction. You have snatched the flag that flew at Mullaghmast from the hands of those who would have delivered it to the minister, and it is owing to your virtue that it does not fly to-day beneath the Union Jack from the walls of Woburn Abbey. You did not support—you did not even tolerate this minister. You are free from the guilt of his policy—you did not leave Repeal " an open question " with him, to be minced by him into scraps and instalments of " justice." This time last year this minister took office. He passed from the Opposition to the Ministerial benches and amid the cheers of the English Radicals and the greedy chatterings of the Irish Liberals, undertook to govern Ireland without the assistance of an Arms Bill. What was then the condition of Ireland? It was poor, but it was not bankrupt. It was hungry, but it was not famished. It was worn with misery, but it was not rotten with the plague. It had its damp, dark cabins, but it had not its reeking fever-sheds. It had its acres of waste lands, but it had not its acres of graves. There were eight millions in Ireland on that day—there are now two millions of them dead. Do not these two million victims cry for vengeance? Will you tolerate the men whose policy has been more sweeping than the blast— more scathing than the lightning? Will you tolerate the men who " tried " them, excused them, begged from them. Perish two millions more, if such be your tameness and debasement. Meet these Whigs upon the hustings—meet them boldly—meet them resentfully, meet them to crush them. Show no mercy to them—they have shown no mercy to the people. Leave them to their resources as they have left you to your resources. Down with these ministers and down with their colleagues of Conciliation Hall. Whilst life is left us they shall have a foe. Not till they have beaten us to the earth and trampled on us in the public streets shall we desist. Then let them hold their jubilee. Then let them celebrate the triumph of their pure, their peaceful, their bloodless policy. Then let them enumerate the political victories they have won without the effusion of one drop of blood. Then let them point in ecstasy to their sacred banner, and with tongues that uttered words of vengeance against their fellow-citizens, let them reiterate their favourite maxim that " He who commits a crime gives strength to the enemy." Fearless of these men, continue to act as you have done —continue to be the friends of truth and enemies of corruption. Be assured of this : that they whom you have stood by so manfully—these whose youth has been no obstacle to your confidence—will stand by you to the last—proud to share the calumnies with which you are sure to be assailed—proud to share the trials it will be your destiny to endure—proud to share the dangers that may await you from within and from without—elated with the dazzling hope that burns above the ruins of the island, that having worked steadfastly, intelligently, honestly together, though the lives of some amongst us may be short, we may celebrate together the inauguration of the Irish Senate.

The Ulstermen

SPEECH DELIVERED IN THE MUSIC HALL, BELFAST,
NOVEMBER 15TH, 1847.

Citizens of Belfast, I appear before you as the advocate of those principles, with the resolute assertion of which the proudest reminiscences of Ulster have been identified. I appear before you as the disciple of that creed which, a few years since, was preached from the pulpit of Dungannon Church, and which the armed apostles that issued from it delivered to the nation. If I am wrong, blame your fathers—blot their names from the records of the north—burn their banners, on which " free trade " was written—brand their arms, which saved the nation, and restored the senate. Blame them—they have taught me the principles which you impeach as treason. Blame them—they have taught me the creed which you anathematise as heresy. Blame them—they have taught me to love the frank, bold voice of freedom—to shun the lazy sanctity of servitude. The sentiments they cherished, I would labour to diffuse. The attitude they assumed, I would have their sons assume. The position to which they raised this kingdom, I would urge this kingdom to regain. Therefore, I demand the Repeal of the Act of Union ; and that this act may be repealed, I invoke the spirit of the North. Not for vote by ballot—not for an extension of the franchise—not for corporate reform amendment acts—not for " eleven comprehensive measures "—do I demand

Repeal. These are not the grounds upon which an
Irish citizen should claim for his country the restitution
of her legislative power. The grievances of a class,
the defects of an institution, may be, in time, removed
by that parliament, the legislation of which has, for
so long a period, been conservative of error and abuse.
Political reform is a question common to both countries ;
and you must bear this in mind, that many politicians
in England believe that an assimilation of the franchises,
and various political institutions, of the two countries,
will confirm rather than disturb the control which
England maintains at present over the taxes, the
produce, and the energies of Ireland. On higher
grounds—on grounds that are immutable—on grounds
that are common to all parties in the state—I take
my stand, and beckon the nation to a new career.
That the taxes of this island may be levied and applied,
by its own decrees, for its own particular use and
benefit ; that the produce of the soil may be at our own
free and full disposal, and be dealt with precisely as
the national necessities require ; that the commerce
of the island, protected by native laws, may spring
into a strenuous activity, and cease to be a mere
Channel trade ; that the manufactures of our towns,
encouraged by the premiums which a native parliament
would not hesitate to grant, may revive, and, with a
generous supply, meet the demand which a resident
gentry, and all the public offices connected with the
seat of legislation, would be sure to create ; that, in
fact, the whole property of this island—the food that
sustains—the skill that clothes—the enterprise that
enriches—the genius that adorns—may belong, per-
manently and absolutely, to itself, and cease to be the
property of any other people : on these grounds, sir,
we insist that Ireland shall be exempt from foreign

rule. Against this project, what objection have you
to urge ? Is what we advocate tainted with sectarian-
ism ? Is it distempered with Whiggery ? Does it
predict the fall of Protestantism ? Does it threaten
the rights of property ? I know that many of you
are the enemies of Repeal. I know full well, that, in
the North, Repeal has been identified with Popery,
whilst the Union'has been identified with Protestantism.
I know full well, that, on this side of the Boyne, it has
been declared antagonistic to Orangeism, and that,
with the principles of 1688, a legislative disconnection
from England has been judged incompatible. Your
fathers did not say so. On the 1st of July, 1779, the
Volunteer companies of Belfast held a different opinion.
On that day the Orange cockades were glittering in
their hats, and the same guns that backed the Declaration of Irish Rights, poured forth their volleys in com-
memoration of the great victory you still so vehemently
celebrate. Why have you foresworn the faith of which
your fathers were the intrepid missionaries ? I will
not urge this question deceitfully. You are frank,
blunt men, in Ulster, and speak your opinions boldly.
You like to hear the plain truth, and shall have it.
That there have been circumstances, connected with
the Repeal movement, which justify in a great measure
your hostility to Repeal, I candidly admit. Until
very lately, the movement has worn the features of
the Catholic movement of 1827. Exclusions of Catholics
from the jury box—exclusion of Catholics from government offices, infidel colleges, Propaganda rescripts,
Bequest Acts, Maynooth grants—questions which could
not be discussed without provoking sectarian strife,
and which could not be decided without originating
factions—these, and similar questions, were frequently
introduced at Repeal meetings, giving to them the

complexion of the meetings that preceded the Act of 1829. Instead of keeping to the one plain question —the question upon which, in 1782, the advocate of Catholic claims and the advocate of Catholic disabilities concurred—the question upon which, in 1799, the Catholic Committee and the Orange Lodge pronounced the same opinion—instead of keeping to this one plain question, the leaders of the movement constantly diverged into those topics, upon which, as I have just said, division was inevitable, and from the discussion of which in a popular assembly, I conceive, the fiercest antipathies must arise. Besides, sir, it seems to me that a predominance in the movement was conceded to the Catholic priests, which the Protestant portion of the community could not recognise, and which, I maintain, it would be an abdication of their civil liberty for Protestants to tolerate. " The Priests and the People "—that was the motto of the Repeal Association. " The Citizens of Ireland "—this is the motto of the Irish Confederation. And by this we mean, the peer, the priest, the merchant, the peasant, the mechanic —every class, trade, creed, race, profession—all the elements that move and act within this island—sustaining its existence, and directing its career. Will you adopt that motto ? But, first of all, tell me, do you believe the Union is essential to Irish interests ? Do you believe that we cannot get on through life unless we are bound by an act of parliament to England ? Do you believe that we have been gifted with no inherent strength, and that, without the help of a neighbouring state, we must limp, and stagger through the world ? Is that your faith ? and if it be, whence comes it ? Is it the result of inspiration, or the result of teaching ? Inspiration ! What—the secret tutorship of God ! What—the instruction which the soul receives amid the mysteries of nature, which comes to it borne upon the black pinion of the wave, and bids it go forth and bring a new world into contact with the old—which comes to it along the burning pathways of the stars, and bids it utter those mighty thoughts which shall echo through all ages—which comes to it, even at this day, across the waste and desolation of the desert—wakes an outcast tribe into brilliant heroism, and gives them strength and skill to cope with the cross and sword of the Christian civiliser ! Inspiration ! Utter not the word. No craven faith ever came from thence. Taught from thence, you would spurn the menial's garb, and snap the vassal's fetter. Taught from thence, you would boldly dare, and nobly consummate. Taught from thence, you would find no enterprise too perilous, no eminence too giddy for your ambition to attempt. Taught from thence, you would step from height to height, bearing aloft your country's flag, until you had reached the summit, whence your voice would be heard, and your glory witnessed, from the furthest confine of the earth. From false teaching your timid faith has come. Look to it, and see if it be not false. You cannot do without the aid of England—the Union Act is your stoutest main-stay ! This you have been taught to say. And how is this sustained ? Mr. Pitt assured you that the Union was essential to the local interests of Ireland. In his speech, on the 31st of January, 1799, he declared, that the measure " was designed and calculated to increase the prosperity, and ensure the safety of Ireland." He declared, moreover, that he wished for it " with a view of giving to Ireland the means of improving all its great national resources, and of giving to it its due weight and importance, as a great member of the empire." Is it not absurd to ask the question—Where

Terence Bellew MacManus

are the evidences of increased prosperity, and how
has the safety of Ireland been ensured ? Thel andlord
swamped—the tradesman bankrupt—the farmer in
the poorhouse—are these the evidences of increased
prosperity ? And tell me is it by the scourge or
famine that the safety of Ireland has been ensured ?
I do not enter into the details of ruin which the history
of the Union contains. Were I to do so, I should have
to detain you for many hours ; and, besides, it is an
inquiry that can be more instructively pursued in
private than in public. The Council of the Confederation will take care to have pamphlets and tracts distributed throughout the country, in which these details will be fully given ; for we desire that from a
conviction of its necessity, and from that alone, you
should unite with us in the demand for self-government.
An intelligent concurrence of opinion is the only sure
basis for a firm political combination. The accession
to a political society of men who do not understand
its object—who have not been convinced of the utility
of that object, and the practicability of its attainment
—such an accession, in my mind, is utterly worthless.
Hence, I say, that the meetings of 1843 failed to promote
Repeal. There was no mind at work within those
gigantic masses. There was faith, trust, heroism. But
that which outlives the tumult of a meeting—that
which dies not with the passion the orator has evoked
—that which survives, though the arm may shrivel,
and the heart grow cold—a free, intelligent opinion
was wanting. What, then, do we propose ? Nothing
more than this—that the question of Repeal should
be honestly considered by the country, and that if
the result of this consideration be a conviction of its
necessity, the country should demand Repeal as the
condition of its allegiance. That the country will be

8

in time, and in a very short time, convinced of the necessity of Repeal, I entertain no doubt. That it is already the growing conviction of many minds, hitherto opposed most decisively to Repeal, I firmly believe. What is the meaning of the Irish Council, sitting in the Rotunda, if it be not this—that the affairs of Ireland having been mismanaged by the parliament of England, the citizens of Ireland have been, at length, compelled to assemble, as an Irish parliament would do, to overlook those affairs, and advise upon them ? In that council many of our best citizens deliberate. What does it report ? That the Union must be repealed ? No ; but that the Union has been an experiment, of which the utter prostration of the national interests attests the terrible fatality. Do you refuse to authenticate this report ? Doctor Boyton must be esteemed an authority in the North. He was a zealous opponent of Catholic claims, and a powerful champion of ultra-Conservatism. In 1835 there was a great Protestant meeting at Morrisson's Hotel, Dublin, and at that meeting, Doctor Boyton delivered an anti-Union speech, from which I will read to you the following extract :—

" The exports and imports, as far as they are a test of a decay of profitable occupation—so far as the exports and imports are supplied from the parliamentary returns—exhibit extraordinary evidences of the condition of the labouring classes. The importation of flax seed (an evidence of the extent of a most important source of employment) was—In 1790, 339,745 barrels ; 1800, 327,721 barrels ; 1836, 469,458 barrels. The importation of silk, raw and thrown, was—In 1790, 92,091 ℔s. ; 1800, 79,060 ℔s. ; 1830, 3,190 ℔s. Of unwrought iron—In 1790, 2,271 tons ; in 1800, 10,241 tons ; in 1830, 871 tons. Formerly we spun all our own woollen and worsted yarn. We imported in 1790, only 2,294 ℔s. ; in 1800, 1,880 ℔s. ; in 1826, 662,750 ℔s.—an enormous increase. There were, I understand, upwards of thirty persons engaged in the woollen trade in Dublin, who have become bankrupts since 1821. There has been, doubtless, an increase in the exports of cottons. The exports were —In 1800, 9,147 yards ; 1826, 7,793,873. The exports of cotton from Great Britain were—In 1829, 402,517,196 yards, value £12,516,247, which will give the value of our cotton exports at something less than a quarter of a million—poor substitute for our linens, which in the province of Ulster alone exceeded in value two millions two hundred thousand pounds. In fact, every other return affords unequivocal proof that the main sources of occupation are decisively cut off from the main body of the population of this country. The export of live cattle and of corn has greatly increased, but these are raw material ; there is little more labour in the production of an ox than the occupation of him who herds and houses him ; his value is the rent of the land, the price of the grass that feeds him, while an equal value of cotton, or linen, or pottery, will require for its production the labour of many people for money. Thus the exports of the country now are somewhat under the value of the exports thirty years since, but they employ nothing like the number of people for their production ; employment is immensely reduced— population increased three-eighths. Thus, in this transition from the state of a manufacturing population to an agricultural, a mass of misery, poverty, and discontent is created."

Thus have Mr. Pitt's predictions been verified ; thus has the prosperity of Ireland increased ; thus have its local interests been protected ; and thus its due weight and importance, as a great member of the empire, has been established! Mr. Staunton, in his able essay—an essay which, for its statistical information, I know would be highly prized in the North—has quoted an opinion of the late O'Conor Don, in which the weight and importance of Ireland, as a great member of the empire, is very respectfully set forth. The opinion is simply this—that " any five British merchants waiting upon the minister, to urge on his attention any public subject, would have more weight than the whole body of Irish representatives." In this opinion is it erroneous to coincide? Do you really believe that Ireland is a great member of the British Empire? You might as well say that the boy Jones was a great member of the royal family. He had no right to the privy purse, and you have no claim to the Imperial Exchequer. So you may boast of your English connection, but you'll get nothing by it. Get nothing by it? No; but depend upon it, you will lose everything you have to lose. See what you have lost already. You have lost your manufactures. You have lost your foreign trade. You have lost several public institutions. The Board of Customs has been transferred to London. So have the Revenue and Excise Boards. The Board of Ordnance, within the last few weeks, has been ordered off. And is it not the fashionable news of the day, that Lord Clarendon will be the last of the English Proconsuls, and that the Castle will be given up to the Board of Works, of whose genius for mischief, upon every road in the country, there have been deposited the most embarrassing testimonials? Depend upon this—the English people love old England, and to make her rich and powerful they will exact from you every treasure you possess, and then commit you, most piously, to

Providence and your own resources. Like proper men of business, they mind their own affairs, and will not entrust them to the Diet of Hungary, or the French Chamber of Deputies. And, in doing so, of course, they will pay very little attention to the affairs of Ireland, or any other despicable province. Thus it is, that the grant in aid of your linen manufacture has been withdrawn. Thus it is, that the grant in aid of the deep-sea fisheries has been withdrawn. Thus it is, that the protective duties have been repealed, in spite of the remonstrance of the principal manufacturers of Ireland. Thus it is, that for the reclamation of your five million acres of waste land, they have refused to vote an adequate advance. Thus it is, as Mr. Grey Porter has stated, in the first pamphlet which he published, that, since the Union Act came into operation, only fifteen local acts have passed for Ireland, whilst four hundred and forty-five local acts have passed for Great Britain. I might proceed with these facts, if you did not interrupt me with the exclamation —" Look to Belfast, if you please ; we have thriven here in spite of England—the industry of the people can thwart the injustice of the parliament—cease your spouting—go to work—leave the old parliament house with the bankers—the cashier's office is just as good as a Treasury bench—build the factory—build the warehouse—learn this, that industry is true patriotism, and that for a nation to be prosperous it must cease to be indolent." Now, sir, this is most excellent advice, and I congratulate Belfast upon its miraculous exemption from the ruin in which every other town in Ireland has been embedded. Your fate has been as singular as that of Robinson Crusoe ; and your ingenuity, in making the most of a desert island, has been no less remarkable. But, in ascribing the indigence of the country to the indolence with which you charge it, how do you explain this fact, that, previous to the enactment of the Union, in thousands of factories, now closed up, there were so many evidences of an industrious disposition ?   I cannot run through all them —but, take one or two.   Dublin, with its ninety-one master manufacturers in the woollen trade, employing 4,938 hands ;   Cork, with its forty-one employers in the same trade, giving employment to 2,500 hands ; Bandon, your old southern ally, with its camlet trade, producing upwards of £100,000 a year ;   were these no proofs of an active spirit, seeking in the rugged paths of labour for that gold out of which a nation weaves its purple robe, and moulds its sceptre ?   I cite those towns—I could cite a hundred other towns—Limerick, Roscrea, Carrick-on-Suir, Kilkenny—I cite them against the Union.   You cite Belfast, and because Belfast has prospered, the Union must be maintained !   Is that your argument ?   I do not deny, that whilst Belfast has been industrious, the other places I have mentioned have been inert.   But how does this admission serve the Unionist ?   He admits the existence of an industrious energy, prevailing all through the country, previous to the Union.   In the English Commons, it was asserted by Mr. Sheridan, Mr. Burdett, and, I believe, also by Mr. Tierney.   Mr. Pitt himself bore testimony to it, but said there was room for improvement.   What then ?   The indolence of the country dates from the passing of the Union ; and the fact is indisputable, that whilst the Union has grown old, the country has grown decrepid.   How could it be otherwise ?   In the history of all nations, you will find that, with the decline of freedom the decay of virtue has been contemporaneous.   Restrict the powers —restrict the functions of a nation—and you check the passions that prompt it to what is noble. The nation that does not possess the power to shape its own course, will have no heart, no courage, no ambition. Like the soul, in which a sense of immortality has been extinguished, it will not look beyond to-day—it will do nothing for the morrow. All its acts will be little, and, for the future, it will have no generous aspiration, and, therefore, no heroic effort. Argue you as you please, the plain fact is this—a nation will be indolent, sluggish, slothful, unless it has a security for its outlay, and this security exists solely in the power to protect, by laws and arms, the riches which its industry may accumulate. Do you dispute the fact? Have you no faith in freedom? If so, let the *Northern Whig* supplant the gospel of Dungannon. Go into the churchyard—write " Fool " upon every tombstone that commemorates a Volunteer—and thank your God that you live in an age of commonsense, Whig philosophy, and starvation. Ay, write the sarcasm upon the tombstone of the Volunteer. It may be sacrilege—but it is commonsense. The citizen soldier of 1782 was a fool! He did not sign petitions for out-door relief, but labelled his gun with " free trade." He did not drive to the Castle to beg " justice for Ireland," but drew his sword in College Green, under the statue of King William ; took the oath of independence, and compelled the Castle to do homage to the Senate. He insisted upon a final settlement between the two countries—declared that Ireland should not be an integral portion of a monopolising empire—declared that Ireland should be an independent sovereignty —and, until that settlement was concluded, he " put his trust in God, and kept his powder dry." I am much mistaken if you do not ambition to imitate this " fool." I believe that you desire to have this country occupy an honourable position, and that of its abilities to be great you have formed no mean conception. But as I have already said, you dread Repeal, which means the restoration of the Constitution of 1782, and you cling to the Union, which is an abdication of that Constitution—an abdication by the country of all control over her resources, her revenue, and her existence. The Union Act, you say, is the great charter of Irish Protestantism. But has that charter been held inviolate? Have those ancient privileges been preserved, which, a few years since, gave to Irish Protestantism an authority so supreme? The corporations—once the citadels of the Williamites—have been surrendered to the Radicals; and though, as yet, the civic chain has never shone as a trophy upon the altar of the Catholic, how often, let me ask you, does it glitter in the Protestant pew, for which its brilliancy has been so fastidiously reserved? The Castle, too, has slipped from your hands. The sleek Catholic slave is a greater favourite in that quarter, now-a-days, than an alderman of Skinner's Alley. The Orange flag is designated by a Conservative minister the symbol of vagabondism—your processions are prohibited—and, when you declaim against the spread of Popery, and pray for the repeal of the Emancipation Act, they knock ten mitres of the Established Church into " kingdom come," and vote £26,000 a year to Maynooth. What say you now to the great charter of Protestant supremacy? What said Dr. Maunsell, in the Dublin Corporation, in 1844, when his motion in favour of rotatory parliaments was under discussion? Speaking upon this very subject, he asked the following question: " What is now the position, and what may be the reasonable expectations of Irish Protestants? Two institutions—and two only

—in which they have a special interest, have been suffered to remain—the University and the Church. Now, I ask any reflecting man will he engage that the Protestant University will not, within a year, be thrown as a sop to the monster of agitation ? On this matter the handwriting of the Premier has but recently appeared upon the wall. The question is no longer a mooted one : the days of the University of Dublin, as an exclusively or special Protestant institution, are numbered ; and I will again ask, when the University shall have been sacrificed, how long do Irish Protestants suppose their Church, as a national establishment, will survive ? Surely, if the history of the last fifteen years be remembered, no one, not the most sanguine truster in statesmen, can in his sober moments fail to see that this establishment is already doomed—that the purses of the great English proprietors of Irish soil gape for the remnant of the patrimony of the Church, to the appropriation of which they have already made a first step, by converting it from an actual property in the land to a stipendiary rent-charge ? No ; let no one hope that a minister whose mind is trained in manœuvres for tiding over political shoals will hesitate to slip these the two only remaining anchors of Irish Protestantism, as a national establishment, if doing so will enable him to escape official wreck, even if it were but for a session." Such were the prospects of Protestantism in 1844 ; and, since then, have those prospects been improved ? Alderman Butt is an authority upon this subject, and wherever integrity is prized, his opinion must have weight. At the second meeting of the Irish Council he delivered a most powerful speech upon the condition of Ireland, and in alluding to that establishment, of which he has been for so many years the gifted champion, he made

the following remarks : " Take any of those interests
for which party has contended. Where will they be
when the country is gone ?   Let us take the question
of the Church establishment—a question, perhaps,
which has excited much of angry discussion.   I am one
of those who thought—I still think—that the Protestant
establishment of Ireland ought to be maintained.   I
see gentlemen in this room who have differed with me
honestly and sincerely, I am sure, upon this question.
We have contended about this, and what is the result ?
The question will be settled without the decision of
our disputes.   The poor-rate has swallowed up the
income of the clergy ; and in many districts the Protestant Church has suffered that which you, its most
determined opponents, never proposed.   The present
incumbents will be left, by the operation of the present
pauperism of Ireland, without the means of actual
support.   Thus, while we have been contending about
the Church, the Church is sharing the ruin of the country.
Need I refer to other instances to prove that, struggle
as we will for party interests, no. party interest can
survive our country ?   There are gentlemen here who
have been advocates of the voluntary system—who
have applauded that system, as carried out in Ireland,
in the support of the clergy of the Church of Rome.
I inquire not now into the reasonableness of your
opinions ; but are not these clergy now in many
districts reduced to actual destitution with the misery
of their flocks ?   What interest, I ask again, for which
party was intended, can outlive the ruin of our native
land ? "   This is the declaration of one of the most
eminent of the Irish Protestants.   Is this declaration
false, and do you still maintain that the Union Act is
your great charter ?   Beggary, insult, the sneers of
English prelates, tithe reductions of twenty per cent.—

are these your ancient privileges ? If so, stand to the
Union, and kiss the hand that has given you gall and
wormwood to drink ! If so, stand to the Union, and
be the history of Irish Protestantism henceforth the
history of debasement ! If so, stand to the Union,
and let the spires of your churches mark the way by
which slaves may crawl, like bruised and bleeding
worms, to the grave ! In the summer of 1845 there
was a purer blood rushing through your veins ; and,
from the hills of the south, there were eyes that strained
and glistened, day after day, from the rising to the
setting of the sun, as they looked towards that river,
into which your forefathers knocked the crown of a
craven king, for there a splendid spectacle had been
predicted. Do you forget the prediction ? Do you
forget the menace which the *Evening Mail* flung in
the face of England, when her Prime Minister was
warned that " a hundred thousand Orangemen, with
their colours flying, might yet meet a hundred thousand
Repealers on the banks of the Boyne, and, on a field
presenting so many solemn reminiscences to all, sign
the Magna Charta of Ireland's independence ? " Why
has that rapturous menace been withdrawn ? Repeal
would deliver you into the hands of the priests—a
penal code would exclude the Protestant from the
privileges of the citizen—the Union has made him a
beggar, but Repeal would make him a slave ! You
might as well predict that there will be a Smithfield
fire in College Green, and a Spanish Inquisition in the
House of Lords, where your victories of Aughrim and
the Boyne are worked in gorgeous tapestry upon the
walls. I say here, what I said in Cork—and I am the
more anxious to repeat it, because it has been censured
—I say, that there is a spirit growing up, amongst
the young Catholics of Ireland, which will not bend to

any clerical authority beyond the sanctuary—a spirit which will not permit the priesthood of any religion to hold a political power greater than that which any other class of citizens possess—a spirit which would raise the banner of revolt against the pulpit, if the pulpit preached intolerance to the people—a spirit which would level the altar to the dust, before the bigot had stained it with the sacrifices of the scaffold. Catholic ascendancy ! It is a ghost that frightens you, and, whilst you stand trembling before it, the Union, which is no ghost, is playing the thief behind your back. The Unionist tells you not to trust the Catholic, and, in your panic, you forget who robbed you of the ten mitres and the corporations. Away with the evil counsellor ! In Rome, the Jew and Christian have embraced. There is a creed which includes all other creeds—a creed common to the synagogue, the cathedral, and the mosque. The genius of the poor weaver of Belfast, whose lyrics are the brightest treasures you possess, has announced it to you :—

> " And though ten thousand altars bear
>   On each for Heaven a different prayer,
>   By light of moon, or light of sun,
>   At Freedom's we must all be one."

This is the creed which we profess—and the place-beggar calls it " infidelity." The place-beggar—that figure with two faces—like the Marquis of Rockingham, described by Grattan—one face turned towards the Treasury, and the other presented to the people, and, with a double tongue, speaking contradictory languages. You disapprove·of place-begging, I understand. And why not ? This country can never be independent, whilst it is a recruiting depot for the English Whigs, or any other English faction, that frets and fights for

salary behind the benches of St. Stephen's. Orangemen of Ireland !—stand to your colours—keep up your
anniversaries—but do not damn the Pope at the skirts
of England. Burn Guy Fawkes, but in the flames let
not the writings of Molyneux be consumed. Radicals
of Ireland !—claim the ballot—claim the household
suffrage—claim annual or triennial parliaments—but
claim them from a native parliament. Of the House
of Russell scorn to be the scavengers. Imitate, in this
respect, that nation from whose corn-law majorities,
sugar-bill majorities, coercion-bill majorities, we struggle
to emancipate ourselves. Be antagonists in religion—
be antagonists in the science of legislation—but combine for the common right—combine for self-government. Is this absurd ? Is this impracticable ? Consult the oracles of Exeter Hall—consult the oracles of
the Catholic Institute. High above them both flies
the ensign of St. George, and though the war of sects
is waged beneath, no hand is ever raised to tear it
down and fling it to a foreign foe. Interrogate the
cotton lord of Manchester—interrogate the corn monopo-
list of Buckinghamshire—and see if they would not link
their forces—artisans and farmers—if a camp, like that
of 1803, threatening an invasion, were descried from
the cliffs of Dover. A union of parties, then, in the
name of national independence, is not impracticable.
But the acquisition of independence is impossible.
What ! the public opinion of Ireland is a feather in the
scales of the British Constitution ! Is that the conclusion you have come to ? Have you tried your
weight at all ? You have not ; and before you assert
that you are not up to the mark, you are bound to make
the experiment. In God's name, then, let the experiment be made ! To raise this kingdom to the position
of an independent state should be the passionate

ambition of all its citizens. Gifted, as she has been, with fine capacities for power, it is a crime to tolerate the influence by which those capacities are restrained. In the profusion of its resources, the will of heaven, that this land should be blessed with affluence, has been nobly signified. Nor have the intimations of that will been less distinctly traced in the character of its people. The generous passion, the vivid intellect, the rapturous faith, are visible through all their vicissitudes, their errors, and their vices. For a destination the most exalted, we behold, in every arrangement, facilities the most adequate. Shall the dispensations of Providence be contravened, through the timorous inactivity of man ? In a sluggish acquiescence to the sword of conquest, and the law of rapine, are we to witness the profane rejection of that charter, which, through these dispensations, instructs us to be free, and empowers us to be great ? A right noble philosophy has taught us, that God has divided this world into those beautiful systems, called nations, each of which, fulfilling its separate mission, becomes an essential benefit to the rest. To this Divine arrangement will you alone refuse to conform, surrendering the position, renouncing the responsibility, which you have been assigned ? Other nations, with abilities far less eminent than those which you possess, having great difficulties to encounter, have obeyed, with heroism, the commandment—from which you have swerved—maintaining that noble order of existence, through which even the poorest state becomes an instructive chapter in the great history of the world. Shame upon you ! Switzerland—without a colony, without a gun upon the seas, without a helping hand from any court in Europe—has held, for centuries, her footing on the Alps ; spite of the avalanche, has bid her little

territory sustain, in peace and plenty, the children to
whom she has given birth ; has trained those children
up in the arts that contribute most to the security,
the joy, the dignity of life ; has taught them to depend
upon themselves, and for their fortune to be thankful
to no officious stranger ; and, though a blood-red
cloud is breaking, even whilst I speak, over one of her
brightest lakes, whatever plague it may portend, be
assured of this, the cap of foreign despotism will never
gleam again in the market-place of Altorff. Shame
upon you ! Norway—with her scanty population,
scarce a million strong—has kept her flag upon the
Categat ; has reared a race of gallant sailors to guard
her frozen soil ; year after year has nursed upon that
soil a harvest to which the Swede can lay no claim ;
has saved her ancient laws, and, to the spirit of her
frank and hardy sons, commits the freedom which she
rescued from the allied swords, when they hacked her
crown at Frederichstadt. Shame upon you ! Greece
—" whom the Goth, nor Turk, nor Time, hath spared
not "—has flung the crescent from the Acropolis ; has
crowned a king in Athens, whom she calls her own ;
has taught you that a nation should never die ; that
not for an idle pageant has the blood of heroes flowed—
that not to vex a school-boy's brain, nor smoulder in
a heap of learned dust, has the fire of heaven issued
from the tribune's tongue. Shame upon you ! Holland
—with the ocean as her foe—from the swamp in which
you would have sunk your graves, has bid the palace,
and the warehouse, costlier than the palace, rear their
ponderous shapes above the waves that battle at their
base ; has outstripped the merchant of the Rialto ;
has threatened England in the Thames ; has swept
the Channel with her broom ; and though, for a day,
she reeled before the bayonets of Dumouriez, she

sprang to her feet again, and with the cry—" Up, up with the House of Orange ! "—struck the Tricolour from her dykes. And you—you, who are eight million strong ; you, who boast, at every meeting, that this island is the finest which the sun looks down upon ; you, who have no threatening sea to stem—no avalanche to dread ; you, who say that you could shield along your coast a thousand sail, and be the princes of a mighty commerce ; you, who by the magic of an honest hand, beneath each summer sky, might cull a plenteous harvest from your soil, and with the sickle strike away the scythe of death ; you; who have no vulgar history to read ; you, who can trace, from field to field, the evidences of a civilisation older than the conquest—the relics of a religion more ancient than the gospel ; you, who have thus been blessed, thus been gifted, thus been prompted to what is wise and generous, and great ; you will make no effort ; you will whine, and beg, and skulk, in sores and rags, upon this favoured land ; you will congregate in drowsy councils, and, when the very earth is loosening beneath your feet, respectfully suggest new clauses and amendments to some blundering bill ; you will strike the poor-rate— ay, fifteen shillings in the pound !—and mortgage the last acre of your estates ; you will bid a prosperous voyage to your last grain of corn ; you will be beggared by the million ; you will perish by the thousand ; and the finest island which the sun looks upon, amid the jeers and hootings of the world, will blacken into a plague-spot, a wilderness, a sepulchre ! God of Heaven ! shall these things come to pass ? What say you, yeomen of the north ? Has the Red Hand withered ? Shall the question be always asked at Innishowen— " Has the time come ? "—and shall no heroic voice reply—" It has. Arise ! " Swear that the rule of

England is unjust, illegal, and a grievance. Swear it, that, henceforth, you shall have no lawgivers, save the Queen, the Lords, and Commons of the kingdom. Swear it, that, as you have been the garrison of England for years, from this out you will be the garrison of Ireland. Swear it, that the flag which floats next summer from the battlements of Derry shall bear the inscription of Dungannon. Swear it, that you shall have another anniversary to celebrate—that another obelisk shall cast its shadow on the Boyne—that, hereafter, your children, descending to that river, may say —" This is to the memory of our fathers ; they were proud of the victory which their grandsires won upon these banks, but they ambitioned to achieve a victory of their own ; their grandsires fought and conquered for a king ; our fathers fought and conquered for a nation—be their memories pious, glorious, and immortal ! "

Mitchel's Policy

Speech in the Pillar Room of the Rotunda, on the Policy of the Irish Confederation, February, 1848.

Sir, I beg leave to say a few words upon the question before the chair. They shall be very few indeed, for I find myself engaged in this debate quite unexpectedly. I arrived from England at rather a late hour this morning, and it was not until my arrival here that I was made acquainted with the proceedings of the last two evenings. Such being the case, I now speak under very unfavourable circumstances, for I speak without that preparation which the importance of the question requires. Previous to my going into the question at issue, however, I beg to express—and I do so sincerely —the same sentiment as that to which Mr. Reilly, in the commencement of his speech, gave utterance. I trust that we who are about to conclude this discussion, may not, by any mishap, disturb the good feelings that have prevailed all through it ; and I fervently pray, that, in this conflict of opinions, we shall preserve those feelings which have so long united us in a sincere and devoted companionship. Now, as to the question before us, I think that Mr. Mitchel has brought it, most conveniently for me, into the smallest possible space. The real question (he says) which we have to decide is, whether we are to keep to constitutional and parliamentary agitation or not ? Precisely so ; you have to decide nothing less, and nothing more than this—whether " constitutional agitation " is to be given up, or to be sustained. This is the one, simple point that we are to determine ; for, upon all other points, connected with the policy and action of the Confederation, there appears to be, amongst us all, perfect concurrence of opinion. At all events, whatever decision you may come to, with regard to the utility of our pursuing, any further, a constitutional course of action, I believe that, by this time, we have become quite agreed, that all this vague talk should cease, with which your ears have been vexed for so long a period. All this vague talk about a " crisis is at hand "—" shouts of defiance "—" Louis Philippe is upwards of seventy "—" France remembers Waterloo " —" the first gun fired in Europe "—all this obscure babble—all this meaningless mysticism—must be swept away. Ten thousand guns, fired in Europe, would announce no glad tidings to you, if their lightning flashed upon you in a state of disorganisation and incertitude. Sir, I know of no nation that has won its independence by an accident. Trust blindly to the future—wait for the tide in the affairs of men which, taken at the flood, may lead to fortune—envelop yourselves in the mist—leave everything to chance— and be assured of this, the most propitious opportunities will rise and pass away, leaving you still to chance— masters of no weapons—scholars of no science—incompetent to decide—irresolute to act—powerless to achieve. This was the great error of the Repeal Association. From a labyrinth of difficulties, there was no avenue opened to success. The people were kept within this labyrinth—they moved round and round—backwards and forwards—there was perpetual motion, but no advance. In this bewilderment are you content to wander, until a sign appears in heaven, and the mystery is disentangled by a miracle ? Have you no clear intelligence to direct you to the right path, and do you fear to trust your footsteps to the guidance of that mind with which you have been gifted ? Do you prefer to substitute a driftless superstition in place of a determined system—groping and fumbling after possibilities, instead of seizing the agencies within your reach ? This, indeed, would be a blind renunciation of your powers, and thus, indeed, the virtue you prize so justly—the virtue of self-reliance —would be extinguished in you. To this you will not consent. You have too sure a confidence in the resources you possess to leave to chance what you can accomplish by design. A deliberate plan of action is, then, essential—something positive—something definite. Now, there are but two plans for our consideration—the one, within the law : the other, without the law. Let us take the latter. And I will, then, ask you—is an insurrection practicable ? Prove to me that it is, and I, for one, will vote for it this very night. You know well, my friends, that I am not one of those tame moralists who say that liberty is not worth a drop of blood. Men who subscribe to such a maxim are fit for out-door relief, and for nothing better. Against this miserable maxim, the noblest virtue that has served and sanctified humanity, appears in judgment. From the blue waters of the Bay of Salamis—from the valley, over which the sun stood still, and lit the Israelite to victory—from the cathedral, in which the sword of Poland has been sheathed in the shroud of Kosciousko—from the convent of St. Isidore, where the fiery hand that rent the ensign of St. George upon the plains of Ulster, has crumbled into dust— from the sands of the desert, where the wild genius of the Algerine so long had scared the eagle of the Pyrennees—from the ducal palace in this kingdom, where the memory of the gallant Geraldine enhances, more than royal favour, the nobility of his race—from the solitary grave which, within this mute city, a dying request has left without an epitaph—oh! from every spot where heroism has had a sacrifice or a triumph, a voice breaks in upon the cringing crowd that cheers this wretched maxim, crying out—" Away with it, away with it." Would to God that we could take every barrack in the island this night, and with our blood purchase back the independence of the country! It is not, then, a pedantic reverence for common law —it is not a senseless devotion to a diadem and sceptre —it is not a whining solicitude for the preservation of the species—that dictates the vote I give this night in favour of a constitutional movement. I do so, not from choice, but from necessity. Gentlemen, I support this constitutional policy, not from choice, but from necessity. My strongest feelings are in favour of the policy advised by Mr. Mitchel. I wish to heavens that I could defend that policy. It is a policy which calls forth the noblest passions—it kindles genius, generosity, heroism—it is far removed from the tricks and crimes of politics—for the young, the gallant, and the good, it has the most powerful attractions. In the history of this kingdom, the names that burn above the dust and desolation of the past—like the lamps in the old sepulchres of Rome—shed their glory round the principles, of which a deep conviction of our weakness compels me this night to be the opponent. And in being their opponent, I almost blush to think, that the voice of one whose influence is felt through this struggle more powerfully than any other, and whose noble lyrics will bid our cause to live for ever—

I almost blush to think, that this voice, which speaks to us in these glorious lines—

" And the beckoning angels win you on, with many a radiant vision,
   Up the thorny path to glory, where man receives his crown— "

should be disobeyed, and that, for a time at least, we must plod on in the old course, until we acquire strength, and discipline, and skill—discipline to steady, skill to direct, strength to enforce the claim of a united nation. To an insurrectionary movement, the priesthood are opposed. To an insurrectionary movement, the middle classes are opposed. To an insurrectionary movement, the aristocracy are opposed. To give effect to this opposition, 50,000 men, equipped and paid by England, occupy the country at this moment. Who, then, are for it ? The mechanic and the peasant classes, we are told. These classes, you will tell us, have lost all faith in legal agencies, and, through such agencies, despair of the slightest exemption from their suffering. Stung to madness—day from day gazing upon the wreck and devastation that surround them, until the brain whirls like a ball of fire—they see but one red pathway, lined with gibbets and hedged with bayonets, leading to deliverance ! But will that pathway lead them to deliverance ? Have these classes, upon which alone you now rely, the power to sweep, like a torrent, through that pathway, dashing aside the tremendous obstacles which confront them ? You know they have not. Without discipline, without arms, without food—beggared by the law, starved by the law, diseased by the law, demoralised by the law— opposed to the might of England, they would have the weakness of a vapour (A voice, " No, no "). Yes, but you have said so ; for what do you maintain ?

You maintain that an immediate insurrection is not designed. Well, then, you confess your weakness; and, then, let me ask you, what becomes of the objection you urge against the policy we propose? The country cannot afford to wait until the legal means have been fully tested—that is your objection. And yet, you will not urge an immediate movement—you will not deal with the disease upon the spot—you will permit it to take its course—your remedy is remote. Thus, it appears, there is delay in both cases—so, upon this question of time, we are entitled to pair off. But, at no time, you assert, will legal means prevail—public opinion is nonsense—constitutional agitation is a downright delusion. Tell me, then, was it an understanding, when we founded the Irish Confederation, this time twelvemonth, that if public opinion failed to Repeal the Act of Union in a year, at the end of the year it should be scouted as a " humbug ? " When you established this Confederation in January, 1847—when you set up for yourselves—did you agree with " public opinion " for a year only? Was that the agreement, and will you now serve it with a notice to quit? If so, take my advice and break up your establishment at once. You have no other alternative, for the house will fall to pieces with a servant of more unruly propensities. After all, look to your great argument against the continuance of a parliamentary or constitutional movement. The constituencies are corrupt—they will not return virtuous representatives—the tree shall be known by its/fruits ! The constituencies are knaves, perjurers, cowards, on the hustings—they will be chevaliers, *sans peur et sans reproche*, within the trenches ! The Thersites of the polling-booth, will be the Achilles of the bivouac ! Your argument comes to this, that the constituencies of Ireland will be saved " so as by fire "—they will acquire morality in the shooting gallery—and in the art of fortification, they will learn the path to paradise. These constituencies constitute the *elite* of the democracy ; and is it you, who stand up for the democracy, that urge this argument ?   To be purified and saved, do you decree that the nation must writhe in the agonies of a desperate circumcision ? Has it not felt the knife long since ?   And if its salvation depended upon the flow of blood, has it not poured out torrents —into a thousand graves !—deep enough, and swift enough, to earn the blessing long before our day ? Spend no more until you are certain of the purchase. Nor do I wish, gentlemen, that this movement should be a mere democratic movement. I desire that it should continue to be what it has been, a national movement not of any one class, but of all classes. Narrow it to one class—decide that it shall be a democratic movement, and nothing else—what, then ? You augment the power that is opposed to you—the revolution will provoke a counter-revolution—Paris will be attacked by the Emigrants, as well as by the Austrians.   You attach little importance to the instance cited by Mr. Ross—Poland is no warning to you. The Polish peasants cut the throats of the Polish nobles, and before the Vistula had washed away the blood, the free city of Cracow was proclaimed a dungeon. So much for the war of classes. But, there is the French Revolution—the revolution of Mirabeau, of La Fayette, of Vergniaud. There, you say, is democracy, triumphant against the aristocracy, winning the liberty of the nation ! How long did that triumph last ? Madame de Genlis took the present King of France, when he was only eighteen years of age, to see the ruins of the Bastile. To read him the lessons of liberty she brought him there. And did the son of Philippe Egalité learn the lessons of liberty from those great fragments, upon which the fierce hand of the French democracy had left its curse? He learnt a very different lesson—he learnt to rebuild the prison—he learnt to plant his throne within the circle of a hundred bastiles—and it is thus that the democracy of the revolution has triumphed. No; I am not for a democratic, but I am for a national movement—not for a movement like that of Paris in 1793, but for a movement like that of Brussels in 1830—like that of Palermo in 1848. Should you think differently, say so. If you are weary of this " constitutional movement "—if you despair of this " combination of classes "—declare so boldly, and let this night terminate the career of the Irish Confederation. Do not spare the Confederation, if you have lost all hope in constitutional exertion. If you despair of the middle classes and the aristocracy, vote its extinction—renounce the principles you have so long maintained—precipitate yourselves into an abyss, the depth of which you know not—and let the world witness the spectacle of your death—a death which shall be ignominious, for it shall have been self-designed and self-inflicted! Yet, upon the brink of this abyss, listen, for a moment, to the voice which speaks to you from the vaults of Mount Saint Jerome; and if you distrust the advice of the friend who now addresses you—one who has done something to assist you, and who, I believe, has not been unfaithful to you in some moments of difficulty, and, perhaps, of danger—if you do not trust me, listen, at least, to the voice of one who has been carried to his grave amid the tears and prayers of all classes of his countrymen, and of whose courage and whose truth there has never yet been uttered the slightest doubt : " Be bold, but wise—be brave, but sober—patient, earnest, striving, and untiring. You have sworn to be temperate for your comfort here and your well-being hereafter. Be temperate now for the honour, the happiness, the immortality of your country—act trustfully and truthfully one to another—watch, wait, and leave the rest to God."

A Reply to the Placehunters

SPEECH AT THE WATERFORD HUSTINGS, MARCH 4TH, 1848.

Mr. Sheriff and gentlemen, electors of the city of Waterford, I stand . before you convicted of a most serious crime. I have claimed the representation of my native city; and, my opponents tell me, I have claimed it with an effrontery which can never be forgiven. I, who have stretched out my hand to the Orangemen of Ulster, and from that spot, where the banner of King James was rent by the sword of William, have passionately prayed for the extinction of those feuds which have been transmitted to us through the rancorous blood of five generations.—I, who have presumed to say, that the God, by whose will I breathe, has given to me a mind that should not cringe and crawl along the earth, but should expand and soar, and, in the rapture of its free will, exultingly pursue its own career.—I, who have dared to assert the sovereignty of this mind, and, ambitious to preserve in it the charter and inheritance I had from heaven, have disdained to be the slave of one, whom, were it not an impious perversion of the noblest gift of God, it might have been no ignominy to serve.—I, who have been spurned from the hearse of the Catholic emancipator, and am stained with the blood which his retinue, with such a decent resentment, have filched from his coffin and dashed in my face.—I, who have rushed through this career of criminality, and have thus

been soiled and stigmatised, have had the daring to
stand here this day, and claim, through your suffrages,
an admission to the senate of empire! This act of
mine has been pronounced to be without parallel in
the records of the most intemperate presumption, has
been so pronounced by those eminent politicians of our
city, who so long have swayed its destinies to their own
account. Should their censure fail to extinguish me,
is there not, in other quarters, an envious ability at
work with which I have not strength sufficient to
compete?   Has not the Loyal National Repeal
Association declared against me?   And is it possible
—possible!—that you will be so degenerate and
seditious as to spurn this attempt to tamper with your
votes?   What, then, inspires me to proceed?   Against
this sea of troubles, what strength have I to beat my
way towards that bold headland, upon which I have
sworn to plant the flag I have rescued from the wreck?
Weak, reckless, bewildered youth!—with those clouds
breaking above my head—with cries of vengeance
ringing in my ears—what sign of hope glitters along
the waters?   There is a sign of hope—the people are
standing on this headland, and they beckon me to
advance!   Yes, the people are with me in this struggle,
and it is this that gives nerve to my arm, and passion
to my heart.   Whilst they are with me, I will face the
worst—I can defy the boldest—I may despise the
proudest.   You who oppose me, look to the generous
and impetuous crowd, in the heart of which I was
borne to the steps of this hall; and tell me—in that
crowd, do you not find some slight apology for the
crime of which, in your impartial judgments, I stand
convicted?   Does not that honest thrift, that bold
integrity, that precipitate enthusiasm, plead in my
defence, and, by the decree of the people, has not my

crime become a virtue ? By this decree, has not the
sentence against the culprit, the anarchist, the infidel,
been reversed ? By this decree, I say, have not these
infamous designations been swept away ? and here,
asserting the independence of the Island, shall I not
recognise, in the justice of the people, their title to
accept an eminent responsibility—their ability to attain
an exalted destination ? You say " no," to all this—
you gentlemen of the Corporation and the Repeal
news-room. Ah ! you are driving the old coach still.
You will not give way to modern improvements—you
are behind your time most sadly—conservative of error,
intolerant of truth. Is it not so ? Is not your cry
still the hackneyed cry—" You have differed with
O'Connell—you have maligned O'Connell." You meet
me, gentlemen, with these two accusations, and to
these accusations you require an answer. The answer
shall be concise and blunt. The first accusation, that
I have differed with O'Connell, is honourably true.
The second accusation, that I have maligned O'Connell,
is malignantly false. It is true that I differed with
Mr. O'Connell, and I glory in the act by which I forfeited the confidence of slaves, and won the sanction
of independent citizens. I differed with him, for I
was conscious of a free soul, and felt that it would be
an abdication of existence to consign it to captivity.
Was this a crime ? Do you curse the man who will not
barter the priceless jewel of his soul ? To be your
favourite—to win your honours—must I be a slave ?
What ! was it for this that you were called forth from
the dust upon which you trample ? What ! was it for
this you were gifted with that eternal strength, by
which you can triumph over the obscurity of a plebeian
birth—by which you can break through the conceits
and laws of fashion—by which you can cope with the

craft of the thief and the genius of the tyrant—by which you can defy the exactions of penury, and rear a golden prosperity amid the gloom of the garret, and the pestilence of the poorhouse—by which you can step from height to height, and shine far above the calamities with which you struggled, and from which you sprung—by which you can traverse the giddy seas, and be a light and glory to the tribes that sit in darkness and the shadow of death—by which you can mount beyond the clouds, and sweep the silver fields, where the stars fulfil their mysterious missions—by which you can gaze, without a shudder, upon the scythe and shroud of death, and, seeing the grave opened at your feet, can look beyond it, and feel that it is but the narrow passage to a luminous immortality. What! was it to cramp, to sell, to play the trickster and the trifler with this eternal strength that you were called forth to walk this sphere—to be, for a time, the guest of its bounty and the idolator of its glory? Gentlemen, from this ground I shall not descend, to seek, in little details, the vindication of my difference with Mr. O'Connell. It was my right to differ with him, if I thought him wrong; and upon that right, in the name of truth and freedom, I take my stand. Let no man gainsay that right. It is stamped upon the throne of the everlasting hills, and the hand that strives to blot it out conspires against the dignity of man and the benevolence of God. And yet, were it my desire to play a petty part upon this day—my desire to vindicate the conduct, in which I glory, upon low and shifting grounds—I might tell you, gentlemen of the old school, that in the career of Mr. O'Connell it is easy to find a justification of the " insubordination " you impugn. The Rev. Mr. O'Shea, who I am very happy to perceive in the " omnibus box " on my right

—he told you, at the meeting in the Town Hall, on last Monday week, that I had just as much right to differ with Mr. O'Connell, as Mr. O'Connell had to differ with Mr. Grattan. The difference between Mr. O'Connell and Mr. Grattan occurred in July, 1813. What was Mr. O'Connell at that time? He was a young man—a man who had done little or no service to his country, and he had certainly advanced a very short way towards that commanding position in which we beheld him a few months since. But what of Henry Grattan? Henry Grattan, at that time, was venerable for his years and services. His grey hairs were encircled with a crown of glory, and, as he sat in the Senate Hall of England, men gazed upon him with a noble pity; for in his weak, and pale, and shrivelled form, they beheld the shadow of that power by which, in 1782, the dead came forth, and the sepulchre was clad in beauty—by which the province became a kingdom, and, stirred by his rushing genius, rose from her bed in the ocean, and got nearer to the sun. And did the young O'Connell blast his prospects by his difference with the great Irish citizen? On this account did vulgar tongues—did poisoned pens assail the daring Catholic? For this, was he scoffed at as an infidel—hooted as a traitor to his country—outlawed as the murderer of her deliverer? No. I tell you, gentlemen—you, who are in that inconvenient corner there, and think you represent the city—I tell you this, that public men were more just and chivalrous in the days of Grattan than they are in yours; and if in the war of parties there might have been a keener enmity, there was assuredly less falsehood, and less cant. I am now done with this accusation, and being done with it, I beg leave to tell you, that this is the last time I shall apologise for having refused to be a slave. Call it vanity—call it ingratitude

—call it treachery—call it, as your prototype, Justice Dogberry, would have called it—call it house-breaking or flat perjury—call it by any name you please—from henceforth I shall but smile at the intolerant dictation that will utter, and the mischievous credulity that will cheer, an accusation so preposterous and fictitious. Nor is it my intention to touch, in the slightest degree, upon the other counts in the indictment that has been preferred against me. The first count is the only one for which I entertain the least respect, so that I deeply sympathise with the reverend gentleman who has taken such profane and profitless trouble to provoke me. However, if he really desires that I should satisfy him upon those points to which, with such priestly decorum, he has so vehemently referred—I may, perhaps, console him by the assurance that, in the statement of the grounds upon which I seek the representation of this city, that satisfaction may be gained. This statement will be very brief. I am an enemy of the Legislative Union—an enemy of that Union in every shape and form that it may assume—an enemy of that Union whatever blessing it may bring—an enemy of that Union whatever sacrifice its extinction may require. Maintain the Union, gentlemen, and maintain your beggary. Maintain the Union, and maintain your bankruptcy. Maintain the Union, and maintain your famine. Tolerate the usurpation which the English parliament has achieved, and you tolerate the power in which your resources, your energies, your institutions are absorbed. Tolerate the rigour of the English Conservatives—their proclamations and state prosecutions—tolerate the English Whigs—their smiles and compliments—their liberal appointments, and modified coercion bills—and you tolerate the two policies through which the statesmen of England have alternately managed,

Patrick O'Donoghue

ruled, and robbed this country. On the morning of the 18th of October, in the year 1172, upon the broad waters of our native Suir, the spears and banners of a royal pirate were glittering in the sun. Did the old city of the Ostmen send forth a shout of defiance as the splendid pageant moved up the stream, and flung its radiance on our walls? No; from these walls no challenge was hurled at the foe; but, from the tower of Reginald, the grey eye of a stately soldier glistened as they came, and whilst he waved his hand, and showed the keys of the city he had won, the name of Strongbow was heard amid the storm of shouts that rocked the galleys to and fro. He was the first adventurer that set his heel on Irish soil in the name of England; and he—the sleek the cautious, and the gallant Strongbow—was the type and herald of that plague with which this Island has been cursed for seven desolating centuries. The historian Holinshed has said of him, that " what he could not compass by deeds, he won by good works and gentle speeches." Do you not find in this short sentence an exact description of that despotism which has held this Island from the days of Strongbow, the archer, down to our own—the days of Clarendon, the green-crop lecturer. By force or fraud—by steel or gold—by threat or smile—by liberal appointments or speedy executions—by jail deliveries or special commissions—by dinners in the Park or massacres at Clontarf—by the craft of the thief or the genius of the tyrant—they have held this Island ever since that morning in October, 1172; seducing those whom they could not terrify—slaying those whom they could neither allure nor intimidate. Thus may the history of the English connection be told—a black, a boisterous night, in which there shone but one brief interval of peace and lustre! Friends and foes!—you who cheer, and you who hiss me (Cries from the Old Ireland party —" No one hissed you."). Well, then, you who cheer, and you who curse me—sons of the one soil—inheritors of the one destiny—look back to that interval, and, for an instant, contemplate its glory. Now, you who quake and quiver when I insist upon the right of this country to be held, governed, and defended by its own citizens, and by them alone—you who are so industrial in your projects, and so constitutional in your efforts —what do you say to your fathers, the actors in that scene? Conservatives of Waterford, who were the officers in the Irish army that occupied our Island on the 16th of April, 1782? Call the muster-roll, and at the head of the regiments levied in Waterford, the Alcocks, the Carews, the Boltons, the Beresfords, will appear. And will you, gentlemen—the grand jurors of the city and the county—forswear the right of which they were the champions? Will that which was loyalty in the fathers be sedition in the sons? Time does not change virtue into vice. Do not scruple, then, to revive the sentiments of those whose name you bear, and to whose principles—if you have any pride of ancestry—you should ambitiously adhere. You have stood aloof too long from the people, of whose integrity in this contest you have had so startling an attestation; and deterred by vague fears and vaguer prejudices, you have leant most cringingly upon England, instead of trusting manfully to yourselves. Identify yourselves with the hopes, the ideas, the labours of your country; make the country your own, and make it worthy of your pride. Form for the future no mean estimate of its powers; assign to it no narrow space for its career; open to it the widest field—conceive for it the boldest destiny. Repealers of Waterford—you who oppose me—is your resentment towards me——(Great confusion, in which the rest of the sentence was lost). Well, then, is "Old Ireland" still your cry? Old Ireland, indeed! I am not against Old Ireland: but I am against the vices that have made Ireland old. The enmity I bear to the Legislative Union is not more bitter than the enmity I bear to those practices and passions from which that Union derives its ruinous vitality. Impatient for the independence of my country—intolerant of every evil that averts the blessing—I detest the bigot, and despise the place-beggar. Who stands here to bless the bigot or to cheer the place-beggar? They are the worst enemies of Ireland. The rancour of the one, and the venality of the other, constitute the strongest forces by which this Island is fettered in subjection. Down with the bigot! he who would sacrifice the nation to the supremacy of his sect. Down with the bigot! he would persecute the courage which had truth for its inspiration, and had humanity for its cause. Down with the bigot! he would banish the genius which, in the distribution of its fruits, was generous to all creeds; and in the circle of its light would embrace every altar in the land. Down with the place-beggar! he would traffic in a noble cause, and beg a bribe in the name of liberty. Down with the place-beggar! he would fawn in private on the men whom he scourged in public, and with his services sustain the usurpation his invectives had assailed. Down with the place-beggar! he would thrive by traitorism; and, in the enjoyment of his salary, he would spurn the people upon whose shoulders he had mounted to that eminence, from which he had beckoned to the minister, and said—"Look here—a slave for hire—a slave of consequence—a valuable slave—the people have confided in me." You have now some notion of the principles upon which I stand.

Do you scout, detest these principles ? Do you think them intolerant, profane, and impure ? Declare your opinion, and decide my fate. If you declare against my principles, you declare against the claim I have this day urged. I can borrow no great name to hide my own insignificance ; I have been the servant of no government—the follower of no house. Without any of those great influences to assist me, upon which public men usually depend, I flung myself into this struggle, trusting to the power of truth and the enthusiasm of the people. It was a daring act, yet there is a wisdom sometimes in audacity. There was a bold spirit slumbering amongst you—it required but one bold act alone to startle it into a resolute activity. I am guilty of that act, and I await the penalty. Punish me, if you desire to retain your past character. Preserve the famous motto of our ancient municipality free from stain. As it was won by a slavish loyalty, so maintain it by a sordid patriotism. Spurn me ! I have been jealous of my freedom, and in the pursuit of liberty I have scorned to work in shackles. Spurn me ! I have fought my own way through the storm of politics, and have played, I think, no coward's part upon the way. Spurn me ! I loathe the gold of England, and deem them slaves who would accept it. Spurn me ! I will not beg a bribe for any of you—I will negotiate no pedlar's bargain between the minister and the people. Spurn me ! I have raised my voice against the tricks and vices of Irish politics, and have preached the attainment of a noble end by noble means. Spurn me ! I have claimed the position and the powers which none amongst you, save the tame and venal, will refuse to demand, and in doing this I have acted as became a free, unpensioned citizen.

Repeal or a Republic

SPEECH IN THE MUSIC HALL, MARCH 11TH, 1848, AT A
MEETING OF THE IRISH CONFEDERATION, IN MOVING
THE ADOPTION OF AN ADDRESS TO THE CITIZENS
OF DUBLIN.[1]

Citizens of Dublin, I move the adoption of that
address. In doing so, I will follow the advice of my
friend, Mr. M'Gee. This is not the time for long
speeches. Everything we say here, just now, should
be short, sharp, and decisive. I move the adoption
of that address, for this reason—the instruction it
gives you, if obeyed, will keep you in possession of
that opportunity which the revolution of Paris has
created. The game is in your hands, at last ; and you
have a partner in the play upon whom you may depend.
Look towards the southern wave, and do you not find
it crimsoned with the flame in which the throne of
the Tuilleries has been consumed ?—and, borne upon
that wave, do you not hail the rainbow flag, which, a
few years since, glittered from the hills of Bantry ?
Has not France proclaimed herself the protectress of
weak nations, and is not the sword of the Republic
pledged to the oppressed nationalities which, in Europe,
and elsewhere, desire to reconstruct themselves ? The
feet that have trampled upon the sceptre of July
have trampled upon the Treaty of Vienna. Henceforth the convenience of kings will be slightly
consulted by France, where the necessities of a people

[1] At this meeting an address to the French Provisional
Government was also adopted ; and the address, which
Meagher moved, called upon the people not to be led into a
premature rising on the 17th of March, for which the Government were formidably prepared.

manifest themselves. But do not wait for France. Do
not beg the blood which, on the altar of the Madeleine,
she consecrates to the service of humanity. Do not
purchase your independence at the expense of those
poor workmen, whose heroism has been so impetuous,
so generous, so tolerant. It is sufficient for us, that
the Republic—to use the language of Lamartine—
shines from its place upon the horizon of nations, to
instruct and guide them. Listen to these instructions
—accept this guidance—and be confident of success.
Fraternise !—I will use the word, though the critics
of the Castle reject it as the cant of the day—I will
use it, for it is the spell-word of weak nations.
Fraternise !—as the citizens of Paris have done ;
and in the clasped hands which arch the colossal car
in that great funeral procession of the 4th of March,
behold the sign in which your victory shall be won.
Do you not redden at the thoughts of your contemptible
factions—their follies—and their crimes ? Do you not
see, that every nation with a sensible head and an
upright heart, laughs at the poor profligate passion
which frets and fights for a straw in this parish—a
feather in that barony—a bubble in that river ? Have
you not learned by this, that, whilst you have been
fighting for those straws and bubbles, the country has
been wrenched from beneath your feet, and made over
to the brigands of the Castle ? And what enables
these sleek and silken brigands to hold your country ?
Have you fought them ? Have you struck blow for
blow, and been worsted in the fight ? Think of it—
you marched against them a few years back, and when
you drew up before the Castle gates, you cursed and
cuffed each other—and then withdrew. Withdrew !
For what ? To repair the evil ? To reunite the
forces ? Ah, I will not sting you with these questions

—I will not sting myself. Let no Irishman look into the past. He will be scared at the evidences of his guilt—evidences which spring up, like weeds and briars, in that bleak waste of ruins. Between us and the past, let a wall arise, and, as if this day was the first of our existence, let us advance together towards that destiny, in the light of which this old Island shall renew itself. Citizens—I use another of the " cant phrases " of the day, for this, too, is a spell-word with weak nations—I speak thus, in spite of circumstances which within the last few days—I allude to the addresses from the University and the Orange Lodges—have darkened the prospect of a national union. I speak thus, in spite of that squeamish morality which decries the inspiration of the time, and would check the lofty passion which desires to manifest itself in arms. But, I will not despair of this union, whoever may play the factionist. The people will act for themselves, and in their hands, the liberty of the country will not be compromised. At this startling moment—when your fortunes are swinging in the balance—let no man dictate to you. Trust to your own intelligence, sincerity, and power. Do not place your prerogatives in commission —the sovereign people should neither lend nor abdicate the sceptre. As to the upper classes—respectable circles of society—genteel nobodies—nervous aristocrats —friends of order and starvation—of pestilence and peace—of speedy hangings and green-cropping—as to these conspirators against the life and dignity of this Island, they must no longer be courted. They are cowards, and when they know your strength, they will cling to you for protection. Do I tell you to refuse this protection ? Were I base enough to do so, you would remind me that the revolution of Paris has been immortalised by the clemency of the people. In my letter, last week, to the Council of the Confederation, I stated it was not my wish to urge any suggestion as to the course we should now pursue. Upon reflection, however, I think I am called upon to declare to you my opinion upon this question, for it would not be honourable, I conceive, for any prominent member of the Confederation to shield himself at this crisis. And I am the more anxious to declare my opinion upon this question of ways and means, since I had not the good fortune of being present at your two previous meetings, and, perhaps, my absence may have occasioned some suspicion. I think, then, that from a meeting—constituted, as the Repealers of Kilkenny have suggested, of delegates from the chief towns and parishes—a deputation should proceed to London, and, in the name of the Irish people, demand an interview with the Queen. Should the demand be refused, let the Irish deputies pack up their court dresses—as Benjamin Franklin did, when repulsed from the court of George III —and let them, then and there, make solemn oath, that when they next demand an admission to the throne room of St. James's, it shall be through the accredited ambassador of the Irish Republic. Should the demand be conceded, let the deputies approach the throne, and, in firm and respectful terms, call upon the Queen to exercise the royal prerogative, and summon her Irish parliament to sit, and advise her, in the city of Dublin. Should the call be obeyed—should the sceptre touch the bier, and she " who is not dead, but sleepeth," start, at its touch, into a fresh and luminous existence—then, indeed, may we bless the Constitution we have been taught to curse ; and Irish loyalty, ceasing to be a mere ceremonious affectation, become, with us, a sincere devotion to the just ruler of an independent State. Should the claim be rejected—

should the throne stand as a barrier between the Irish
people and their supreme right—then loyalty will be
a crime, and obedience to the executive will be treason
to the country. I say it calmly, seriously, and deliberately—it will then be our duty to fight, and
desperately fight. The opinions of Whig statesmen
have been quoted here to-night—I beg to remind
you of Lord Palmerston's language in reference to the
insurrection at Lisbon, last September—" I say that
the people were justified in saying to the government,
If you do not give us a parliament in which to state
our wrongs and grievances, we shall state them by
arms and by force." I adopt those words, and I call
upon you to adopt them likewise. Citizens of Dublin,
I know well what I may incur by the expression of
these sentiments—I know it well—therefore, let no
man indulgently ascribe them to ignorance or to idiotcy.
Were I more moderate—as some Whig sympathiser
would say—more sensible—as he might add, without
meaning anything personal, of course,—more practical
—as he would further beg leave to remark, without
at all meaning to deny that I possessed some excellent
points—in fact, and in truth, were I a temperate trifler,
a polished knave, a scientific dodger—I might promise
myself a pleasant life, many gay scenes, perhaps no
few privileges. Moderate, sensible, practical men, are
sure to obtain privileges just now. Paid poor-law
guardianships are plentiful, now-a-days, and the invitations to the Castle are indiscriminate and innumerable.
But, I desire to be, neither moderate nor sensible,
neither sensible nor practical, in the sense attached to
these words by the polite and slavish circle, of which
his Excellency is the centre. It is the renunciation of
truth, of manhood, and of country—the renunciation
of the noblest lessons with which the stately genius

of antiquity has crowned the hills of Rome, and sanctified the dust of Greece—the renunciation of all that is frank, and chivalrous, and inspiring—it is the renunciation of all this which makes you acceptable in the eyes of that meagre, spectral royalty, which keeps " open house " for reduced gentlemen upon the summit of Cork Hill. Better to swing from the gibbet, than live and fatten on such terms as these. Better to rot within the precincts of the common jail—when the law has curbed your haughty neck, young traitor ! —than be the moderate, sensible, practical villain, which these Chesterfields of the Dublin promenades and saloons would entreat you to be, for the sake of society, and the success of the Whigs. But the hour is on the stroke when these conceits and mockeries shall be trampled in the dust. The storm which dashed the crown of Orleans against the Column of July, has rocked the foundations of the Castle. They have no longer a safe bedding in the Irish soil. To the first breeze which shakes the banners of the European rivals they must give way. Be upon the watch, and catch the breeze ! When the world is in arms—when the silence, which, for two and thirty years, has reigned upon the plain of Waterloo, at last is broken—then be prepared to grasp your freedom with an armed hand, and hold it with the same. In the meantime, take warning from this address—" do not suffer your sacred cause to be ruined by stratagem or surprise." Beware of the ingenuity, the black art, of those who hold your country. By your sagacious conduct, keep them prisoners in their barracks on the 17th. There must be no bloody joke at your expense amongst the jesters and buffoons in St. Patrick's Hall upon that night. Citizens of Dublin, you have heard my opinions. These opinions may be very rash, but it would not be honest

to conceal them. The time has come for every Irishman to speak out. The address of the University
declares, that it is the duty of every man in the kingdom
to say, whether he be the friend, or the foe, of the
government. I think so, too, and I declare myself
the enemy of the government. But if I am rash—it
was Rome, it was Palermo, it was Paris, that made
me rash. Vexed by the indiscretion—the fanaticism—
of these cities, who can keep his temper—dole out
placid law—and play the gentle demagogue? When
the sections of Paris were thickening, like the clouds
of a tempest, round the Tuilleries, in 1793, Louis XVI
put on his court dress, and, in his ruffles and silk
stockings, waited for the thunderbolt. Is it thus that
you will wait for the storm now gathering over Europe?
Shall the language of the nation be the language of
the Four Courts? Will the revolution be made with
rose-water? Look up!—look up!—and behold the
incentives of the hour. By the waves of the Mediterranean the Sicilian noble stands, and presents to you the
flag of freedom. From the steps of the Capitol, the
keeper of the sacred keys unfurls the banner that was
buried in the grave of the Bandieras, and invites you
to accept it. From the tribune of the French Republic
where that gallant workman exclaimed—" Respect the
rights of property !—the people have shown that they
will not be ill-governed—let them prove they know
how to use properly the victory they have won "—
from this tribune, where these noble words are uttered,
the hand of labour—the strong hand of God's nobility
—proffers you the flag of independence. Will you
refuse to take it? Will you sneak away from the noble,
the pontiff, and the workman? Will you shut your
eyes to the splendours that surround you, and grope
your way in darkness to the grave? Ah, pardon me

this language—it is not the language which the awakening spirit of the country justifies. Taught by the examples of Italy, of France, of Sicily, the citizens of Ireland shall, at last, unite. To the enmities that have snapped the ties of citizenship, there shall be a wise and generous termination. Henceforth, the power of the Island shall be lodged in one head, one heart, one arm. One thought shall animate, one passion shall inflame, one effort concentrate, the genius, the enthusiasm, the heroism of the people. Thus united—to repeat what I have said before—let the demand for the reconstruction of the nationality of Ireland be constitutionally made. Depute your worthiest citizens to approach the throne, and, before that throne, let the will of the Irish people be uttered with dignity and decision. If nothing comes of this—if the constitution opens to us no path of freedom—if the Union will be maintained in spite of the will of the Irish people—if the government of Ireland insists upon being a government of dragoons and bombardiers, of detectives and light infantry—then, up with the barricades, and invoke the God of Battles ! Should we succeed—oh ! think of the joy, the ecstasy, the glory of this old Irish nation, which, in that hour, will grow young and strong again. Should we fail—the country will not be worse than it is now—the sword of famine is less sparing than the bayonet of the soldier. And if we, who have spoken to you in this language, should fall with you—or if, reserved for a less glorious death, we be flung to the vultures of the law—then shall we recollect the words of France—recollect the promise she has given to weak nations—and standing upon the scaffold, within one heart's beat of eternity, our last cry upon this earth shall be—" France ! France ! revenge us ! "

Famine and Felony

Speech at the Soiree, Given by the Confederates
of Limerick to Messrs. O'Brien, Meagher,
and Mitchel, Previous to their Trials for
Sedition, May, 1848.

Mr. Chairman, Ladies, and Gentlemen, the occurrences of this evening do not dishearten me. I am
encouraged by your sympathy, and can, therefore,
forgive the rudeness of a mob. Nor do I conceive
that our cause is injured by these manifestations of
ignorance and immorality. The mists from the marshes
obscure the sun—they do not taint—they do not extinguish it. Enough of this. The wrongs and perils
of the country must exclude from our minds every
other subject of consideration. From the summer of
1846 to the winter of 1847, the wing of an avenging
angel swept our soil and sky. The fruits of the earth
died, as the shadow passed, and they who had nursed
them into life read in the withered leaves that they,
too, should die ; and, dying, swell the red catalogue
of carnage in which the sins and splendours of that
empire—of which we are the prosecuted foes—have
been immortalised. And, whilst death thus counted
in his spoils by the score, we, who should have stood
up between the destroyer and the doomed—we, who
should have prayed together, marched together, fought
together to save the people—we were in arms !—drilled
and disciplined into factions !—striking each other
across the graves that each day opened at our feet,
instead of joining hands above them, and snatching

victory from death ! The cry of famine was lost in the
cry of faction, and many a brave heart, flying from
the scene, bled as it looked back upon the riotous
profanation in which the worst passions of the country
were engaged. You know the rest—you know the
occurrences of the last few weeks. At the very hour
when the feud was hottest, a voice from the banks of
the Seine summoned us to desist. That voice has
been obeyed—we have trampled upon the whims and
prejudices that divided us—and it is this event that
explains the sedition in which we glory. The sudden
re-construction of that power which, in 1843, menaced
the integrity of the empire, and promised liberty to
this island, dictated the language which has entitled
us to the vengeance of the minister, and the confidence of
the people. Nor this alone. It is not in the language of
the lawyer, or the police magistrate, that the wrongs and
aspirations of an oppressed nation should be stated.
For the pang with which it writhes—for the passion
with which it heaves—for the chafed heart—the burning
brain—the quickening pulse—the soaring soul—there
is a language quite at variance with the grammar and
the syntax of a government. It is bold, and passionate,
and generous. It often glows with the fire of genius—
it sometimes thunders with the spirit of the prophet.
It is tainted with no falsehood—it is polished with no
flattery. In the desert—on the mountain—within the
city—everywhere—it has been spoken, throughout all
ages. It requires no teaching—it is the inherent and
imperishable language of humanity! Kings, soldiers,
judges, hangmen, have proclaimed it. In pools of
blood they have sought to cool and quench this fiery
tongue. They have built the prison—they have
launched the convict-ship—they have planted the
gallows tree—to warn it to be still. The sword, the

sceptre, the black cap, the guillotine—all have failed.
Sedition wears the crown in Europe on this day,
and the scaffold, on which the poor scribes of royalty
had scrawled her death-sentence, is the throne upon
which she receives the homage of humanity, and
guarantees its glory. Therefore, it is, I do not blush
for the crime with which I have been charged. Therefore, it is, you have invited a traitorous triumvirate to
your ancient and gallant city, and have honoured
them this evening. In doing so, you have taken your
stand against the government of England, and I know
of no spot in Ireland where a braver stand should be
made than here, by the waters of the Shannon, where
the sword of Sarsfield flashed. Whilst that old Treaty
stone, without the Thomond gate, attests the courage
and the honour of your fathers, the nerve and faith
of Limerick shall never be mistrusted. No, there
could be no coward born within those walls, which,
in their old age, instruct so thrillingly the young hearts
that gaze upon them with reverence—whispering to
them, as they do, memories that drive the blood, in
boiling currents, through the veins—telling those
young hearts, not to doubt, not to falter, not to fear
—that in a sunnier hour the Wild Geese shall yet return
from France. These sentiments are, no doubt, seditious,
and the expression of them may bring me within the
provisions of this new Felony Bill—the bill, mind you,
that is to strike this nation dumb! Yes, from this
day out, you must lie down, and eat your words!
Yes, you—you starved wretch, lying naked in that
ditch, with clenched teeth and staring eye, gazing
on the clouds that redden with the flames in which
your hovel is consumed—what matters it that the
claw of hunger is fastening in your heart—what matters
it that the hot poison of the fever is shooting through

your brain—what matters it that the tooth of the lean dog is cutting through the bone of that dead child, of which you were once the guardian—what matters it that the lips of that spectre there, once the pride and beauty of the village, when you wooed and won her as your bride, are blackened with the blood of the youngest to whom she has given birth—what matters it that the golden grain, which sprung from the sweat you squandered on the soil has been torn from your grasp, and Heaven's first decree to fallen man be contravened by human law—what matters it that you are thus pained and stung—thus lashed and maddened—hush !—beat back the passion that rushes from your heart—check the curse that gurgles in your throat—die !—die without a groan !—die without a struggle !—die without a cry !—for the government which starves you, desires to live in peace ! Shall this be so ? Shall the conquest of Ireland be this year completed ? Shall the spirit which has survived the pains and penalties of centuries—which has never ceased to stir the heart of Ireland with the hope of a better day—which has defied the sword of famine and the sword of law—which has lived through the desolation of the last year, and kept the old flag flying, spite of the storm which rent its folds—what ! shall this spirit sink down at last—tamed and crippled by the blow with which it has been struck—muttering no sentiment that is not loyal, legal, slavish, and corrupt ? Why should I put this question ? Have I not been already answered by that flash of arms, which purifies the air where the pestilence has been ? Have I not already caught the quick beating of that heart, which many men had said was cold and dull, and, in its strong pulsation, have we not heard the rushing of that current, which, for a time, may overflow the land—overflow it, to fertilise, to

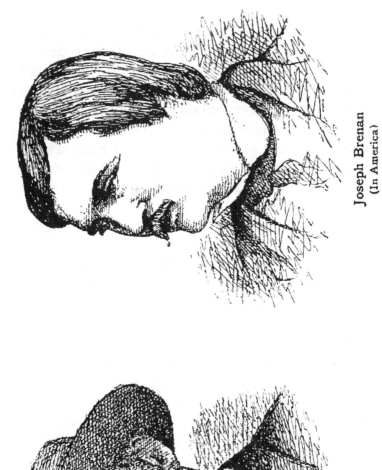

Joseph Brenan
(In America)

Michael Kavanagh
(In America)

restore, and beautify ? The mind of Ireland no longer wavers. It has acquired the faith, the constancy, the heroism of a predestined martyr. It foresees the worst—prepares for the worst. The cross—as in Milan—glitters in the haze of battle, and points to eternity ! We shall no longer seek for liberty in the bye-ways. On the broad field, in front of the foreign swords, the soul of this nation, grown young and chivalrous again, shall clothe herself, like the Angel of the Resurrection, in the white robe, and point to the sepulchre that is void ; or shall mount the scaffold —that eminence on which many a radiant transfiguration has taken place—and bequeath to the crowd below a lesson for their instruction.

II

John Mitchel

SPEECH IN THE MUSIC HALL, JUNE, 1848, AT A MEETING OF THE IRISH CONFEDERATION, UPON THE TRIAL AND TRANSPORTATION OF JOHN MITCHEL.

Citizens of Dublin, since we last assembled in this Hall, an event has occurred which decides our fate. We are no longer masters of our lives. They belong to our country—to liberty—to vengeance. Upon the walls of Newgate a fettered hand has inscribed this destiny—we shall be the martyrs or the rulers of a revolution. "One, two, three—ay, hundreds shall follow me," exclaimed the glorious citizen who was sentenced to exile and immortality upon the morning of the 27th of May. Such was his prophecy, and his children will live to say it has been fulfilled. Let no man mistrust these words; whilst I speak them I am fully sensible of the obligations they impose. It is an obligation from which there is no exemption but through infamy. Claiming your trust, however, I well know the feeling that prevails amongst you—doubt—depression—shame! Doubt, as to the truth of those whose advice restrained your daring. Depression, inspired by the loss of the ablest and the boldest man amongst us. Shame, excited by the ease, the insolence, the impunity with which he was hurried in chains from the island to whose service he had sacrificed all that he had on earth—all that made life dear, and honourable, and glorious to him—his home, his genius, and his liberty. In those feelings

of depression and shame I deeply share; and from
the mistrust with which some of you, at least, may
regard the members of the late Council, I shall not
hold myself exempt. If they are to blame, so am I.
Between the hearts of the people and the bayonets of
the government, I took my stand, with the members
of the Council, and warned back the precipitate devotion which scoffed at prudence as a crime. I am
here to answer for that act. If you believe it to have
been the act of a dastard, treat me with no delicacy,
treat me with no respect—vindicate your courage in
the impeachment of the coward. The necessities and
perils of the cause forbid the interchange of courtesies.
Civilities are out of place in the whirl and tumult of
the tempest; and do not fear that the forfeiture of
your confidence will induce in me the renunciation of
the cause. In the ranks—by the side of the poorest
mechanic—I shall proudly act, under any executive
you may decree. Summon the intellect and heroism
of the democracy, from the workshop, the field, the
garret—bind the brow of labour with the crown of
sovereignty—place the sceptre in the rough and
blistered hand—and, to the death, I shall be the subject and the soldier of the plebeian king. The address
of the Council to the people of Ireland—the address
signed by William Smith O'Brien—bears witness to
your determination; it states that thousands of confederates had pledged themselves that John Mitchel
should not leave these shores but through their blood.
We were bound to make this statement—bound in
justice to you—bound in honour to the country.
Whatever odium may flow from that scene of victorious
defiance, in which the government played its part
without a stammer or a check, none falls on you. You
would have fought, had we not seized your hands, and

bound them. Let no foul tongue, then, spit its sarcasms upon the people. They were ready for the sacrifice ; and had the word been given, the stars would burn this night above a thousand crimsoned graves. The guilt is ours—let the sarcasms fall upon our heads. We told you in the clubs, four days previous to the trial, the reasons that compelled us to oppose the project of a rescue. The concentration of 10,000 troops upon the city—the incomplete organisation of the people—the insufficiency of food, in case of a sustained resistance—the uncertainty as to how far the country districts were prepared to support us—these were the chief reasons that forced us into an antagonism with your generosity, your devotion, your intrepidity. Night after night we visited the clubs, to know your sentiments, your determination—and to the course we instructed you to adopt, you gave, at length, a reluctant sanction. Now, I do not think it would be candid in me to conceal the fact, that the day subsequent to the arrest of John Mitchel, I gave expression to sentiments having a tendency quite opposite to the advice I have mentioned. At a meeting of the Grattan Club, I said that the Confederation ought to come to the resolution to resist by force the transportation of John Mitchel, and if the worst befel us, the ship that carried him away should sail upon a sea of blood. I said this, and I shall not now conceal it. I said this, and I shall not shrink from the reproach of having acted otherwise. Upon consideration, I became convinced they were sentiments which, if acted upon, would associate my name with the ruin of the cause. I feel it my duty, therefore, to retract them—not to disown, but to condemn them—not to shrink from the responsibility which the avowal of them might entail, but to avert the disaster which the enforcement of them would ensure. You have now heard all I have to say on that point ; and, with a conscience happy in the thought that it has concealed nothing, I shall ex-ultingly look forward to an event, the shadow of which already encircles us, for the vindication of my conduct, and the attestation of my truth. Call me coward—call me renegade. I will accept these titles as the penalties which a fidelity to my convictions has imposed. I will be so for a short time only. To the end I see the path I have been ordained to walk, and upon the grave which closes in that path I can read no coward's epitaph. Bitterly, indeed, might the wife and children of our illustrious friend lament the loss they have sustained, if his example failed to excite amongst us that defiant spirit which, in spite of pains and penalties, will boldly soar to freedom, and from the dust, where it has fretted for a time, return in rapturous flight to the source from whence it came. Not till then—not till the cowardice of the country has been made manifest—let there be tears and mourning round that hearth, of which the pride and chivalry have passed away. I said, that in the depression which his loss inspired, I deeply shared. I should not have said so. I feel no depression. His example—his fortitude —his courage—forbid the feeling. All that was perish-able in him—his flesh and blood—are in the keeping of the privileged felons who won his liberty with their loaded dice. But his genius, his truth, his heroism— to what penal settlement have these immortal influences been condemned ? Oh ! to have checked the evil promptly—to have secured their crown and govern-ment against him and his teachings—to have done their treacherous business well, they should have read his mission, and his power, in the star which presided at his birth, and have stabbed him in his cradle. They seized him thirty years too late—they seized him when his steady hand had lit the sacred fire, and the flame had passed from soul to soul. Who speaks of depression, then ? Banish it ! Let not the banners droop—let not the battalions reel—when the young chief is down. You have to avenge that fall. Until that fall shall have been avenged, a sin blackens the soul of the nation, and repels from our cause the sympathies of every gallant people. For one, I am pledged to follow him. Once again they shall have to pack their jury box—once again, exhibit to the world the frauds and mockeries—the tricks and perjuries—upon which their power is based. In this island, the English never—never, shall have rest. The work begun by the Norman never shall be completed. Generation transmits to generation the holy passion which pants for liberty—which frets against oppression ; and from the blood which drenched the scaffolds of 1798, the " felons " of this year have sprung. Should their blood flow—peace, and loyalty, and debasement may here, for a time, resume their reign—the snows of a winter, the flowers of a summer, may clothe the proscribed graves—but from those graves there shall hereafter be an armed resurrection. Peace, loyalty, and debasement, forsooth ! A stagnant society !—breeding, in its bosom, slimy, sluggish things, which to the surface make their way by stealth, and there, for a season, creep, cringe, and glitter in the glare of a provincial royalty. Peace, loyalty, and debasement ! A mass of pauperism !—shovelled off the land—stocked in fever sheds and poorhouses—shipped to Canadian swamps—rags, and pestilence, and vermin. Behold the rule of England !—and in that rule, behold humanity dethroned, and Providence blasphemed. To keep up this abomination, they enact their laws of felony. To sweep away the abomination, we must break through their laws. Should the laws fail, they will hedge the abomination with their bayonets and their gibbets. These, too, shall give way before the torrent of fire which gathers in the soul of the people. The question so long debated—debated, years ago, on fields of blood —debated latterly in a venal senate, amid the jeers and yells of faction—the question, as to who shall be the owners of this island, must be this year determined. The end is at hand, and so, unite and arm! A truce to cheers—to speeches—to banquets—to " important resolutions " that resolve nothing, and " magnificent displays," which are little else than preposterous deceptions. Ascertain your resources in each locality— consolidate, arrange them—substitute defined action for driftless passion—and in the intelligent distribution and disciplined exercise of your powers, let the mind of the country manifest its purpose, and give permanent effect to its ambition. In carrying out this plan, the country shall have the services of the leading members of the Council, and from this great task— the organisation of the country—we shall not desist until it has been thoroughly accomplished. When it is accomplished, the country may resume its freedom and its sovereignty. To the work, then, with high hope and impassioned vigour. There is a black ship upon the southern sea this night. Far from his own, old land—far from the sea, and soil, and sky, which, standing here, he used to claim for you with all the pride of a true Irish prince—far from that circle of fresh young hearts, in whose light, and joyousness, and warmth, his own drank in each evening new life and vigour—far from that young wife, in whose heart the kind hand of heaven has kindled a gentle heroism, sustained by which she looks with serenity and pride upon her widowed house, and in the children that girdle her with beauty behold the inheritors of a name which, to their last breath, will secure for them the love, the honour, the blessing of their country—far from these scenes and joys, clothed and fettered as a felon, he is borne to an island where the rich, and brilliant, and rapacious power, of which he was the foe, has doomed him to a dark existence. That sentence must be reversed—reversed by the decree of a free nation, arrayed in arms and in glory. Till then, in the love of the country, let the wife and children of the illustrious exile be shielded from adversity. True—when he stood before the judge, and with the voice and bearing of a Roman, told him that three hundred were prepared to follow him—true it is, that, at that moment, he spoke not of his home and children—he thought only of his country—and to the honour of her sons bequeathed the cause for which he was doomed to suffer. But, in that one thought, all other thoughts were embraced. Circled by the arms and banners of a free people, he saw his home secure—his wife joyous—his children prosperous. This was the thought which forbade his heart to blench when he left these shores—this the thought which calls up to-night, as he sleeps within that prison ship, dreams full of light and rapturous joy— this the thought which will lighten the drudgery, and reconcile his proud heart to the odious conditions of his exile. Think! oh, think! of that exile—the hopes, the longings, which will grow each day more anxious and impatient. Think! oh, think! of how, with throbbing heart and kindling eye, he will look out across the waters that imprison him, searching in the eastern sky for the flag that will announce to him his liberty, and the triumph of sedition. Think! oh, think! of that day, when thousands and tens of thousands

will rush to the water's edge, as a distant gun proclaims
his return—mark the ship as it dashes through the
waves and nears the shore—behold him standing there
upon the deck—the same calm, intrepid, noble heart—
his clear, quick eye runs along the shore, and fills with
the light which flashes from the bayonets of the people
—a moment's pause!—and then, amid the roar of
cannons, the fluttering of a hundred flags, the pealing
of cathedral bells, the cheers of millions—the triumphant
felon sets his foot once more upon his native soil—
hailed, and blessed, and welcomed as the first citizen
of our free and sovereign state!

Sentenced to Death

SPEECH IN THE DOCK AT CLONMEL, OCTOBER, 1848.

My Lords, it is my intention to say only a few words. I desire that the last act of a proceeding which has occupied so much of the public time, shall be of short duration. Nor have I the indelicate wish to close the dreary ceremony of a State prosecution with a vain display of words. Did I fear that hereafter when I shall be no more, the country which I have tried to serve would think ill of me, I might indeed avail myself of this solemn moment to vindicate my sentiments and my conduct. But I have no such fear. The country will judge of those sentiments and that conduct in a light far different from that in which the jury by which I have been convicted have viewed them ; and, by the country, the sentence which you, my Lords, are about to pronounce, will be remembered only as the severe and solemn attestation of my rectitude and truth. Whatever be the language in which that sentence be spoken, I know my fate will meet with sympathy, and that my memory will be honoured. In speaking thus, accuse me not, my Lords, of an indecorous presumption. To the efforts I have made, in a just and noble cause, I ascribe no vain importance, nor do I claim for those efforts any high reward. But it so happens, and it will ever happen so, that they who have tried to serve their country, no matter how weak the efforts may have been, are sure to receive the thanks and blessings of its people. With my country then I leave my memory—my sentiments—my acts—proudly feeling that they require no vindication from me this day. A jury of my countrymen, it is true, have found me guilty of the crime of which I stood indicted. For this I entertain not the slightest feeling of resentment towards them. Influenced, as they must have been, by the charge of the Lord Chief Justice, they could have found no other verdict. What of that charge? Any strong observations on it, I feel sincerely, would ill befit the solemnity of the scene ; but, earnestly beseech of you, my Lord, you who preside on that bench, when the passions and the prejudices of this hour have all passed away, to appeal to your conscience and ask of it, was your charge, as it ought to have been, impartial, and indifferent between the subject and the Crown ?

My Lords, you may deem this language unbecoming in me, and perhaps it might seal my fate. But I am here to speak the truth, whatever it may cost. I am here to regret nothing I have done—to retract nothing I have ever said. I am here to crave with no lying lip, the life I consecrate to the liberty of my country. Far from it ; even here—here, where the thief, the libertine, the murderer, have left their foot-prints in the dust—here on this spot, where the shadows of death surround me, and from which I see my early grave, in an unanointed soil open to receive me—even here, encircled by these terrors, the hope which has beckoned me to the perilous seas upon which I have been wrecked still consoles, animates, and enraptures me. No, I do not despair of my old country, her peace, her glory, her liberty ! For that country I can do no more than bid her hope. To lift this island up—to make her a benefactor to humanity, instead of being the meanest beggar in the world—to restore her to her native power and her ancient constitution—this has been my ambition, and my ambition has been my crime. Judged by the law of England, I know this crime entails the penalty of death ; but the history of Ireland explains this crime, and justifies it. Judged by that history I am no criminal—you [addressing MacManus] are no criminal—you [addressing O'Donoghue] are no criminal : I deserve no punishment—we deserve no punishment. Judged by that history, the treason of which I stand convicted loses all its guilt ; is sanctified as a duty, will be ennobled as a sacrifice ! With these sentiments, my Lords, I await the sentence of the court. Having done what I felt to be my duty—having spoken what I felt to be truth, as I have done on every other occasion of my short career, I now bid farewell to the country of my birth, my passion, and my death—the country whose misfortunes have invoked my sympathies—whose factions I have sought to still—whose intellect I have prompted to a lofty aim—whose freedom has been my fatal dream. I offer to that country, as a proof of the love I bear her, the sincerity with which I thought, and spoke, and struggled for freedom—the life of a young heart, and with that life all the hopes, the honour, the endearments of a happy and an honourable home. Pronounce then, my Lords, the sentence which the law directs—I am prepared to hear it. I trust I shall be prepared to meet its execution. I hope to be able, with a pure heart, and perfect composure, to appear before a higher tribunal—a tribunal where a Judge of infinite goodness, as well as of justice, will preside, and where, my Lords, many—many of the judgments of this world will be reversed.

A Personal Narrative of 1848

[This narrative was written by Meagher in Richmond Prison, Dublin, in 1849, and addressed to Gavan Duffy, who published it subsequently in the *Nation*. It is incomplete.]

On Sunday evening, July the 16th, I came down from Slievnamon, and remained at home until the following Thursday, superintending the organisation of the Waterford Confederates.

The Thursday I refer to brought us the proclamation of the Arms Act ; copies of which, during the early part of the day, were posted upon the walls of my native city.

Not wishing to act upon my own judgment—which, at such a moment, it would have been assuming too serious a responsibility to do—I resolved to leave at once for Dublin, with a view to ascertain there the intentions of the principal Confederates, so that the proclaimed districts might act in concert. Previous to my leaving, I issued a counter-proclamation, exhorting the people to firmness, and entreating them to complete the organisation of the Clubs.

In several places, this proclamation was posted over the Government manifesto ; and wherever the latter was not superseded in this way, it was torn down and flung about the streets.

In the evening, between seven and eight o'clock, I ordered a covered car ; intending to drive to Kilkenny, sleep the night there, and take the first coach to Carlow in the morning ; so that I might arrive in Dublin, by three o'clock in the afternoon of Friday, the 21st of July.

Whilst the car was getting ready, I ran up to the drawing-room, where my father and aunt were sitting at the time to wish them good-bye. I put on my tri-colour sash—green, white and orange—buckled on my sword-belt, cross-belt, cartouche-box—and flourishing a very handsome old sword, which belonged to a grand-uncle of mine in the days of the Merchant Corps of the Waterford Volunteers, gave myself up to the gay illusion of a gallant fight, a triumphal entry, at the head of armed thousands, into Dublin, before long!

I was full of liveliness and hope at that moment, and welcomed the struggle with a laughing heart. But, I recollect it well, my father was far otherwise. He seemed to me mournfully serious, and impressed with the saddest anticipations. In the Confederate Move-ment, however, he never had the slightest faith. More than once—particularly when I met him in London, on my way, with Eugene O'Reilly, O'Gorman, and Holly-wood, to present the congratulatory address to its Provisional Government of the French Republic, in the month of April—he warned me against being led away, by the success of the Continental Revolutionists, to trust the fortunes of our cause to the desperate chances of insurrection.

That evening—Thursday, July the 20th, 1848—I saw my home for the last time.

The car having come, I drove off to Kilkenny, and arrived there a few minutes before midnight.

Very early next morning, I sent a messenger to —— with a note requesting him to step over to me with as little delay as possible. Shortly afterwards he met me in Walshe's Hotel, where I was staying, and, whilst I was at breakfast, we had an anxious conversation upon the subject of the contemplated rising.

He was strongly adverse to any move being made,

for several weeks to come ; urging the fact, that it was within the last few weeks only the country parts had caught the flame from Dublin : hence, that it would take a considerable time to have the provincial Clubs organised, disciplined, and equipped ; and that, to give the signal before this time had expired, would be to rush, with naked hands, upon the bayonets of the police and soldiery.

He further added—indeed, he urged this consideration more earnestly than any other—that, as yet, the Catholic Priests had not given their sanction to the movement, and that, so long as they stood aloof, the people, outside of Dublin, would make no vigorous, hearty effort.

I could not but assent in great measure to these views ; yet, in parting from my friend, I stated to him my conviction, that, in the face of every difficulty, we would be driven to the last plank before many weeks, and would have to fight for it.

At six o'clock I left by the day mail for Carlow, and arrived in Dublin between two and three o'clock, p.m.

From the railway station I drove to the *Nation* office, and there met Dillon, O'Gorman, and Smyth, with whom I proceeded to the Council Rooms.

Having stated the reason which induced me to hurry up to Dublin, I learned from them that the Delegates of the Clubs had met in D'Olier Street, the day before, and had come to the resolution of offering no active resistance to the carrying out of the provisions of the Arms Act ; that, however, the members of the Clubs, and the people generally, had been instructed to conceal their arms and ammunition, and hold themselves in readiness for any collision which might take place.

Being so far satisfied, I told them I had pledged myself to be back in Waterford next morning, and should, therefore, leave Dublin that night. They pressed me to remain until the morning, insisting it was of importance I should attend a meeting of the Club Delegates, to be held that evening, for the purpose of electing an Executive Committee of Five. My presence, they added, was the more necessary at this meeting, since, in consequence of some misrepresentations, a want of confidence had been expressed, or, rather, murmured, against O'Brien, Dillon, and O'Gorman.

I consented to stay, and at five o'clock went down to Richard O'Gorman's house on Merchant's Quay, where, with the exception of those who were in Newgate, I met all the members of the late Council of the Confederation.

The conversation during dinner turned, of course, upon the movement ; our progress, difficulties, and prospects of success. So confident were we upon this occasion—the last upon which we met each other, and drank prosperity to the good old Irish Cause !—so confident were we, that we had some three or four weeks more to devote to the organisation of the country, and so little did we suspect that we should be taken unawares, and be driven to the field before our plans had been matured, that, during dinner, O'Gorman determined upon leaving, by the mail train, for Limerick with a view to superintend the formation of the Clubs in Limerick and in Clare.

O'Brien, too, little dreaming that a special warrant was at that very moment prepared for his arrest, announced his intention of starting early next morning for Wexford, and, in shaping out the course of his excursion through the country, fully calculated upon a month of uninterrupted agitation.

The opening of the Commission at Newgate was

fixed for the 8th of August. On that day, Duffy, Martin, Williams, and O'Doherty, were certain to be brought up for trial.

Now, in calculating the time that still remained to us for the organisation of the clubs, we counted up to the 13th of August, and for this reason :—

In case one or more of our friends were brought to trial on the 8th of August, five days would be allowed for pleading to the indictment, and four days, at least, were sure to elapse before the trial could terminate. Hence you will perceive, that the arrangements we made upon this evening of July the 21st had direct reference to the Confederates in Newgate.

Whatever opinions might have been previously expressed elsewhere, there existed but the one determination amongst the leading members of the Confederation at this, our last, meeting ; the determination, that not one of the Political Prisoners, in case of an adverse verdict and sentence of transportation, should be permitted to leave the country, without an attempt being made to resist the execution of the sentence.

It is true, we felt convinced it would be much wiser to wait until the cutting of the harvest, the time originally proposed. But, a consideration of the serious extent to which the spirit and reputation of the country would be affected by the loss of another leading man, forced us to the determination I have just stated.

And yet, this was no rash and hopeless conclusion ; though none of us subscribed to it without feeling it was hazardous in the extreme.

In coming to it, however, we derived confidence from an anticipation of the excitement which another conviction, similar to that of Mitchel's, was calculated to produce, and felt ourselves sustained by the deep persuasion, that, in such an event, the passions of the people would compensate for any deficiency which might exist in their organisation and equipment.[1]

At eight o'clock, O'Gorman left us for the Dublin and Cashel Railway. It was the last time I saw him. When wishing him good-bye that evening, I was far from thinking it would have been for ever.

O'Brien, at the same time, returned to his lodgings in Westland Row. He did not attend the meeting in D'Olier Street, being, in some measure, opposed to the election of an Executive Committee for the Clubs, and having, moreover, to make preparations for his departure to the South next morning.

Within a few minutes of nine o'clock, Dillon and I arrived at the Confederation rooms. About thirty of the Club Delegates were assembled there.

This, you will recollect, was the meeting sworn to by the spy, Dobbyn ; who, by-the-bye, I did not

---

[1] After Mitchel's transportation, a few of the leading Confederates thought the cause had received such an impetus by the rage against jury-packing, which sprung up universally in the country, that another victim ought to be offered to the Government. " There is no tribune," they exclaimed, " like the dock of Green Street ; let us keep it occupied." The principal advocate of this course proffered himself as the next Felon. But cooler heads warned them that the result would disappoint their expectations ; that the people would become accustomed to the transportation of their leaders, as they had become accustomed to murder by famine, till, in the end, the Government, might make a *battue* of Confederates with impunity. Let there be no seeking of martyrdom, they said ; on the contrary, wherever it can, with honour, let it be shunned, till the harvest is ripe : for the next victim must not be yielded without a struggle. This counsel was finally adopted. Accordingly, when a warrant was issued against John Martin, he evaded it for some days, for the express purpose of postponing his trial for an entire commission. He succeeded, but, nevertheless, his trial, and that of Mr. Duffy, and Messrs. Williams and O'Doherty, were fixed for a period much earlier than the Council contemplated, when they resolved not to yield another victim. It was, however, a period four months nearer the harvest than Mitchel's trial.—[Charles Gavan Duffy.]

recognise once during the proceedings ; who, in fact, I never saw, until he kissed the Gospel, before me, in the Court House of Clonmel ; although he swore I shook hands with him, and wished him good-night. In the main, however, his swearing tallied with the facts ; and my belief is, he must have been present at the meeting.

The object of the meeting was, as I have already intimated, the formation of a Directory or Committee, the members of which, being chosen by ballot, should be entrusted with the control and guidance of the Clubs in and about Dublin.

The necessity for the formation of such a body arose from the fact that the Clubs were now left to themselves, and had no source of instruction to look to in the difficulties which were thickening round them.

After the first meeting of the Irish League, the Council of the Irish Confederation had been dissolved. Now, the Council of the Confederation, up to the time I allude to, had acted as the Executive of the Clubs. This Executive having ceased to act, it became necessary to appoint another.

The new one was to succeed the old, in the same place, but with a more serious responsibility, and with larger powers. With the Executive Committee of Five was to rest the responsibility of giving the signal for insurrection, or withholding it, just as it appeared most fit ; the proceedings were to be strictly secret, and the instructions issued from it were to be obeyed implicitly.

The authority of the Executive Committee, in short, was declared wholly irresponsible and absolute ; was declared so by the several Delegates present at the meeting, on behalf of their respective Clubs ; and these same Delegates pledged themselves, moreover, that the obedience of the Clubs, to the orders of the Executive, would be prompt, strict, and zealous.

Dillon was in the chair. A resolution, after a little discussion, passed, to the effect, that the new Council should consist of five, and be entitled the *Executive Council of Five.*

The balloting then took place. Previous to it, however, I stated to the Delegates, that O'Brien, having conceived some objection to the appointment of the new Council, it would be useless to vote for him ; the more particularly, since he was to start in the morning for the South, where, for a few weeks, he would be engaged in the organisation and inspection of the Munster Clubs.

I have no recollection of a word being said in reference to the Rev. Mr. Kenyon, or any other priest. Of this I am certain, that the spy, Dobbyn, swore a falsehood, when he stated that an objection was raised to the election of any priest whatever. Indeed, I do not hesitate to tell you, that a very strong desire existed quite the other way. We were sensible enough to perceive, that a Roman Catholic clergyman, sitting in the Executive Council of Five, would have more power over the people than twenty or fifty laymen, and be enabled to lead them to acts of daring, more surely and irresistibly, than the bravest and most sagacious soldier. " Oh ! if you had seen them "— said Dillon to me, the evening I met him on the Commons of Boulagh—" if you had seen them when the old priest blessed them, you'd have thought they could have swept the country from sea to sea, and done the business with a blow."

The following were elected members of the Executive Council of Five. I give the names in the same order as they were announced. by the Tellers—Thomas

Francis Meagher, Rev. John Kenyon, John B. Dillon, Thomas D. Reilly, Richard O'Gorman, Jun.[1]

When the balloting had taken place, MacD., addressing the meeting, declared, that, since there were one or two upon the Council in whom he had but little confidence, he would, previous to assuring his obedience to it, exact from each member of it a distinct pledge to the effect, that in or about the harvest there should be an insurrection. I stepped forward when he had concluded, and replied, that, for my part, I would reject any such pledge ; that it was a pledge which the Executive Council could not adopt, since it was not in their power to guarantee its fulfilment ; that five men, however gifted or authoritative they might be, could not make an insurrection ; that such a business was for the entire people, or, at all events, for a considerable portion of the people, to decide upon ; the Executive Council could only urge them to it, and, if taken in hand, superintend its execution. Yet, I felt it my duty to add that as far as I could exercise any influence, nothing should be left undone by me to get the country under arms before the cutting of the harvest.

---

[1] The spy swore that a letter was read, before the election, from Mr. Duffy, then a prisoner in Newgate, recommending that three priests should be put on the Executive Council of Five, and that the discussion arose out of this circumstance. What gives some probability to his statement is the fact, that Mr. Duffy did write a letter, enclosing five names unanimously adopted by the political prisoners in Newgate, to be recommended by them as an Executive, and that one of them was a priest. The names so recommended were those of John B. Dillon, Thomas Francis Meagher, Rev. John Kenyon, T. D. M'Gee, and T. D. Reilly. These were the five actually elected, with the exception that the Rev. John Kenyon was left off, and either Richard O'Gorman, or James Fintan Lalor (we believe the latter) substituted. Meagher's list is therefore erroneous in including Mr. Kenyon, and omitting Mr. M'Gee.
—[Charles Gavan Duffy].

MacD. expressed himself satisfied at this, and, after some further conversation, the meeting broke up.

It now appears strangely unaccountable to me, that at this meeting—the most serious, perhaps, of any that was held in connection with the national movement of 1848—whilst a consideration of our position, our project, and resources, was taking place—whilst the stormy future, upon which we were entering, formed the subject of the most anxious conjecture, and the dangers of it fell like wintry shadows round us—it seems strangely unaccountable to me, that not an eye was turned to the facilities, for the counteraction of our designs, which the Government had at their disposal; that not a word was uttered in anticipation of that bold, astounding measure—the Suspension of the Habeas Corpus Act—the announcement of which broke upon us next day, so suddenly; driving us, headlong and bewildered, into a system of resistance for which the country was very far from being sufficiently prepared.

I seek not to exculpate the leaders of the Confederation from the responsibility of this grievous mistake. The Suspension of the Habeas Corpus was a resource in the hands of the English Government which should have entered prominently into the consideration of the question which, for three years, we had laboured to explain and illustrate, and the settlement of which, at this time, we ambitioned, at any cost and sacrifice, to effectuate.

The overlooking of it was a fatal inadvertence. Owing to it, we were routed without a struggle, and have been led into captivity without glory. We suffer not for a rebellion, but for a blunder.[1]

---

[1] Some leading members of the Council, of whom Meagher was one, had repeatedly urged the necessity of providing against all contingencies, by being prepared for action. But some of

When the meeting was over, I drove out with my old friend and school-fellow, Smyth, to his father's house, Mount Brown, Old Kilmainham, and slept there that night. Before going to my room, I desired him to call me in time for the eight o'clock train, so as to enable me to arrive in Waterford early next evening.

The following morning, however, owing to the fatigue of the previous day, I felt too sleepy to get up as early as I had wished, and remained in bed until twelve o'clock nearly, when Smyth came in to me with the *Freeman's Journal*, and read for me the announcement of the intended Suspension of the Habeas Corpus Act, and the report of a special warrant having been issued from the Home Office for the apprehension of Smith O'Brien.

Death itself could not have struck me more suddenly than this news. I had fully calculated—and so had O'Brien, O'Gorman, Dillon, and the rest of us, the evening before—that nothing would occur, for three or four weeks at least, to precipitate a rising ; and I had reckoned, with certainty, upon so much time, for the further extension and arming of the Clubs in Dublin and throughout the country.

their honestest and bravest colleagues had a strange reluctance to commit themselves prematurely to the necessary measures. Accordingly, it is said, that when ————————— was despatched across the Atlantic, his credentials were signed only by four of the leaders of the Confederation ; two of whom are now in Van Dieman s Land, one in America, and one in Ireland. And it is even believed, in well-informed quarters, that so late as the day before Mr. Duffy's arrest, when Mitchel was transported, and a warrant out for Martin, a motion to despatch an accredited agent to France was defeated in the Council, by a majority of one, as " a premature measure." This reluctance to take the necessary means to the end contemp'ated was one of the greatest moral impediments to success. How the same agent was huddled off on his mission, when it was too late, Meagher tells in a subsequent part of his memoir.—[Charles Gavan Duffy.]

Now I saw we were driven, by a master-stroke, to the last point upon the board ; and that, either we must surrender without a parley, or fight without arms and arrangement. " We are driven to it "—I said to Smyth " there is nothing for us now but to go out ; we have not gone far enough to succeed, and yet, too far to retreat." He thought so too, and at once made up his mind to share the worst with me.

After a hurried breakfast, we drove rapidly into town. We called, first of all, at Merchant's Quay, and learned from Richard O'Gorman, Sen., that the news of the Suspension Act was confirmed by a private letter he had received that morning from England, in which it was positively stated that the special warrant for the apprehension of Smith O'Brien had been issued from the Home Office.

Nothing could be more embarrassing than the position in which I found myself at this moment. I was left completely to myself ; deprived of all companionship and advice. O'Brien had started, five hours previously, for Wexford. O'Gorman had gone down to Limerick the night before. Doheny was in Cashel. Duffy, Martin, Williams, and O'Doherty, were shut up in Newgate ; and any access to them, except by their immediate relatives, was strictly prohibited.

Dillon and Reilly, however, were in town ; and, in the hope of finding them, I drove down to the *Nation* office, and from thence to the Council Rooms, in D'Olier Street. In neither place did I find them ; and what was still worse, could learn no tidings of them.

Having consulted with Halpin—who was then acting as Corresponding Secretary to the Clubs—I hurried off to Merrion Street, with the hope of finding Dillon.

I was passing up the east side of Merrion Square, when Dillon beckoned to me from a covered car. I ran over, and found Charles Hart and John Lawless, Secretary of the Sandymount Club, with him. They had been in search of me, and were on their way to the Council Rooms, at the moment I fell in with them.

Having got into the car, Dillon proposed that he and I should start by the night mail for Enniscorthy, and on then, without delay, to Ballinkeele, the residence of Mr. John Maher, where Smith O'Brien had purposed to remain a few days ; and that, in case O'Brien conceived the time had come for making a stand, we should throw ourselves into Kilkenny, call the people to arms, barricade the streets, and proclaim the separation of the countries.

In reply to a question I put to him, he told me that, a day or two before I came up from Waterford, the leading men of the Dublin Clubs had determined upon not making Dublin the head-quarters of the insurrection ; the garrison in the city—exceeding 11,000 men —being thought too formidable a body to contend with ; whilst the number of inhabitants, well-affected towards the Government, or disinclined, at all events, to join the people, was calculated, in their opinion, to counteract or, in great measure, weaken the efforts of the latter.

That the Dublin Clubs would have fought with courage and enthusiasm, not one of us ever doubted. In none of the Continental cities, from the citizens of which, during the course of a most eventful year, we had received so many lessons of exalted heroism, I sincerely believe, would there have been displayed an amount of bravery greater than that which the Dublin Clubs were prepared to exhibit, had they been called upon to pile the barricades in the streets of their noble city, and sack the English Castle.

Acting amongst them for upwards of two years ;

knowing them familiarly; knowing them, man for man; I have good reason to speak of them with confidence, and, I may truly add, with the most affectionate admiration.

Honest, intelligent, high-minded, they had conceived a proud notion of what their country's destiny should be; and having weighed well the labours and the sacrifices it was necessary to undergo, to the end that this high destiny might be attained, they remained faithful, in the face of much calumny and persecution, to their convictions, at a time when a majority of their countrymen were of a different way of thinking; and subsequently trod, with a step that never faltered and a heart that never quailed, the dangerous path to which we led them; exulting in the thought, as they fearlessly hastened on, that by such paths have all brave nations mounted to their freedom and become immortal.

The Dublin Clubmen were, in fact, the very pick and pride of the population, and I shall never cease to pray that Ireland may be made worthy of them. Nothing could pain me more deeply than to think that they supposed, for an instant even, we had the slightest reason to distrust them. It was far otherwise. In their quick, generous, courageous nature, our faith was deeply fixed.

But the power immediately opposed to them was too ponderous; too skilfully disposed; and, withal, too heartily supported by the adherents of the Castle, to justify us in committing them against it. The blood which would have flowed from so terrible a collision, appeared to us too costly a treasure to account for.

By commencing the insurrection elsewhere—commencing it in some town or district, where a force less considerable than that which was distributed through

Dublin happened to be stationed—it seemed to us that the chances of success would be greatly increased.

In the first place, it struck us that the smallest victory, however unimportant it might be—considering merely the position won, or the numbers overcome—would have a very great influence upon the spirit of the country at large—kindling it, as it surely must have done, into the brightest hopefulness, and tempting it to still more daring exploits.

In the next place, an outbreak, in a thinly garrisoned district—and the more especially, a successful outbreak —would have surely led to the diminution of the larger garrisons, and, in this way, enabled the Confederates of Dublin, of Cork, of Limerick, of Waterford, and other towns, to rise with effect, and make good their ground.

These were the views which principally induced the leading men of the Confederation to abandon the design of commencing the revolution in Dublin, and in these views I fully concurred. Since the events of July, 1848, I have seen nothing, I have heard nothing, that was calculated to convince me those views were wrong. On the contrary, the more I have reflected upon the events of that time, the more deeply impressed have I become with the correctness of those views, and the propriety of having acted in compliance with them.

Not a doubt of it ; had we taken a different course, a desperate fight would have been made in the streets of Dublin ; as desperate a fight as that of the Rue St. Méry, in the Parisian insurrection of 1831 ; but in like manner, it would have been stifled in a pool of squandered blood. This, indeed, our generous and heroic followers might not have deplored. But it is one thing to offer to the cause of liberty the tribute of our own life, and another, to exact the lives of others. To justify the exaction, there must be clear grounds for the belief, that the outlay will be repaid by an equivalent result.

And what is the equivalent of a nation's blood? The gratification of a just revenge? The vindication of the public spirit? The attainment of heroic fame?

I recollect well the dreary evening I put these questions to a fond and gallant friend, who had followed me from Dublin, and was at that moment sharing with me the fortunes of an outlaw's life. Calmly, seriously, and I can sincerely say, in the most truthful, conscientious spirit, we discussed them; for a circumstance had just occurred to force them, in the most urgent and impressive manner, upon our attention.

What this circumstance was, I shall mention in the proper place. Here, it is sufficient for me, so far, to anticipate the order of my little narrative, as to say, we came to the conclusion, that, not for the gratification of a just revenge, not for the vindication of the public spirit, nor for the attainment of heroic fame, would we be justified, as Christian men, in demanding the blood of the smallest section of the people; that, for the liberty of our island—that is, for the power which would enable her to shape her own course through the world, and build up an honourable renown and fortune out of her own soil and genius—for this, and this alone, would we be justified in requiring so great a treasure; and that, not even for this high and sacred purpose would so solemn a requirement be authorised, unless it appeared clear, to our inmost consciences, that the probabilities were in favour of such a purpose being wholly or to a great extent fulfilled.

Thus much I have written in explanation of the motives which governed us in transferring, at the outset, the scene of our revolutionary proceedings from the capital to the Southern counties.

PART II

When we reached the Council Rooms, we found —— and M'Gee there, and, after a short conversation with them it was arranged that the former should leave in the evening for Paris, put himself immediately into communication with the most influential Irishmen residing in that city, and leave nothing undone to procure a military intervention, in the event of the insurrection we contemplated taking place.

In a few hours he sailed from Kingstown ; and I have lately heard, from a trusted source, that the duties he undertook were performed by him with great ardour, intelligence, and success ; that, in fact, owing to his earnest representations, the armed intervention of the French Government would have taken place, had we made a good beginning, and shown ourselves worthy of so honourable an assistance.

As for M'Gee, he volunteered to start that same evening for Belfast, cross over to Glasgow, and lie concealed there until he heard from Dillon. Should he receive any favourable information, he was to summon the Irish population of that city to rise and attack whatever troops were entrusted with its defence. In case of these troops being overpowered, he should seize two or three of the largest merchant steamers lying in the Clyde ; with pistols at their heads, compel the engineers and sailors to work them out ; steer round the north coast of Ireland ; and, at the head of two thousand men, or more, if he could get them, make a descent on Sligo ; fight his way across the Shannon, and join us in Tipperary.

This project may now appear a monstrously absurd one. At the time, however, many circumstances concurred to give it a rational, sober, practicable character.

Adventurous, bold, dangerous in the highest degree, it certainly was, to the individual who proposed and ventured to conduct it. But, once taken in hand by our countrymen in Glasgow, no doubt could have been entertained of its accomplishment. Not alone, that the Irish there numbered several thousands; not alone, that Chartism was on the watch there, and panting for an outbreak; but the city was almost wholly defenceless; the troops of the line had been drafted off to other places; and, as a substitute, an awkward Militia force had been hastily patched up, and strapped together.

The project, however—whether it was good or bad— did not originate exclusively with M'Gee. In proposing it to us, he was acting in obedience to the wishes of three Delegates who had arrived in Dublin the previous evening, and had been instructed by a large body of Irishmen, resident in Glasgow, to lay the project in question before the chief men of the Clubs, and urge them to sanction, encourage, and direct it.

That evening, M'Gee started for Belfast; and, next day, crossed over to Scotland; where, I have since learned, from a Catholic clergyman of high integrity and intellect, he went through the difficult and perilous business he had undertaken, with singular energy, tact, and firmness; and, for several days, stood fully prepared to carry out the views just stated, had Dillon or I sent him word to do so.

Why we failed to communicate with him will be easily learned from the sequel of this letter.

Yet, upon a moment's reflection, I think it may be more satisfactory for me to state at once, that, in consequence of no decisive blow having been struck in Tipperary, we felt we would not be justified in bringing our friend, and the men under him, into collision with the Government. He was to take the field in the event of our establishing a good footing in the South ; and, this not having been accomplished, it would have been treacherous on our part to have written a line directing him to explode the conspiracy he had organised.

Having parted with —— and M'Gee, Dillon and I went upstairs to the room used for private committees, took down the large map of Ireland which hung there, and folding it up, with the intention of bringing it with us to the country, returned to the room in which Halpin and his assistants were at work.

We desired the former to let Duffy, Martin, and the other Confederates in Newgate, know of our going to the country, and our resolution of commencing the insurrection, if possible, in Kilkenny.[1]

We further desired him to communicate, in the course of the evening, with the officers of the Clubs ; inform them of our intentions ; and desire them to be in readiness to rise, and barricade the streets, when the

---

[1] If Meagher does not mistake the person to whom he gave this charge, it raises a serious imputation against Mr. Halpin. For he communicated no such message to the State Prisoners. Not a syllable of it. On the contrary, he was despatched by them to the south, two days afterwards, to ascertain from O'Brien what was about to be done there. For several days he sent them no communication. At length he returned to Dublin (having been sent back by Meagher on a special mission) ; but the first thing the prisoners heard of his arrival was a letter he published in the newspapers on some personal subject. The same morning he was arrested. They instantly sent a professional gentleman to him to afford him every necessary advice or assistance, and to get his report from the South. The professional gentleman (who was a Confederate) was also arrested ; and the prisoners never received a word from Mr. Halpin on the subject of his mission. These facts are not irreconcilable with his perfect fidelity, if Meagher entrusted him with no such message as he states ; but, if he did, the non-delivery of it is a serious fact, and must give a colour to all the rest.—[Charles Gavan Duffy.]

news of our being in the field should reach them ; and when, as an inevitable result, three or four regiments from the Dublin garrison had been drawn off to reinforce the troops of the Southern districts.

We had wished good-bye to Halpin, and were going out, when young R——H—— and Smyth came up. We told them the arrangements we had made ; entreated them to go round to the different Clubs that evening—state openly to the members what we purposed doing—communicate to them our wishes ; and exhort them to observe a calm, patient attitude, until the moment we designed for their coming into action had arrived.

They promised faithfully to do so.

We arrived at the Kingstown Railway Station, just in time to catch the five o'clock train.

The carriages were crowded, and the conversation very noisy about the Suspension Act. I retain a vivid picture of one gentleman in particular ; a very stiff, cold, sober gentleman, with red whiskers and a gambouge complexion ; who took occasion to remark, in quite a startling and fragmentary style, that " the Government had done the thing—the desirable thing— at last—time for them—should have been done long ago—country had gone half-way to the devil already— Whigs always infernally slow—had given those scoundrels too much rope—but—they'd hang themselves —he'd swear it—that he would."

I nudged Dillon at the conclusion of these consoling observations. He threw a quiet, humorsome look at the loyal subject with the red whiskers and gambouge complexion, and burst out laughing. He was joined by some gentlemen, and two or three ladies, who recognised us, but little suspected, I should say, the errand we were on.

John Mitchel
(Paris, 1861)

At Kingstown we got upon the Atmospheric Railway, and rattled off to Dalkey. Half an hour after, we were at dinner in Druid Lodge, Killiney, where Mrs. Dillon was staying at the time.

I should have mentioned, before this, that whilst Dillon and I were at the Council Rooms, in D'Olier Street, Lawless went to the office of the Wexford Coach, and engaged for us two inside seats, as far as Enniscorthy, in that night's mail ; leaving word with the clerk, that the gentlemen, for whom he had engaged the seats, were to be taken up at Loughlinstown ; a little village, seven miles from Dublin, and little more than two from Druid Lodge.

The places were taken in the name of Charles Hart, with a view to conceal our departure from the Police, who were on the alert ; picking out, in every nook and corner, information relative to our movements.

At half past eight, we left Druid Lodge for Loughlinstown. We did not enter the village, however ; but drew up at the tree, opposite, I believe, to Sir George Cockburn's demesne.

There, underneath that fine old tree, we remained for above twenty minutes, until the coach came up ; and, whilst we were standing in silence under it, surrounded by the darkness, which the deepening twilight, mingling with the shadow of the leaves, threw round us, I could not but reflect, with something of a heavy heart, upon the troubled future, within the confines of which I had set my foot, never to withdraw it.

The evening, which was cold and wet, the gloom and stillness of the spot, naturally gave rise to sentiments of a melancholy nature. But, above all, a feeling, which, for many days, had more or less painfully pressed upon my mind, and which, in some of the most exciting scenes I had lately passed through, failed not

to exercise a saddening influence upon my thoughts
and language—the feeling that we were aiming far
beyond our strength, and launching our young resources upon a sea of troubles, through which the
Divine Hand alone could guide and save them ; this
feeling, more than all, depressed me at the moment of
which I speak, and I felt far from being happy.

At that moment, I entertained no hope of success.
I knew well the people were unprepared for a struggle ;
but, at the same time, I felt convinced that the leading
men of the Confederation were bound to go out, and offer
to the country the sword and banner of Revolt, whatever
consequences might result to themselves for doing so.

The position we stood in ; the language we had
used ; the promises we had made ; the defiances we
had uttered ; our entire career, short as it was, seemed
to require from us a step no less daring and defiant
than that which the Government had taken.

Besides, here was an audacious inroad upon the
liberty of the subject ! The utter abrogation of the
sacred personal inviolability, guaranteed by sound old
law, to all people linked by rags or golden cords to the
Brunswick Crown ! Was it not the choicest ground of
quarrel, upon which a people, provoked and wronged
like the Irish people had been for years and years,
could fling down the gage of battle ?

Was it not said, too, by the most peaceable of our
Repealers, that the moment the Constitution was
invaded, they would sound the trumpet, and pitch
their tents ? Was it not said, over and over again,
by these sensitive, scrupulous, pious, poor men—by
these meek, forbearing, mendicant Crusaders—that
they would stand within the Constitution ? On both
feet, within it ? But that, the very instant the soldier
or the lawyer crossed it, they would unsheathe the

sword of Gideon, and, with a mighty voice, call upon the Lord of Hosts, and the Angel of Sennacherib !

I hold that the leaders of the Confederation were bound to give these men an opportunity to redeem their pledges ; bound to give the people, who honestly and earnestly desired to change their condition, an opportunity to attempt such a change, if it so happened that all they required was the opportunity to make the attempt ; ¯bound at all events, and whatever might be the result to themselves, to mark, in the strongest and most conclusive manner, their detestation of an act which left a great community to be dealt with, just as the suspicions of a police magistrate, a detective, or a Viceroy, might suggest.

And what is the befitting answer of a people to the Parliaments, the Cabinets, or Privy Councils, that deem it " expedient " to brand the arms, and gag the utterance of a nation ?   There is but one way to reply to them, and that is, by the signal-fire of insurrection.

Then again, had we not gone out upon the Suspension Act, and written our protest against that measure upon the standard of Rebellion, the English officials would have been led to believe that the privileges of Irish citizens might be abused, not only with perfect impunity, but without one manly symptom of resentment. We preferred risking our lives, rather than suffer this contemptuous impression to go abroad.

Thoughts such as these crossed my mind—as hastily and irregularly as I have now written them—whilst we were waiting for the coach. In giving them to you, I have made no effort to mould them into anything like an accurate and graceful form. Yet, misshapen as they are, you may, perhaps, glean from them the motives that prompted me to an enterprise which I felt convinced would fail, and learn the views I took, at the last moment, of our position and its duties, the difficulties by which it was surrounded, and the sacrifices which it exacted,

At nine o'clock the coach came up; and, having wished Charles Hart, who had accompanied us from Druid Lodge, an affectionate farewell, Dillon and I took our places; the guard sung out " All right ! " and, in a second or two, we were dashing away, in gallant style, along the road to Bray.

We were the only inside passengers, and we had the good fortune not to be interrupted until we came to Enniscorthy.

At Rudd's hotel we dismounted, and ordered a car for Ballinkeele. It was little more than five o'clock, and the morning was bitterly cold. A clear, bright sun, however, was melting the thin frost which had fallen in the night, and changing into golden vapour the grey mist which arched the gentle current of the Slaney. Not a soul was stirring in the streets; the hotel itself was dismally quiet; the fowls in the stable yard, and the gruff old dog, beside the soft warm ashes of the kitchen fire, were all at rest.

Whilst the car was getting ready, I sat down before the fire, and taking out the last number of the *Felon*, read for Dillon the beautiful, noble appeal—written, as I have understood since, by James Fintan Lalor—which ended with this question : " *Who will draw the first blood for Ireland ? Who will win a wreath that shall be green for ever ?* "

Passing out of the town, the first object which struck us was Vinegar Hill, with the old dismantled windmill, on the summit of it, sparkling in the morning light. You can easily imagine the topic upon which our conversation turned, as we passed it by.

Alas ! it is a bitter thought with me, whilst I write

these lines—more bitter far, a thousand times, than the worst privations of prison life—that, unlike those gallant Wexfordmen of '98, we have left behind us no famous field, within the length and breadth of our old country, which men could point to with proud sensation, and fair hands strew with garlands.

After an hour's drive we arrived at Ballinkeele, and, having asked for Smith O'Brien, were shown, by the servant, to his room.

We found him in bed. He did not seem much surprised at the news we told him, and asked us what we proposed to do? Dillon replied, there were three courses open to us. The first to permit ourselves to be arrested. The second, to escape. The third, to throw ourselves upon the country, and give the signal of insurrection.

O'Brien's answer was just what we had expected.

As to effecting an escape, he was decidedly opposed to it; whatever might occur, he would not leave the country; and as to permitting ourselves to be arrested, without first appealing to the people, and testing their disposition, he was of opinion we would seriously compromise our position before the public were we to do so. The Suspension of the Habeas Corpus Act was an event, he conceived, which should excite, as it would assuredly justify, every Irishman in taking up arms against the Government—at all events, he felt it to be our duty to make the experiment.

I told him we had come to the same conclusion previous to our leaving Dublin, and were prepared to take the field with him that day.

He then got up, and having sent for Mr. Maher, informed him of the news we had brought. It was arranged we should breakfast immediately, and leave Ballinkeele with as little delay as possible.

At ten o'clock we were seated in Mr. Maher's carriage, and on our way back to Enniscorthy. Whilst we drove along, different plans of operation were discussed, of which the one I now state to you was, in the end, considered to be the best.

From all we had heard, we were of opinion it would not be advisable to make our first stand in Wexford ; very few Confederates having been enrolled from that county, and our political connection with it, consequently, being extremely slight. Indeed, there was scarcely a single man of influence in the county, with whom we could put ourselves in communication ; and, without taking other circumstances of an unfavourable nature into consideration, it appeared to us, that, this being our first visit amongst them, it was too much to expect that the Wexfordmen would rally round us with the enthusiasm which the people, in other parts of the country, where we were better known, would be sure to exhibit. It was absolutely necessary to commence the insurrection with heart and vigour, and, at a glance, we saw, that, in Waterford, in Kilkenny, in Tipperary, we might calculate upon the manifestation of the warmest and boldest spirit.

At first, O'Brien was strongly in favour of going to New Ross. I was opposed to this, and argued against it with no little anxiety ; urging upon him the serious disadvantage it would be to us—in case the people of New Ross responded to our appeal—to commence the fight in a town so helplessly exposed to the fire of the war-steamers then lying in the Barrow, and the number of which, in little more than two hours, would certainly be increased by a contingent from the larger ones which were anchored in the Suir, abreast of Waterford.

The like objection prevailed against our selection of

the latter place; and we finally determined upon making for Kilkenny. The same plan, in fact, which Dillon and I thought of, the day before, was agreed to by O'Brien.

It seemed to him, as it had seemed to us, that Kilkenny was the very best place in which the insurrection could break out. Perfectly safe from all war-steamers, gunboats, floating batteries; standing on the frontiers of the three best fighting counties in Ireland—Waterford, Wexford, and Tipperary—the peasantry of which could find no difficulty in pouring in to its relief; possessing from three to five thousand Confederates, the greater number of whom we understood to be armed; most of the streets being extremely narrow, and presenting, on this account, the greatest facility for the erection of barricades; the barracks lying outside the town, and the line of communication, between the principal portions of the latter and the former, being intercepted by the old bridge over the Nore, which might easily be defended, or, at the worst, very speedily demolished; no place, it appeared to us, could be better adapted for the first scene of the revolution, than this, the ancient " City of the Confederates."

In making this selection, there were one or two considerations, of temporary interest, which influenced us to some extent.

The railway from Dublin was completed to Bagnalstown only, leaving fourteen miles of the ordinary coach road still open between the latter place and Kilkenny. The thick shrubberies and plantations; the high bramble fences, and at different intervals, the strong limestone walls which flank this road; the sharp twists and turns at certain points along it; the alternations of hill and hollow, which render a journey by it so broken and diversified; its uniform narrowness, and the steep embankments, which, in one or two places, spring up where its width measures scarcely sixteen feet ; everything was in favour of its being converted, by an insurgent population, with almost perfect security and ease, to the most successful enterprises. Along this road, as they left the station house at Bagnalstown and marched upon Kilkenny, whole regiments, drafted off from Dublin and Newbridge garrisons, might have been surprised and cut to pieces, had the country once been up.

Then, the Royal Agricultural Society was on the eve of holding its annual Cattle Show in Kilkenny ; specimens of the choicest beef and mutton had already arrived, and, in full clover, were awaiting the inspection of the highest nobles and the wealthiest commoners of the land. Many, too, of these proud gentlemen had themselves arrived ; and carriages might have been met, each hour, along the different avenues to the town, freighted with the rank, the gaiety, and fashion of the surrounding country. In case of a sustained resistance, here was a creditable supply of hostages and provisions for the Insurgents !

With some hundred head of the primest cattle in the island, we could have managed admirably behind the barricades for three or four days ; whilst with a couple of Earls, from a half a dozen to a dozen baronets, an odd marquis, or " the only duke " himself, in custody, we might have found ourselves in an excellent position to dictate terms to the Government.

We arrived in Enniscorthy between eleven and twelve o'clock. Dillon and I drove up to the chapel, just as Mass was commencing.

After Mass, we were joined by O'Brien and the Rev. Mr. ——[1] A large crowd collected round us in a few

[1] Father Parle.

minutes, and, placing ourselves at the head of it, we proceeded to the house of one of the Confederates.

Here we had a long conversation respecting the number of men enrolled in the local Clubs, and the extent to which they were armed. The information we received upon both these points, confirmed us in the resolution we had come to, of not attempting any insurrectionary movement in Wexford, at the outset. We were assured, however, by the Rev. Mr. ———, that, in case an attempt were made by the police to arrest us, the people, ill-prepared as they were, would certainly resist it.

We left the house then ; and mounting the car which was to take us to Graigue-na-mana, spoke a few words to the people. We told them the time had come when they should determine whether it were better to give in quietly to England, or go out, like men, and make a stand against her, once for all. And having asked them, would they pledge themselves to take the field, in case they heard of the people of any neighbouring county doing so, they replied, with a ringing shout : *" that they would ; and with God's blessing, too ! "*

This pledge having been given, we told them to lose no time in providing themselves with arms and ammunition, and making every other arrangement for turning out ; so that, the moment they heard of fighting going on in Kilkenny, in Tipperary, or else-where, they might be prepared to strike a blow in their own county ; and, by this means, keeping the Government forces employed at different points, prevent them from concentrating to any formidable extent, upon any one town or district.

Of course, I do not mean to give lengthened " reports " of what we said to the people along our route. The topics we touched upon, the sentiments we expressed, the appeals we made, you can very easily conceive.

The versions of our Speeches, produced upon the trials in Clonmel, and sworn to by the police, have in them a large degree of truthfulness ; though, what with bad grammar, bewildered metaphors, sentences prematurely cut off, or wedged into one another, without the slightest regard to commonsense, the rules of rhetoric, or poetic euphony, it is no easy task to make out their meaning. An eloquent speech is enough, of itself, to disorganise the police force of Ireland. A metaphor brings on giddiness of the brain ; an allusion to the shield of Achilles, or the trumpet of Alecto, induces the worst symptoms of suffocation ; blank verse bogs them ; an antithesis starts a sinew ; and as for an apostrophe ! it is sure to give them sciatica, or the lock-jaw.

It wanted but a few minutes of one o'clock when we started from Enniscorthy. Two hundred of the Clubmen, marching in column, four deep, escorted us beyond the town. A car, containing five more of them, drove on before us, keeping about a quarter of a mile in advance. This was done with the view of preventing any party of police coming upon us by surprise. There was not much fear of this, to be sure ; O'Brien, however, thought it better to adopt the precaution.

The day was exceedingly cold, and frequently heavy falls of rain compelled us, at different intervals, to take shelter in the cabins along the road. Whenever this occurred, we made it a point to enter into conversation with the poor people who owned them ; and though not in as direct a way as we might have done, yet sufficiently so for our purpose, we asked them various questions, with a view to elicit their feeling respecting the " great rising," concerning which we perceived, in

every instance, a vague impression floating through
their minds.

It depressed us sorely, to observe amongst them but
little inclination to welcome and support it.   And here,
at the very outset, we had evidence of the truth which a
short time afterwards we learned to estimate more
clearly, more painfully, and with hearts less able to
bear up against it bravely—the truth, that cold and
nakedness, that hunger and disease, to the last extremity, had done their work ; had not only withered
up the flesh and pierced the marrow in the bone ; had
not merely preyed upon the physical resources of the
man, until they wore away his substance and his form,
leaving him, beside his poor turf fire, with sunken eye
and wrinkled arm, with faltering tongue and crouching
gait, the flickering shadow of what he was ; but worse
than all—oh ! worse, a thousand times, than death by
the bayonet, or the gibbet—had eaten their way into
the soul itself, killing there the most sensitive, the most
powerful and vital of all instincts ; that instinct, which,
even in the poor worm, the lowest of all God's creatures,
teaches it to turn upon the foot by which its humble
life is perilled.

Hunger, I had thought, would break through gates
of brass and walls of granite ; would rush through
fire, or like the bayed tiger in his last desperate
extremity, spring upon the spears which hemmed it
in !

Nor was I altogether wrong.   For the hunger, which,
like the earthquake, or the whirlwind, hath been sent in
sudden wrath upon a people, has done these things, and
done them with the fury of the fiercest elements that
bend the pillars of the sky or shake the foundations of
the sea.

But the hunger of the Irish land was no such visitation. It had not come yesterday; nor a week ago; nor yet, for the first time, in the autumn of '45.

On the greyest headstone, in the loneliest and oldest churchyard, the spectre had sat down, years and years before; and from thence had looked out, with cold and bloodless eyes, upon the land, over the homes and fruits of which it had been made supreme. Years upon years—years upon years—it had walked the land; some few blessing it as a serene angel, sent by God to chastise and purify; the multitude cursing it as a foul fiend, yet falling down before it—acknowledging it lord and master!

Years ago, amid the fruits and flowers of radiant summer, the destroyer had stood concealed, watching the young soft hands that worked garlands for the pride, beauty, and gallant boyhood of the land—muttering to himself, that the flowers would shortly fade, and the fruits decay, and that all that pride, and beauty, and gallant boyhood would soon be his—and his, for many a long day to come!

Years ago, from the peak of the loftiest mountain in the South, at an hour when the heavens canopied the island with their white and azure banners, and that peak glittered beneath them like a crown of virgin gold, the phantom had looked down upon the life, and sweetness, and glory, at his feet—boasting like the devil of the wilderness, that all was his, and delivered unto him!

Years ago, in the golden fields of a most joyous harvest time, he had stood amongst the reapers; smiling at the thought, that the curse which had accompanied the fall was at length revoked, and that the children of Adam should no longer eat their bread by the sweat of their brows, as it had been promised!

Everywhere for years and years; in the valley;

on the mountain ; amid the roses and the violets of many a radiant summer ; in the golden fields of many a joyous harvest-time ; on the hearth-stone, by the side of the wrinkled and the silver-haired, mumbling to her words of abject resignation, and pointing to the grave, so that it were not wet with blood as the sweetest home beneath the heavens ; everywhere, for years and years, hunger had been upon our soil ; had ceased, a generation or two ago, to be a stranger ; was no longer shunned ; no longer fought with ; no longer cursed ; it was the eternal destiny of the land, and heaven's will be done !

It was, indeed, a sweet relief to us, when, the rain passing off, and the warm sun shining down upon its track, enabled us to leave these poor cabins, and pursue our journey.

We arrived in Graigue-na-mana about three o'clock, and drove to the little hotel, a few hundred yards above the bridge, in the main street. Though none of us had been there before, we were recognised almost immediately. Some of the lightermen, whose boats were lying in the Barrow close at hand, and who had seen me frequently in Waterford identified me as I stood looking out of one of the windows, and the news of our arrival spread at once from one end to the other of the town.

A large crowd collected before the hotel at Graigue-na-mana ; the chapel bell was set a-ringing ; cheers broke out in wild, glad chorus with it ; girls and women, from doors and windows, waved handkerchiefs and green boughs ; old men hobbled out, and propped themselves against the walls, to listen to the speeches ; old women shook their aprons, clapped their hands, and prayed aloud for God's blessing upon the scene.

We presented ourselves to the people ; stated to

them the object of our visit ; and were borne with loud hurrahs to the residence of the parish priest.

He was not at home. His curate, however, was within ; and having expressed a wish to see him for a few minutes, we were shown into the parlour where he was seated.

O'Brien told him we had come with the hope of meeting the parish priest, conceiving it our duty to state to him, personally the purport of our visit. He then communicated to the Rev. Mr. M——; that, if I mistake not, was the name of the curate—the news of the Suspension Act, and our intention, if the country would support us, to make that act the immediate cause and justification of the armed rising.

O'Brien added, that he and his friends were deeply sensible of the necessity there existed for having the sanction and co-operation of the Catholic priests in such an undertaking, and expressed to the Rev. Mr. M—— his apprehension, that unless the priests concurred with us, any attempt at insurrection, for the present, would prove abortive.

The Rev. Mr. M—— said very little, and that little was of so indecisive a nature as to be somewhat discouraging. The most conclusive sentence we could elicit from him, was simply this : " *That the whole affair was a very difficult subject to decide upon.*"

O'Brien changed the conversation ; and asked about the crops. Dillon inquired the amount of the population in Graigue-na-mana, and wished to know whereabouts General Clooney lived. The Rev. Mr. M—— pointed to the house, with evident sensations of relief ; and shook hands with us, complacently, at parting.

During this interview, the people were waiting for us in the street, and anxiously expecting the result. Our looks conveyed it to them. The frank and merry

smile upon every face before us, changed in an instant—
as though a black cloud were crossing it—into a dull,
cold, sullen gloom.

O'Brien must have marked the change, for, as he
moved in amongst them, he exclaimed—" Now, boys,
to the old General of '98 ! " [1]

There was kindling sunshine, there was kindling music,
in those words. The frank and merry smile broke out
afresh ; the glad, wild hurrah rang, clear and heartily,
through the air once more ; the bell pealed forth anew,
with strokes as wild and glad as that hurrah ; and in the
warm heart of that gallant throng, we were carried to
the house of the venerable, dear old man, who still
enjoys upon this earth the homage and the title won, in
earliest manhood. beneath the insurgent flag of Ireland.

The image of this old man ; his venerable looks ; his
words ; his manner towards us, on that day ; all are
vivid to my mind, and I think of him at this moment,
as I beheld him then, with feelings of tender, tearful,
loving admiration.

The moment O'Brien approached him, he threw his
arms round his neck, and embracing him with all the
fondness of a father, dropped warm tears upon his
cheek. He then took Dillon and me by the hands, and
affectionately welcomed us to his house.

We entered with him ; sat down for a few minutes ;
explained to the old General what had occurred, and
what we purposed doing. [2]

The conversation over, we went out to the doorway,

[1] General Clooney.

[2] It will be sad news to Meagher and his fellow-exiles, that
the noble old man is in his grave. We had the satisfaction of
meeting him a year after the events described above. His
heart was heavy ; two failures such as he had shared (with half
a century between them) quenched the light of hope ; and,
perhaps, life itself, which cannot exist without it.—[DUFFY.]

and from thence addressed the people, who, by this time, had considerably increased in numbers, and were occupying the gardens in front of the house, the streets outside, the walls, and trees and windows all about.

We told them we were on our way to Kilkenny, where we expected to be able to make a stand ; and that, in case we succeeded in doing so, the men of Graigue-na-mana should be prepared to act in our support by cutting up the roads in the neighbourhood, knocking down bridges, intercepting, in every possible way, the passage of the police and soldiers through the country.

We entreated them to lose no time in shaping themselves into something like organised bodies ; to form, for instance, one or two Clubs ; to procure any and every description of arms ; and at once elect the most intelligent and daring men of the place, as their leaders.

Here, as in Enniscorthy, our appeals were responded to with evident sympathy and enthusiasm ; and, I firmly believe that had the Graigue-na-mana men been called upon, that moment, to follow us to Kilkenny, or any other place, they would have armed themselves with stones, scythes, pitchforks and anything else they could lay their hands upon, and have tramped the road, whithersoever it might have led, with the gladdest heart, and the stoutest spirit.

As we drove off, two hundred of them accompanied, and saw us a mile or two upon our road. Most of them were boatmen, and finer fellows I have seldom seen. Square-built, light-limbed, muscular ; they seemed to me, as it were, cut out and rigged for the roughest work, and were just the sort of men to have commenced the business with.

But, it was a weary drive to the city of the Butlers ! A cold, wet, dismal drive ! Far pleasanter, to have

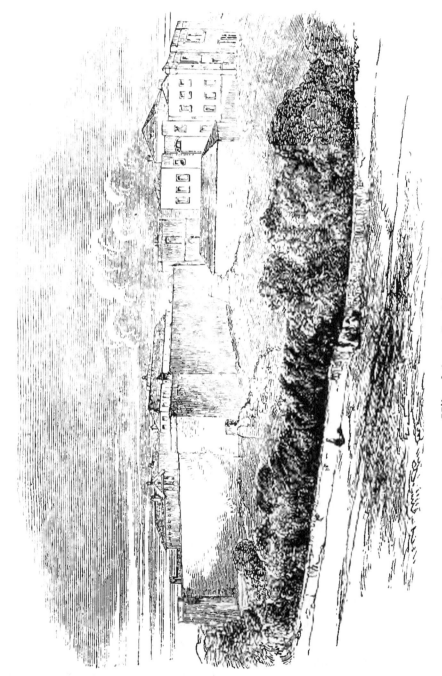

Kilmainham Gaol in 1848

been mounted in the stirrups, dashing away, along the splashing road, at the head of a hundred young and gallant horsemen ; and, as the vesper-bell was ringing out from old St. Canice, to have crossed the Nore, and cleared our course, with flashing sabres, to the aisles, where burgher, priest, and noble, once held high conference in armed and bannered splendour ! [1]

Some place along the road, between Gowran and Kilkenny—I forget exactly where—O'Brien, having learned that a parish priest resided there, suggested

[1] The question, whether the movement should begin in Kilkenny or Dublin, had long agitated the Confederate counsels. One section declared for Dublin, affirming that it was only in the vital parts a single blow was mortal, and that the seat of Government was the brain of the system. The opportunity of seizing upon the mails, and disseminating the first proclamation of the Provisional Government over the whole country in a single day, was insisted upon ; and it was affirmed that the position of Dublin, lying between the Grand and Royal Canals, was a complete military fortification. The other section maintained that Dublin could not be won at a blow, choked as it was with the troops and the friends of the Government ; that the Irish Movement did not resemble the French Revolution either in its ways or means, and must not, like it, aim exclusively at the capital. That, for success, some Authority, which the people would respect and obey, was essential, and that with this view the Council of Three Hundred must be called together, representing the whole country. That each member selected should be required to have for his constituency a certain number of men (say, a thousand), regimented into Clubs, and to bring with him a certain sum of money (say £100, a shilling from each man enrolled). In this way, it was contended, a fund of thirty thousand pounds (or some approach to it) would be secured— and the will of three hundred thousand armed and organised men be consolidated in one Council—which could negotiate with the Crown with authority, or give the signal for insurrection with effect. Kilkenny or Limerick, it was contended, was the proper place to assemble this Council, in the midst of a friendly population—and the former was generally preferred. This controversy had turned attention on Kilkenny from the beginning. But when it was hastily chosen for the last act of the drama, the previous acts, which would have made the selection judicious, were all wanting.—[Charles Gavan Duffy.]

to Dillon and me the propriety of paying him a visit. We saw no necessity for it, and little impropriety in leaving it undone ; we yielded, however, to O'Brien's wish.

At the furthest corner of the field which faced the house, we observed three priests, taking their evening walk. As we approached, one of them came to meet. us.

He was a very old, feeble, venerable man ; his walk was slow and timid ; his voice, faint, gentle, almost sorrowful ; his eyes lit up with a soft, tranquil, modest kindliness. He had entered upon the last hour of the evening of life, and the clouds and stillness of the longest night which poor mortality shall know were closing and deepening round him. Yet, one could catch a glimpse of the Eternal Light behind those clouds, and the repose of the Good and Blessed was in that deepening stillness.

He seemed to take little interest in what O'Brien said ; indeed, seemed hardly sensible of anything around him. He was gliding softly towards another land, and leaving the struggles and the sorrows of this injured one of ours behind him, a long, long way.

I felt glad when we parted from him. My heart was sad and heavy whilst I gazed upon him ; for it was a cruelty, I thought, thus to call him back from the tranquil, shaded path, through which he was descending to the grave, and ask him to take part in the cares and tumults of living men. What his name was, I have never learned.

We arrived in Kilkenny about eight o'clock, and stopped at the house of our friend. Mrs. —— met us in the hall, and gave us the warmest welcome. Her husband, she told us, was out, attending a meeting of one of the Clubs, but would shortly return. O'Brien thought it better to see him at once, and asked the eldest son—a fine, sprightly, handsome boy—to go to where the Club was sitting, for his father. He did so, and returned with him in a few minutes.

O'Brien, Dillon and I went up then with him to the drawing-room, and, for half an hour, and upwards, were engaged in conversation with him. To the plan we laid before him, he hesitated to assent. He did not consider it. advisable to commence in Kilkenny; at all events, not for a few days. The Clubs, he informed us, were insufficiently armed; miserably so, indeed. The Club with which he was connected, for instance, out of five hundred members, had but one hundred armed.

The result, however, of the conversation was an understanding, that O'Brien, Dillon and I were to leave Kilkenny the next morning; drive into Tipperary; visit Carrick, Clonmel, and Cashel; summon the people of those towns to arms; and, in three or four days, return to Kilkenny—at the head of an armed force, if possible—call out the Clubs, barricade the streets, and, from the Council Chamber of the Corporation, issue the first Revolutionary Edict to the country. —— was also obliged to leave Kilkenny in the morning, having been subpœnaed to attend on an important trial at the Cork assizes.

Whilst we were engaged in this deliberation, the people, hearing of our arrival, had flocked from all parts of the city, and were now blocking up the entire length of William Street. O'Brien, having been enthusiastically called for, went to the Citizens' Club-house, from the balcony of which he delivered a noble speech.

As at Enniscorthy and Graigue-na-mana, he told the people the time had come for an appeal to arms, and that he appeared amongst them, to share, with the poorest of his countrymen, the perils and the honours of a righteous war.

In concluding his speech, he begged of the Clubmen not to lose a moment in procuring arms, since it was more than probable, that, before the lapse of five days, they would be called upon to test their strength with the English Government. This announcement they hailed with deafening cheers, and cries of: " *We'll stand to you; We'll die for you!* "

Neither Dillon nor I spoke. We felt too much fatigued to do so. Two or three local gentlemen, however, addressed the crowd; but what they said, I altogether forget.

The following morning we breakfasted at eight o'clock; after which, O'Brien went out, and paid a couple of visits. —— had started, some hours previously, for Cork. Dillon and I remained within, and had an interview with five or six of the principal Confederates. They were the Presidents, and Vice-Presidents, and Secretaries of the different Clubs. We stated to them the resolution we had come to, the night before. They approved of it heartily, and promised to work, day and night, to procure and distribute arms among the Clubmen, so as to be fully prepared to support us on our return from Tipperary.

We then arranged with them the streets that were to be barricaded; the houses that were to be occupied; the number of men to be stationed on each barricade; the proportion of pikemen to each musketeer; and several other details. A complete programme, in fact, was sketched out and determined upon. The men with whom we held the interview were young, intelligent, active fellows; evidently in thorough downright earnest, and full of ardour. So much so, indeed, that Dillon and I parted from them in the highest spirits, and with the belief that, by the end of the week, the " faire citie " would be in the hands of her own brave people, and the Green Flag flying, in defiance to all strangers, from the walls of Ormond Castle !

At one o'clock we left Kilkenny for Callan. On entering this town, we were surprised to find a large concourse of people, headed by the Temperance Band, waiting to receive us. We learned afterwards, that —— in passing through on the Cork mail, had told them we were coming.

A large bon-fire blazed in the centre of the main street. The door-ways of the houses were decked out with laurel boughs ; whilst, from many of the windows, small green flags, decorated with flowers and ribands, were flying gaily. As we drove a little further on, hundreds of fine young fellows rushed towards us, waving their hats, cheering to the top of their voices, and passionately grasping us by the hands. Lively, handsome girls—with flashing black eyes and cheeks of the brightest bloom—bounded through the crowd, threw their arms about our necks, and kissed us, amid the smiles and merry loud applause of their own brave boys.

The latter compelled us to dismount, and fall in behind them. The band struck up " The White Cockade," and with a light step, and hearts as light, we swept on to the Market house.

Arriving at this place, we found it occupied by a party of the 8th Hussars ; a troop of which had come in that morning from Fethard, and were on their way, with the rest of the regiment, to Newbridge from Ballincollig.

At the moment we entered, they were busy cleaning their bridles, saddles, carbines, sword-belts, and other accoutrements. Seeing the crowd approach the Market-house, some of them were for starting off, at first, and leaving the position in the hands of the " enemy." Just as I made my appearance at the door, a tall Englishman, with a shirt speckled all over with blue miniature-likenesses of Jenny Lind, was on the point of bolting down the stone steps which led from the top room to the street ; having managed to coil his saddle girths, saddle-cloth, and every other appurtenance— round one arm, whilst from the other, as from a projecting show-rod over the door-way of a Jew's shop, there dangled a variety of articles, in an aggregate of the most complicated disorder. There was, for instance, a cloak, a pair of short boots, a shako, a brown pocket-handkerchief, and a glazed stock of the most suffocating inflexibility. Most of his comrades were Irish, and burst out laughing at him. One fine lad wanted to know " where the blazes Jim was flying to in that helter-skelter style, as if a mine had knocked the feet from under him."

I told them there was no necessity for their leaving the building ; that no advantage would be taken of them ; that their arms were just as safe there as they would be in Dublin Castle ; perhaps more so.

" We know that, sir," replied the young corporal, " we know well you wouldn't take an unfair advantage of the poor soldiers ; at any rate, you wouldn't do it to the Irish Hussars."

" Three cheers," I cried, going to the door, and calling upon the people, " three cheers, boys, for the 8th Royal Irish Hussars ! "

The tall Englishman with the Jenny Lind shirt, who was standing close to me, grasped his traps again, and swore he'd stand it no longer, but be off. Upon consideration, however—seeing, I presume, it would be no easy matter to cut his way through the crowd which surrounded the Market-house—he adopted, with strong reluctance apparently, the alternative of remaining where he was.

During the entire time we were addressing the people the Hussars stood behind us, inside the door-way, and listened to us, with deep interest and satisfaction. Dillon told me, that whilst I was speaking, he was particularly struck by the appearance of the corporal ; " His eye was full of fire ; his lips set ; his clear, frank features, lit up with a glow of pleasure and enthusiasm, betrayed the gallant treason of his heart ; and when," continued Dillon, " alluding to the police—who were scattered, here and there, all through the crowd—you told them, that ' in a day or two, you were to mount the Green yourself,' he looked as if he would have leaped down amongst the people, and pledged his love and courage to their cause."

Here, too—as we had already done in Enniscorthy, in Graigue-na-mana, and Kilkenny—we called upon the people to provide themselves at once with arms, for we had come to the determination, if the country would support us, to bring, at length, the old quarrel between England and Ireland to an issue, and, it was probable, that, before the close of the week, a thousand Tipperary-men would be in full march, along that road, upon Kilkenny.

Had you heard the thrilling cheer with which this announcement was received, you would have believed with us, that no rash experiment was on the eve of being made ; you would have believed that the spirit of the country had been stirred from its most secret depths, and that a torrent, which would sweep all before it, had been struck from the rock, and was bounding through the land !

With this belief we left the little town of Callan on

that day—Monday, July the 24th—and pursued our
road to Carrick.

At Nine-mile-house we stopped to change horses;
and whilst we were waiting for the fresh relay, twenty
or thirty of the country people, who happened to be
about the place at the time, flocked round us. We
entered, of course, into conversation with them; told
them the business we were on; the resolution we had
come to; the plan of operations we proposed to carry
out; and asked them could we depend upon that part
of the country? Were the people, about there, favourable to a rising? Were they armed? To what extent?
Had any Clubs been formed in the neighbourhood?
How were the priests disposed?

In answer to all these questions, except the last, we
received the most encouraging assurances.

We might depend upon them; there wasn't a man
among them that wasn't true; they were long expecting
it would come to this, and a pity it hadn't been done
five year ago, when Mr. O'Connell had the people and
the priests at their head; they were armed well enough;
if they all hadn't guns, they had their hooks, and their
spades, and their forks, at any rate; and though they
weren't as smart as the guns, they'd stand to them well
enough when it came to close quarters. As for the
Clubs, there were one or two in the neighbourhood,
and the people a-bouts were enrolling themselves as
fast as they could. But as for the priests—there was
only an odd one or two up to the mark; and they
could not do much, owing to their being the curates,
and the parish priests were agin them intirely; yet if
they had a priest, at all, at all, it wasn't much matter
about the rest, for the people were tired of keeping so
quiet, and dying from day to day.

After this conversation, we desired two or three fine

young fellows, whose appearance greatly struck us, and whose earnestness and enthusiasm it was impossible not to detect in every look, and word, and gesture—we desired them to disperse through the adjoining country that night, and let the people know we had determined upon taking the field ; and it was more than probable we would be marching, at the head of an armed body, by that very place, before the end of the week ; and, if this should be the case, it would be well we were met at Nine-mile-house by the Clubs and peasantry of the neighbourhood ; indeed, it was absolutely necessary we should be reinforced at every town, village, and house along the road, since our project was to attack and take possession of Kilkenny.

The moment we had given them these instructions, they started off ; and, a few days afterwards, I learned, that, the whole of that night, these three young peasants were on foot, travelling from house to house, from cabin to cabin, passing, in every direction, within a circuit of seven miles and more, the word we gave them—never once resting, never taking a drop to drink, nor a bit to eat, until the morning woke.

I forget what hour it was when we reached Nine-mile-house. It could not have been, however, very far from our usual dining hour, for we felt extremely hungry ; the consequence of which was that, previous to our starting for Carrick, O'Brien proposed we should have some dinner.

If I remember rightly, there are only two public-houses at this place ; and into one of them—the one on the right-hand side of the road, as you come up from Carrick—we made our way forthwith. The good-humoured-looking woman behind the counter made a courtesy as we entered, and asked us wouldn't we walk into the parlour and sit down a-while ? O'Brien thanked her, and said that, as we were anxious to leave for Carrick with as little delay as possible, we preferred taking anything she had, in the way of dinner, where we were.

"Oh, then, dinner, indeed!" she replied, "it's a poor dinner we can give you; all we have are a few hard eggs, a little salt butter, some bread, and a cup of new milk, if you won't have the spirits."

"That will do admirably," said O'Brien; "we must learn to put up with worse before long, I expect."

"Indeed, then," rejoined the poor woman, "it's the best they've got you'll have from the people at any rate, wherever you go, your honour; and proud they'll be, if you take it; little as it'll be, God help them!"

The eggs and the milk and the salt butter and the bread, were laid out upon the counter, and we set to work with great heart and the keenest appetite; our good, kind hostess blushing very hard all the time, and now and then exclaiming, as she turned away her head, and pretended to be very busy looking for something on the shelves behind the counter, that "Sure it was a pity and a shame to see such gentlemen taking such fare, and they with their own comfortable homes."

When we had done, I went out to see that the luggage was all right, and settle with the driver who had brought us from Kilkenny.

A number of policemen were lounging about the car, and one of them, on my moving towards him, touched his cap, and expressed a hope "that Mr. Meagher was in good health, and wouldn't come to any trouble, as he knew his family well."

I asked him, "How was that? Was he ever in Waterford?"

"Yes, sir," he said, "I was in Waterford, but a long time ago; not for these twenty years, or more."

"Well," I replied, "if so, you could hardly have seen me."

"That's true enough," he continued to observe, "that's true enough. I never seen yourself till now; but I seen your father and the rest of the family, at your grandfather's funeral—that is, your mother's father's funeral—and a splendid funeral it was—it covered the length of the Quay."

This was no other than the respectable old sergeant of police, of whose evidence Mr. Whiteside, upon cross-examination, made so much fun that the solemn Chief Justice, was obliged to interpose, and threaten to have the court-house cleared if another laugh was heard. I recollect the scene well.

"You say, sir," inquired Mr. Whiteside, "that you had a conversation with Mr. Meagher at the Nine-mile-house?"

"Yes."

"Well, sir, pray may I ask you, if it is not intruding too much upon your confidence, what may have been the purport of that conversation?"

"Why, nothing at all," replied the poor sergeant, "only I told him I was at his grandfather's funeral."

"Then, sir," resumed Mr. Whiteside, "the sum total of your connection with Mr. Meagher amounts to this, and this only—that you were at his grandfather's funeral?"

A perceptible suppression of violent convulsions here took place.

"Why then," said the sergeant, "that's all; and I agree with the learned Counsel, that same is not much."

Here the convulsions broke out, and were threatening to put an end, for the rest of the day, to everything like order and sobriety, when, as I have already mentioned, the inexorable Chief of the Queen's Bench vigorously interposed—instructing the High Sheriff to clear the court, in case any such improper levity occurred for the future.

Finding that the sergeant had nothing else of importance to communicate, I wished him good-bye, and took my seat on the car. O'Brien and Dillon were already seated ; so, we took off our hats to the poor fellows who were standing round us, and joining in the cheers they gave for " The Green above the Red," dashed away for Carrick.

I think it was within five miles of the latter place, that, seeing some men working in a field, we pulled up, and beckoned them to come to us. There were cross-roads, at all events, where we stopped ; and this circumstance will serve to indicate the distance we were from Carrick, at the time I speak of, should you ever pass along our line of road, and feel a curiosity to ascertain the different points at which any particular incidents connected with our movement occurred.

The men threw down their spades, and, running across the field, leaped the ditch by the road-side, and came up to us immediately. O'Brien introduced himself, first of all, to them ; and then introduced Dillon. In my case, no introduction was required. They knew me beforehand.

" You're welcome ! You're welcome, Mr. Meagher ! " they exclaimed ; " and we hope your honour has been well since you were on Slievenamon with us ? "

I asked them had they been at the great meeting there ?

" Faith, then, we were," they said, " and we'll be up there again if you want us."

O'Brien intimated it was probable we would, and that they could easily guess the reason we had called them over from their work,

" Well, sure enough, we might," one of them replied, " for there's talk this morning in Carrick—so they tell us—about the Government arresting you ; and if they do, you may depend upon us. We let them know a bit of our minds the other day, when there was a report of Father Byrne's being arrested."

" Oh ! " said O'Brien, " I heard something of that before, but I should like to hear something more about it."

" Why, the short and the long of it is, that, when the report spread, the chapel-bell was set ringing, and all the people of the town turned out, most of them with pikes ; and when the news came out here, why, there wasn't a man nor a boy of fifteen that didn't take the road ; but, it so happened, there was no truth in the report, and Father Byrne quieted the people, and we came back, when we were within a couple of mile of the place, for, your honour, there was nothing for us to do in Carrick ; and that's all about it."

" Then," resumed O'Brien, " I conclude we may reckon upon you, in case we are compelled to take the field ? "

" Indeed, then, you may," they replied, " and upon hundreds besides, round about here ; for we have two Clubs in the neighbourhood, and Mr. O'Mahony—as noble a young gentleman as ever you laid your eyes upon—is President of one of them."

" Does Mr. O'Mahony," inquired Dillon, " live near here ? "

" Quite convanient, your honour," was the reply, " and one of us will run up and fetch him down, if you'd like to see him."

" Certainly," said O'Brien, " by all means ; he is just the man we want to see."

Away went one of them, then, up one of the cross-roads ; and whilst he was absent, O'Brien, Dillon, and I, mingled with the country people who had collected round the car, and quietly conversed with them.

There were some noble-looking girls in the little group, and the enthusiasm with which they spoke of the coming fight I shall never forget. It had no terrors for them ; it wore, in their frank and beautiful eyes, no fiendish aspect. Far otherwise, indeed !

Encircled with a wreath of crimson light, crowned with the sweet wild flowers and the golden fruitage of their native soil, the armed spirit of the nation's liberty approached them as a warrior angel, and they hailed the vision with blessings, and songs of welcome !

Think not that I write this in a mood of idle, driftless exaggeration, and that such sentiments have no deeper birth than those meaningless, insincere, and wanton compliments, with which our public men, at dinners, *soirees*, and meetings, consign to contempt and profanation some of the finest sensibilities, and one of the loftiest adorations of the human heart. Sickened at this disfigurement of a noble theme, I have, at all times, in my speeches and my writings, abstained from giving expression to sentiments such as it is now my pride to vindicate, lest, failing to utter them with due delicacy and decorum, I should myself participate in the vulgar impropriety I here condemn.

But, my mind would feel ill at ease, indeed, if in this little narrative—graceless and unstudied as it is—I refrained from uttering one poor, simple, word in recognition of that pure, sweet, earnest, dauntless spirit, which, during the course of the proceedings I relate, shone out, and, even in the cloudiest seasons of our misfortune, clothed in radiant loveliness the daughters of our native land.

Should these pages ever come to light, let no frivolous,

dull, or withered heart ; let no heart whose blood has
turned to gall amid the insincerities and cruelties of the
world, or whose diviner aspirations—driven back by
the cold and jewelled hand of a faithless and irreverent
society—have died, in paltriest cowardice, within the
field of that rich nature from whence they sprung ; let
no such heart scan with distrust, with levity, or scorn,
this, the humble tribute I have offered up to the fond,
brave sisterhood of our sad old island.

In the proudest moments of our career, when
thousands stood around us, and the chivalrous passion
of our country arose and burned, like a signal-fire
upon the hills, at the bidding of our invocation ; in
the darkest and most desolate moments of our outlaw's
life, when house and hearth were barred against us,
and we knew not where to lay our heads ; in the loneliest
and most abject moments of our imprisonment, when
not a ray of hope or honour flickered above our cells ;
when the pimps and scribes of our triumphant foe were
busy with their jibes and sarcasms, and slander showered
her venom upon our acts, our failure, and our sacrifice ;
when treachery broke loose beneath us, and those whom
we had thought would have had the decency to be
silent, since they had not the courage to befriend us,
stood up amongst our enemies, and fawned upon them ;
when vulgar Pharisees, garbed in civic ermine, voted
from their Council-rooms thanks to the special providence of the English Castle, which had, to use their
silken dialect, " with so much sagacity, and above all,
with so much leniency," averted the event they had
themselves not shunned, not fought against—not they,
the Loyalists !—but had urged on, by Repeal Debates,
and Rotunda Levees, and congratulatory addresses to
the Government of France, and the coming of which
they had hailed, and panted for so greedily in the

recesses of their hearts, and the veiled sanctuaries of their dwelling-places; when the public voice was hushed, and the honest heart could find no vent for all its anguish but through muttered throbbings; in this, as in every vicissitude of our career—in the saddest as in the brightest—we were cheered, inspired, ennobled, by the sympathy of that fair, courageous, faithful sisterhood.

Oh! whilst the songs and sympathies of a choir so glorious vibrate through these skies of ours let no true son of the Irish land despair! From such a choir will come the Brides of a gallant soldiery—the mothers of another Grachii!

We had not been more than twenty minutes in conversation with this little group, when the clatter of horse's hoofs was heard. On looking up the crossroad to our right, we saw a tall, robust, gallant-looking fellow, mounted on a strong black horse, coming at full speed, towards us.

This was O'Mahony—one of the noblest young Irishmen it has been my pride to meet with during the course of my short public life.

His square, broad frame; his frank, gay, fearless look; the warm, forcible, headlong earnestness of his manner; the quickness and elasticity of his movements; the rapid glances of his clear, full eye; the proud bearing of his head; everything about him, struck us with a brilliant and exciting effect, as he threw himself from his saddle, and, tossing the bridle on his arm, hastened to meet and welcome us.

At a glance, we recognised in him a true leader for the generous, passionate, intrepid peasantry of the South. As we clasped his hand, the blood dashed in joy and triumph through our veins; for a moment, every sensation, approaching to disquietude or despondency, vanished from our minds; and, in a dazzling trance of exultation, we became sensible, in his presence, of no emotions, save those of the most joyous confidence.

Strange it is, the influence which a man of a fine and soldierly appearance, flinging himself into a revolutionary movement, has upon the feelings of the most utter stranger. I had never seen O'Mahony previous to this interview; had heard of him but once before, and that in a very slight way indeed; yet, I greeted him at this moment with a warmth of expression, which, I had thought, would have escaped me only in conversation with the oldest and most trusted companion.

A thousand glowing pictures, too, flashed across my mind, as I looked into his open, manly, well-traced features, and read there the force and daring of his courageous heart.

They are still before me :—

Armed columns of the peasantry, pouring down through gap and river-course, scaring, with their tramp and shout, the eagle from his solitude, and waking the echoes from their enchanted sleep in the shadowy mountains far off——

Camp-fires, quivering through the mist and star-light, along the hills——the rude challenges of the out-posts——the signal-shots and pass-words of the scouts.

The grey morning breaking, and the flag of the proud old Irish race flying out from rath and round tower, from bridge and belfry, kindling into rapture the morning-hymn of many a young and gallant spirit——

Then, the red ensign, in some lone defile——hedged in by lines of crossed and matted steel——bending, and splitting, and scattering into scorched and blackened shreds, beneath the volleying clouds, which, from tree

15

and rock, swept down, and broke, in thunder peals, around it !

With somewhat of a firm hand I have traced them here ; yet, with how mournful a light do the lingering recollections of such visions abide with me, in these clouded days of solitude, silence, and captivity ! How vain, senseless, and boyish, as they say, must seem these visions to you ; now that the summer warmth from which they expanded into glory has departed, and a bleaksome winter has come upon the land !

Willingly, in truth, would I draw a black veil over these beautiful, sunlit pictures ; concealing them from every eye, until the splendour descending from the uplifted forehead of our transfigured nation, should beautify and render them immortal prophecies.

But, I am not confining myself to a recital of mere incidents.

As far as my memory enables me, I am telling you sincerely what I thought, and felt ; what hopes, affections, fears, crossed my mind, almost in every scene we passed through ; and, anxious as I am, that you should know the whole truth, I think it would be uncandid—weak and timorous it would be, certainly—to make, with regard to my conjectures—nay, even with regard to my infatuations—the slightest reservation.

From what I have already said, you will easily conceive that our conversation with O'Mahony was full of hopefulness.

He represented to us that the country all about Carrick, on towards Clonmel, and along the Suir on the Tipperary side, was thoroughly alive, and ready to take the field at once.

Producing a couple of leather-covered books from his pocket, he ran over the names of the Clubmen of whom he was the President ; enumerated the sections into which he had divided them ; mentioned who the captains of the sections were ; the number that were armed ; and then, entered into larger details, as to the prevalence of the insurrectionary spirit, and the zeal with which the people, in his neighbourhood, were providing themselves with pikes, and every other description of arms.

Never, never, can I forget the enthusiasm of this gallant, glorious fellow, as he spoke to us, and ran through these details. It was the enthusiasm of a heart, which, fearless itself of danger—panting to meet and grapple with the deadliest peril—lost sight of every difficulty ; and, borne aloft upon its own impetuous faith, exultingly believed that the country had but to strike to prove herself invincible.

The plan of action we had adopted in Kilkenny—and which had been stated openly to the people in Callan and at the Nine-mile-house—we communicated, of course, to O'Mahony. Though strongly of opinion we should commence, that very night in Carrick, he gave way to our suggestions, and promised to meet us, at the head of his Club, and any number of peasantry he could collect in the meantime, at any place, day, and hour we specified.

We then drove off, and, in little more than half an hour, entered Carrick.

I know not how to describe the scene we witnessed on entering this town.

Though many months have passed away since, I am still as perplexed about that strange scene as when I stood in the midst of it, and felt myself up-borne by the mighty passions it disclosed. It was then more like a dream to me than an actual occurrence ; and it now seems to me the same.

A torrent of human beings, rushing through lanes

and narrow streets ; surging and boiling against the white basements that hemmed it in ; whirling in dizzy circles, and tossing up its dark waves, with sounds of wrath, vengeance, and defiance ; clenched hands, darting high above the black and broken surface, and waving to and fro, with the wildest confusion, in the air ; eyes red with rage and desperation, starting and flashing upwards through the billows of the flood ; long tresses of hair—disordered, drenched, and tangled—streaming in the roaring wind of voices, and, as in a shipwreck, rising and falling with the foam ; wild, half-stifled, passionate, frantic prayers of hope ; invocations, in sobs, and thrilling wailings, and piercing cries, to the God of Heaven, His saints, and the Virgin Mary ; challenges to the foe ; curses on the red flag : scornful, exulting, delirious defiances of death ; all wild as the winter gusts at sea, yet as black and fearful, too ; this is what I then beheld—these the sounds I heard—such the dream which passed before me !

It was the Revolution, if we had accepted it.

Why it was not accepted, I fear I cannot with sufficient accuracy explain. For, as I have already said, of that whole scene I remember nothing clearly, save the passion, the confusion, and the tumult.

As a dream it came ; and so it passed before me. As such, alone, I now remember it.

Would to heaven ! that, with these words, I could here lay down my weary pen, and write no more of that mournful past, amid the wreck of which—amid the trampled laurels, the soiled and torn banners, the broken shields, the drooping plumes, the extinguished lamps, the cold and crownless altar-stones of which—I sit imprisoned !

But this cannot be ! The love I bear my country ; the proud love with which I recognise, assert, and worship, her ancient name, descent, and glory; the jealous love with which I sit in sorrow by her tomb, awaiting the morning of her resurrection; this love will not exonerate me from the task I have undertaken.

I must resume, then—distasteful and dispiriting as it is—the line of my broken story.

Extricating ourselves from the immense crowd which hemmed us in on every side, we made our way to the house of Mr. P——; which house, if I recollect rightly, is situated somewhere about the middle of the main street, opposite to Shannahan's hotel.

It was from one of the front windows of this house that, on the Sunday week previous, I addressed upwards of 15,000 people, on my coming down from Slievena-mon. Mr. P—— had been for some time an ardent Confederate, and having, on many occasions, given very striking evidence of his earnest sympathy with our movement, we did not hesitate to select his house as the fittest one for any consultation it might be necessary for us to hold.

On entering the hall, we met several of the more prominent members of the Carrick Clubs, and two or three gentlemen, residing in the vicinity of the town, whose identification with us, in purpose as well as sentiment, was well known, and to be relied on thoroughly.

I missed, however, the Rev. Mr. Byrne, one of the Catholic Curates of the town; a young and gallant clergyman, who had, from the commencement, shown a bold front in the national movement. He was too good a man to be absent. As the trusted guide and leader, too, of the local Clubs, I conceived it was his duty to be with us at so critical a moment; and that, whether it declared for peace or war, his opinion should be sought for.

Having learned that he was at the residence of the

parish priest, the Very Rev. Dr. Connolly, I sat down and wrote him a note, earnestly begging of him to come over, and give us the benefit of his honest and affectionate advice.

Whilst waiting for the answer, we remained in the drawing-room, anxiously conversing with the officers of the different Clubs, of which, in this little town, there had been organised, within the last six weeks, no less than twelve.

A confused and distracted conversation it was, as well as a truly anxious one !

Everyone was giving his favourite opinion ; setting forth, with boisterous impetuosity, his own peculiar views ; urging, with broken phrases and impatient utterance, a plan of action, isolated from, and, in the end, utterly hostile to and contradictory of all the rest.

One was for commencing there and then. Another proposed that the night should be spent in preparation, and that the morning should be ushered in with the volleying of guns and the gleaming of pike-heads. A third suggested—altogether overlooking the Suspension Act—that the elections for the Council of Three Hundred should take place with as little delay as possible, and that the Delegates should proceed, immediately upon their election, to the Rotunda, each escorted by one thousand armed men, selected from the constituents of his electoral division. A fourth was in favour of a camp on Slievenamon. A fifth for taking to the loughs and glens of the Commeragh, and there holding out until the country had armed herself more formidably. There was a sixth proposition, too, and a seventh, and an eighth ; and, for all I remember to the contrary, there may have been as many as the First Book of Euclid contains.

Never did I behold so perplexing and bewildering a

tumult ! Never did there occur to me a scene less susceptible of repose, of guidance, of any clear, steady, intelligible control !

Within, there was this confusion and uproar of tongues ; without, there was the tossing and surging of the mighty throng, whose deep vibrations shook the walls of the house in which we were assembled. Add to this, that hundreds were blocking up the stair-case ; crowding and crushing on the landing-places ; crowding and crushing round the table at which we sat ; pressing down upon us, in their hot anxiety to see and hear us ; and, for this very reason, and urged on by this same vehement and generous passion, were overpowering every exertion we strove to make—drowning completely every word we uttered—exhausting our strength, and rendering us incapable of guiding with a firm hand the elements that swept and roared around us.

NOTE BY GAVAN DUFFY

The history of what was done, and omitted to be done, at Kilkenny, has been an earnest subject of inquiry with us. A Kilkenny Confederate, perfectly familiar with the entire business, furnished this account of O'Brien's visit, which throws additional light on Meagher's narrative :—

" Kilkenny was ill prepared to begin so important a struggle, and one wherein it was of the most para-mount consequence that the first blow should not be a failure. There were four Clubs, one in each of the parishes of Kilkenny, but they were not Confederate Clubs, and had never been in union with the Confedera-tion. They were Clubs of what were called ' United Repealers.' That is, Young and Old Irelanders blended under a new name ; and the officers of some of them were strictly Old Irelanders. These Clubs were only newly formed, and, as Clubs, were neither drilled nor armed. Within the previous week they had given in their adhesion to the ' Irish League,' then formed, which they joined in a body, numbering seventeen hundred. Now in the report of the League meeting, the seventeen hundred were returned in the *Freeman* newspaper as seventeen thousand ; and this error was copied by all the papers, so that Kilkenny was thus reputed to have had enrolled in its Clubs tenfold the number that really were in those associations. Then again, this seventeen hundred included old men and mere boys, as well as adults, so that the real affective strength of the Clubs might have been somewhere about six hundred men.

" Of these, not one-third were armed, and not one-sixth armed with guns, while the quantity of powder and ball was most meagre indeed, and the remainder of the arms consisted of bayonets, swords, and pike heads without handles. In fact, there was no expectation of an immediate outbreak, and matters were far removed from being in a state of readiness to meet so prompt a call. The bulk of the shop-keepers had not joined the movement at all, so the Clubs consisted chiefly of tradesmen, operatives and labourers. There was no means within reach for the immediate arming of the people. There were four arms' shops in the town but they would not supply above sixty stand of arms of the range of carbines or muskets.

" The garrison consisted of one thousand infantry, with two troops of cavalry and some slight ordnance. The wall surrounding the garrison was ten feet high, well looped, supplied inside with ' banquets,' and admirably fitted to resist an attack from a body of three or four thousand infantry. Unless with cannon to make a breach in its walls, it would be most difficult to take it.

" When O'Brien, Meagher and Dillon reached Kilkenny, they were of opinion that that city was the ground to begin on, and that a rapid surprise of the garrison would succeed. The true state of Kilkenny's strength was laid before them, with the certainty of the failure of such an attempt. Cannon there was none ; and neither men nor arms sufficient for such a fight ; an escalade was, therefore, out of the question ; a street barricade to tempt the military out was equally impossible, the more especially as the houses along the lines of street were mostly those of neutrals—nay, of enemies, few of friends.

" John Dillon, who weighed all with the coolness of a practised and calculating soldier, offered to attempt the garrison, if five hundred armed men would be got to follow him. But this was out of the question, though Meagher, with that gallantry so markedly his own, offered to start instantly for Waterford, and by morning to return with one hundred armed men, and whom he proposed to bring up in cars ; but it was considered, that even this addition, supposing it was able to leave Waterford and reach Kilkenny without interruption, would not make a force adequate to so bold a blow.

" Kilkenny being impracticable, attention was now turned to Carrick-on-Suir, where it was stated there were two thousand Clubmen nearly all armed, mostly men of desperate enterprise, and with a garrison in the town of only two hundred soldiers—where men and arms were vastly more numerous on the side of the Confederation than on that of the army—in fine, where matters were in the inverse condition of Kilkenny, and where if the people moved they must have succeeded.

Thus the gain would have been not merely victory, but the *prestige* of the first blow being victorious, which would have lit all Ireland ; whereas, the failure of the first blow would have ruined everything. And that then, having succeeded at Carrick, they might march from thence upon both Clonmel and Kilkenny, both of which would be sure to fall into the hands of the national army, they would be able to lead from Carrick ; and that, when that army reached Kilkenny, the Clubs would respond effectively to their call.

" There were present at this discussion two Presidents of Kilkenny Clubs, and on the following morning, previous to O'Brien and his friends leaving Kilkenny, several of the most determined of the Clubmen waited on them.

" While Dillon and Meagher were for immediate and prompt attack, O'Brien was most desirous that arrest or attempt at arrest, and then rescue, should precede actual war, and that when so rescued they should head the people. However, he offered no opposition to the views of his associates."

Narrative of the Penal Voyage to Tasmania.

[This narrative of Meagher's was contained in a letter to Gavan Duffy written from Campbell Town in February, 1850.]

On Saturday, October 28th, 1849, between eight and nine o'clock in the evening, we reached our destination. The voyage was what they call an average one, having been accomplished in a hundred and some odd days. The weather, during it, was, generally speaking, extremely fine. From Kingstown Harbour to the Cape not more than a fortnight's rain occurred ; and that, not all at once, but at intervals ; three days at a time being the longest succession of wet weather with which we were troubled.

The passage across the Indian Ocean, however, was, on the whole, exceedingly unpleasant. Heavy falls of rain, accompanied by the wildest gales, frequently occurred ; the latter driving us considerably to the south, and introducing us—at a distance, to be sure, but unmistakably enough—to the white bergs and icebergs of the bleak Antarctic. Add to this, that, for the six weeks we were fighting through these cold, wild waves, not a sail appeared, nor had we the faintest glimpse of land.

Yet, what with our little library, and pens, and logbooks—M'Manus's backgammon box, and other harmless resources—the time went by less irksomely than you might suppose, and left us nothing very serious to complain of. Indeed, somehow or other—in sunshine and in storm—running before the wind, ten knots an hour—or rocking sluggishly in a calm—in all weathers, and with every motion of our little ship, we managed to keep alive most cheerfully, and bid defiance to all the shades of Tartarus.

Occupations like these served in great measure to relieve the monotony of our sea-life, and render it something more than endurable. Were it not for them, indeed, the voyage would have been most tiresome and insipid. Except in the coasting-trade, or for an odd cruise in the Mediterranean, I would not be a sailor for all the world. The sameness of the life would be my death before long. " As to the sea," observed Mr. Solomon Gills to his nephew, " that's well enough in fiction, Wally, but it don't do in fact : it won't do at all."

With regard to our accommodations on board, nothing could have been better. We had an excellent saloon, in which we breakfasted, dined, took tea, read, wrote, and got through a variety of other agreeable pursuits. Our berths ran along two sides of it, and were shut off from the saloon by means of sliding-doors and panellings of open work.

The regulations laid down for our observance were but few, and far from being strict.

In the first place, we were forbidden to have any intercourse with the ship's company, save and except with the captain and the surgeon. In the next place, only two of us, at a time, were permitted to be on deck together. At nine o'clock, p.m., we were obliged to retire to our berths ; at which hour the sergeant of marines extinguished the lamp in the saloon, saw that we were all safe and four in number, then locked the door of the saloon on the outside, and reporting " All

right," delivered the key to the captain. Outside of
our quarters, a marine was stationed, night and day,
whose duty it was to report our presence every four
hours, and cut off all communication between the
aforesaid quarters and the rest of the lower deck.
Another marine was appointed to wait on us, and
perform a variety of domestic duties ; so that, in a
peculiar way, and to a certain extent, he became a
modern edition of Proteus ; assuming different characters, presenting various appearances, and exhibiting
divers accomplishments and faculties in the course of
every four-and-twenty hours ; passing, with astonishing
facility through the most startling transitions—from
cook to butler, and from butler to chambermaid. He
was an honest, active, respectable, good man, and his
name was Spriggs.

As for the *Swift* herself—she was a sprightly, handsome, little brig—as steady as a rock, but as graceful
as a swan. I wish you could have seen her in a storm :
at no other time did she look to such advantage. With
a broken, scowling sky above her, and a broken, scowling
sea beneath, she gallantly dashed on. Glancing down
the steepest valleys, she seemed to gather fresh force
and daring from the steepness of the fall ; then breasting
the highest waves, she would top them with a bound, and
flinging their white crests in sparkling atoms, right and
left before her, spring further on—her beautiful light
spars quivering like lances in the gale.

As for the officers, they were fine, generous, gallant
fellows. Owing to the restrictions imposed by the
Home Office, our intercourse with them, as you may
easily suppose, was extremely limited ; but, limited
as it was, we soon were led to conceive the truest esteem
for them. England may well feel proud as long as she

has such brave, upright, noble hearts to serve her. Their frank, generous, warm nature—their manly, gallant bearing—form a striking contrast, indeed, to the cold, cramped rigidity of some of the officials here.

The captain was a most courteous, gentle, amiable, good man ; strict, to be sure, in carrying out, in our regard, the instructions he had received ; but never, in the slightest degree, inquisitive, exacting, or officious. Far from it.   Wherever it was in his power to be so— wherever his instructions left him to his own discretion —we found him always willing and anxious to grant us any little indulgence we asked for.   I do not think that a better man could have been selected to discharge the painful duty with which he was entrusted.

Very probably, you may have heard, long before this, that we were not permitted to remain more than a few hours at the Cape.   On the evening of Wednesday, September 11th, between seven and eight o'clock, we dropped anchor in Simon's Bay ; but had hardly done so, when orders came from Commodore Wyvil, the officer in command of the station, directing us to be off about our business next day, at twelve o'clock precisely ; and, furthermore, prohibiting the slightest communication between the *Swift* and the shores.

These orders were issued in consequence of the storm which was raging at Cape Town, and which threatened to sweep Sir Harry Smith, his government and house-hold, mounted riflemen and all, right into the sea, should any convict, political or otherwise, be permitted to set foot within the immaculate territory of the Hottentot and Boer.   The result of which, so far as we were concerned, was simply this, that, next day, precisely at twelve o'clock, we were running out to sea again, in a very disconsolate condition, indeed ; having a very scanty supply of fresh provisions on board, and ten weeks' accumulation of soiled linen in our portmanteaus and bags.

From that day, September 12th, until Saturday, October 27th, we saw no land ; not so much as would sod a lark, as they say at home. It is true, we should, by right, have passed between St. Paul's and Amsterdam, two volcanic islands, inhabited by wild goats and pigs, lying midway between the Cape and Van Diemen's Land, and included in the dependencies of the Mauritius. The gale, however, which took us out from Simon's Bay, bore us so far astray from the direct course that we were obliged to leave the more southerly of these islands sixty miles to the north.

Well, so much for the *Swift*, and our voyage out ; of which, as you cannot help remarking, I have said little. It would, however, have been difficult for me to have said much more. One day's sailing is just the same as a three months' voyage, and from a sketch of one an excellent outline of the other may be easily conceived. Breakfast—tea, without milk, dry biscuit, and brown sugar ; dinner—salt-beef, preserved potatoes, bottled porter, a joint of mutton, perhaps, and a bowl of pea-soup ; shifting of sails—yarn-spinning, rope-splicing, hands-to-quarters, hammock-scrubbing, singing, drumming, dancing, fifing at the forecastle : the first watch, lights extinguished—there's a complete history of a voyage round the world ! so far, at all events, as my experience enables me to decide.

But, for all the dreariness of those six weeks, in our passage up the Derwent we enjoyed a delightful compensation. Nothing I have seen in other countries—not even in my own—equals the beauty, the glory, of the scenery through which we glided up from Tasman's Head to Hobart Town.

To the left were bold cliffs, compact and straight-built as the finest masonry, springing up, full two hundred feet and more, above the surface of the water, and bearing on their broad and level summits the forests of the gum-trees. To the right, eight miles away, lay the green lowlands of Tasman's Peninsula, sparkling in the clear, sweet sunshine of that lovely evening.

Then, as the little ship glanced quietly and gracefully along, a signal-tower, with the red flag floating from it, appeared in an open space among the trees. Still further on, a farmhouse, with its white walls and green verandah shone out from some cleft or valley close at hand ; and the fresh, rich fragrance of flowers, and ripening fruits, and waving grass, came floating to us through the blue, bright air. By-and-bye, the trees became more scarce, and handsome houses rose up in quick succession, and, forming into graceful terraces, told us, by many a sign of life and comfort, that the town was near at hand, and that we should be soon at rest. Last of all, Mount Wellington, a majestic mountain, towering to the height of four thousand feet behind the town, and wearing a thin circlet of snow upon its head, disclosed itself in all its greatness, grandeur and solemnity.

These were the principal features of the scenery— the beautiful, glorious scenery—within the shade of which we passed up to Hobart Town. You can easily imagine the delight they inspired, and the influence they had upon us. Gazing at them, we lost sight of our misfortunes, and the dull, cold destiny which at that moment, like the deepening twilight, fell upon our path. Gazing at them, we forgot for the while we were prisoners, destined for life to sojourn in a land in the growth of which we could take no interest—the prosperity of which would claim from us no proud congratulation—the glory of which could never stir within our hearts one glad emotion, nor win from our lip or hand the faintest recognition.

It was nearly nine o'clock when we cast anchor. The night had fallen, and all we could see of Hobart Town were the lamplights—up there, a lonely couple—down there, a misty group—along there, a twinkling line—beyond there, an odd one, flickering like a candle in a wine-vault, and doing its best to keep in.

Through the darkness, however, there came a variety of sounds. Now, the clatter of a bell; a moment after, a voice exclaiming, " Peter, where are you ? " then a chorus of loud laughs, shrill whistlings, and the cracking of whips ; all round us, the soft sighs and murmurings of the river, the creaking of cordage, the dip and splash of oars ; by-and-bye, the bugle-call, filling the çalm night with clear, strong notes, and the crashing of the drums in the barrack-square.

Next morning, when we went on deck, the sun was shining warmly ; and in its soft radiance, the town, the noble mountain close behind it, the ships and boats, the trees, the gardens, cottages and villas all about, looked charming in the extreme. It was a beautiful, bold picture ; and, it being Sunday, there seemed to be a sweet tranquillity diffused all through it, which rendered it still more enchanting.

For a good part of the day, we amused ourselves with the glasses, making the most minute observations, and curiously inspecting every object within sight. Horses, cabs, policemen, bonnets, soldiers, sign-boards, sailors, warehouses, chimney-tops, street-door knockers, wheel-barrows, church spires, flower-pots—nothing was omitted in our search. The smallest trifle became the subject of the deepest interest ; and even the poor dog we caught playing amongst the bales and baulks, the casks and spars, upon the wharf in front of us, was followed through all his windings, tumblings, twists, and twirls, with the keenest curiosity.

The whole of this day, we had the *Swift*, I may say, to ourselves ; most of the officers, and, towards evening, most of the men, being ashore, enjoying themselves in every direction ; as well they might, poor fellows ! after their four months' weary work.

Of course, no communication of an official nature was made to us this day. The following morning, however, the Assistant-Comptroller, accompanied by a clerk, arrived in a whale-boat, and shortly after their arrival, we were requested to attend the captain in our saloon. Here we found the fashionable arrivals ; and, as an indispensable part of the lugubrious ceremony of transportation, we were introduced to them in due rotation by Captain Aldham. Whereupon the chairs were taken, and Mr. Nairn, the Assistant-Comptroller, in a smooth, neat speech, opened the proceedings.

First of all, he disengaged a yard or so of thin red tape from a bundle of long, thick wove, blue paper ; and in so doing exhibited an easy dexterity of finger, and a deep-water placidity of look. Having separated the papers, and placed them in a line along the table, one after the other, just as if he were arranging a set of dominoes, he gently fixed his elbows upon the documents, and joining his hands in a meek and devotional manner before him, begged leave to observe :—

" That he was directed by his Excellency, Sir William Denison, to communicate with William Smith O'Brien, Thomas Francis Meagher, Terence Bellew M'Manus, and Patrick O'Donoghue, prisoners of State on board her Majesty's sloop-of-war, the *Swift*. The object of his visit was to inform the aforesaid prisoners, that Sir William Denison had received certain instructions relative to them from the Secretary of State for the Home Department ; that, by these instructions, Sir William Denison was authorised to grant ' tickets-of-leave ' to each and all the aforesaid prisoners, provided that, in the first place, the Captain under whose charge they had been during the voyage was enabled to speak favourably of their conduct, and that, in the second place, they pledged their honour to not make use of the comparative liberty which ' tickets-of-leave ' conferred, for the purpose of escaping from the colony."

Mr. Nairn begged leave to add :—

" He was happy to inform us, that Captain Aldham had reported favourably of our conduct, and, such being the case, it only remained for him now to receive our *parole* not to attempt an escape from the colony."

This speech being ended, a profound silence ensued, during which the Assistant-Comptroller delicately fiddled with his documents, and glided off into a serene abstraction.

I never met, in gaol or in courthouse, in the Queen's Bench or the Henry Street Police Office[1], so sleek, so tranquil, so elaborate an official. His motions were most delicately adjusted, even to the opening of an eye-lid, or the removal from his forehead of a fly. His voice flowed richly and softly from his lips, like a glass of Curaçoa into an India-rubber flask. His fingers appeared to have been formed for the express purpose of writing with the finest steel pen, pressing the clearest-cut official seal, and measuring out, for despatches on the public service, the neatest and narrowest red tape. The knot of his neck-tie was an epitome of the man. It struck one as having been put on by means of the most minute and exquisite machinery. To have accomplished such a knot by

[1]A Police Court existed in Henry Street, Dublin, in 1848.

the aid of manual labour seemed at first sight impossible.

The silence was broken by O'Brien, who begged to state that he, for one, was not prepared to accept a " ticket-of-leave " on the conditions specified by the Assistant-Comptroller ; he certainly had little or no intention of escaping, but felt strongly disinclined to pledge his word to the observance of an arrangement which would preclude his availing himself of any opportunity to escape that might occur hereafter.

I took a different view of the matter. It appeared to me that, whether we pledged our honour to the fulfilment of the conditions proposed by the Government or withheld it, an escape was out of the question.

In the former case, our *parole*, of course, would bind us more firmly than the heaviest irons to the island. In the latter case, it was clear, the authorities would adopt such measures as to render it absolutely impracticable. It seemed to me, then, that the point at issue resolved itself simply into a choice between two evils. Our detention, in either case, being certain, I thought it much more desirable to accept a small amount of liberty, fettered only by my word of honour, than surrender myself to the confinement of a prison, and the vexatious surveillance of turnkeys and constables.

Moreover, the condition annexed to our holding " tickets-of-leave " appeared to me a fair and an honourable one ; it exacted no compromise of conduct or opinion ; exacted no hypocrisy, no submission ; it simply required of us not to make use of certain privileges for the purpose of effecting an escape ; and going thus far, and no farther, I felt convinced, that in pledging myself to the fulfilment of it, I would do no unworthy act. In other countries, better and nobler men have not hesitated, as prisoners-of-war, to accept and fulfil a similar condition.

O'Donoghue and M'Manus took the same view, and we three, consequently, agreed to pledge ourselves to remain in the colony so long as we retained the " ticket-of-leave."

Having come to this determination, the Assistant-Comptroller requested us to put our opinions in writing, in the shape of letters addressed to him. " It would be his duty," he observed, in conclusion, " to lay them before Sir William Denison, and receive his Excellency's reply in reference to them."

I accepted the " ticket-of-leave," on the condition proposed to us, for six months only. I was unwilling to pledge myself for an indefinite period ; so that, at the expiration of the six months, I would be at liberty to surrender myself as a prisoner, or renew the contract.

M'Manus and O'Donoghue wrote letters to the same effect.

Two hours later, Mr. Nairn returned, and informed us that his Excellency had been pleased to grant " tickets-of-leave " on the condition hereinbefore specified to Thomas Francis Meagher, Terence Bellew M'Manus, and Patrick O'Donoghue ; that the official papers authorising this arrangement would be sent on board next day ; and that William Smith O'Brien was to be sent to the probation-station of Maria Island, and be there detained, in strict custody, during the pleasure of his Excellency.

Having made this announcement, the Assistant-Comptroller drew in his lips, economised a smile, slightly bowed, and, drawing back his hat as he inclined his head, withdrew.

Hardly had he disappeared, when another official came on board, and solicited the pleasure of our com-

pany. This gentleman was no less a personage than the
Assistant-Registrar, and his business was to take an
inventory of our respective heights, ages, pursuits, and
families ; also, the shape of our noses, the complexion
of our cheeks, the colour of our eyes and hair, the
character of our chins, and our general appearance as
human beings. " A delicate, a very delicate business,"
he whispered to me as I entered, " and one, which,
considering our position in society, he wished to get
through as delicately as possible."

Whereupon he begged of me to see that the door was
shut, and in a very mild manner—the mildest manner
possible—commenced his observations. One would
have thought we were made of down or gossamer, he
looked so gently at us ; and then he noted down the
results of his inspection so softly, that one might have
also imagined he wrote upon velvet. While this was
going on, I could not help remarking to O'Donoghue
that it forcibly reminded me of Mr. Pickwick's introduction to the Fleet, and the bewilderment with which
he sat in the armchair whilst his portrait was
taken.

The likeness finished, the Assistant-Registrar shut
up his portfolio, expressed his regret at having troubled
us so much, and backing to the door with two or three
scrapes—expressive, no doubt, of high consideration
and esteem—betook himself to the wharf, and from
thence to his office, there to make out and distribute
copies of the performance he had so nimbly and ex-
peditiously completed.

The rest of the evening we had to ourselves. And a
lovely evening it was. There we were, pacing the
quarter-deck, disconsolately gazing at the poor little
Swift, which had been unrigged and dismantled in the
morning, and now lay like a mournful wreck upon the

breast of the calm and noble river. Oftentimes we looked out far ahead, watching every sail that made up towards us, for the news had just reached us that the *Emma*, from Sydney, with O'Doherty and Martin on board, was hourly expected. At other times we turned our eyes to the shore, and found, in the passing to-and-fro of sailors, cabs, and waggon-loads, and a hundred other things, a pleasant relief from the monotony of our wooden walls.

The following day we received our instructions. I was directed to proceed next morning at half-past three o'clock, by coach, to Campbell Town—the principal town of the district which had been assigned me. M'Manus was to start at a later hour for New Norfolk. O'Donoghue was to leave in the course of the day, and take up his quarters in Hobart Town. O'Brien was to be ready to sail for Maria Island by seven o'clock.

This was Tuesday, the 30th of October. After nightfall, just as we had retired to our berths, the *Emma* dropped up the river and cast anchor close beside us.

Next morning at three o'clock, the guard-boat came alongside the *Swift*; and having wished good-bye to O'Brien, M'Manus, O'Donoghue, and the officer on watch, I got into it, and was soon on dry land once more. I arrived at the hotel as the coach was on the point of starting, and five minutes after was rattled away at a magnificent pace from the town; of which, owing to the darkness at the time, I saw little more than half-a-dozen lamplights, two or three constables, and the sentry-box of the Government House.

As the morning dawned, the fresh and beautiful features of the country gradually disclosed themselves. One by one they seemed to wake up, and, shaking off the dew and mist, scatter smiles and fragrance all along our road. There was the river breaking into sparkling life, and flowing cheerfully away, as if it had been pent up and worried all the night, and was glad to feel the warm sun once more. There were farm-houses, cozy hay-ricks close behind them, and fowls spreading out their wings, and, with many a light and nimble effort, shaking off their drowsiness. There was the green corn waving, and the grey clouds melting in the silver sunshine along the hills before us. There were handsome villas next, like those we had seen coming up the Derwent, with their gardens and verandahs, and the blue smoke rising from their chimney tops. There was, by-and-bye, a waggon, painted blue and red, with its ponderous market-load, its fine team of horses, and a large white dog chained to the axle-tree of the hind wheels, rumbling past us, and leaving, in the yellow dust, broad deep tracks, and straws behind it. There was, just a few yards ahead, a clean white turnpike, and the keeper tumbling out to open it, with his woollen nightcap on, and his braces clattering at his heels. Then came carts, and cows, and shepherds, with their kangaroo-skin knapsacks on their backs, and the night-coach, with the windows up, and a thick steam upon them, hindering the faintest sight of the cramped and stifled passengers within. At last, there was the heart of the country itself, with its beautiful hills, rising in long and shadowy tiers one above the other, and the brown foliage of its woods, and the blackened stumps of many a tough old tree, and mobs upon mobs of sheep, and the green parrots, and the wattle birds, and broad lagoons, and broader plains, and ten thousand things besides!

For a long, long time I was in raptures with my drive, and almost forgot I was hurrying away still further from my own poor country, and journeying amid the scenes of a land in the fate of which I could take no interest—for the glory of which I could breathe no prayer.

About three o'clock I arrived in Campbell Town, and was set down at the hotel " where the coach dined," along with my portmanteau and hat-case. After dinner, I strolled out to inspect the institutions of the place, and make myself acquainted in a general way, with its various attractions and resources.

Twenty minutes rendered me fully conversant with the subject of my inquiry. A glance, indeed, was sufficient to inform me that this celebrated town consisted of one main street, with two or three dusty branches to the left ; and, at right angles with these, a sort of boulevard, in which the police-office, the lock-up and the stocks are conveniently arranged.

The main street has one side to it only. The ribs of this side consist of four hotels ; a warehouse ; a board-and-lodging house, with Napoleon upon a green lamp, just as you go in ; half-a-dozen private residences, furnished with a ground floor and a back and front entrance ; a jeweller's shop ; butcher's stall ; a sign post ; and two sheds. Opposite to this line of edifices, and parallel with it, at an interval of fifty feet, runs a wooden paling, which, mid-way up the town, is broken by three cottages, a hay rick and the post-office. Aloof, at the uttermost extremity in a straight line with the paling at the post-office and the hay rick, stands the Established Church—a gaunt structure, compiled of bricks, with facing of white stone.

Having seen so much, I thought I might as well go to bed. To bed, then, I went, and dreamed all night of Eden. Not the Eden of the Scriptures, but that social and stirring Eden so agreeably described in the history of " Chuzzlewit."

Three days having elapsed, I woke up, gave a great

yawn, and drove off to Ross—a little apology of a town, seven miles nearer than Campbell Town to the seat of Government.

The visit I paid it, short as it was, convinced me that Ross was a far more preferable place to take up my quarters in than Campbell Town; the latter place has too much of the vulgar, upstart village in it; contains too much glare, dust, and gossip, and it would be hard, I think, to do anything else than yawn, catch flies, and star-gaze in it. Here one can be more to himself; therefore, more free; consequently, more happy.

To Ross, then, I removed in all haste, and lost no time in looking out for a little cottage, or half a one, if a whole one was impracticable.

I was not long in fixing upon the one in which I now write this letter. The appearance of it was most prepossessing and the interior arrangements singularly inviting. Just fancy a little lodge, built from head to foot with bright red bricks; two flower-beds, and a neat railing in front; a laburnum bush in each bed; a clean smooth flagway, eighteen inches across, from the outer gate to the halldoor; two stone steps to the latter; a window, containing eight panes of green glass, on each side of the same; and then, four rooms inside, each fourteen feet by twelve, and an oven in the kitchen; just fancy all this, and you will have a pretty correct picture of the establishment in which, with a domestic servant of all work, and a legion of flies, I have now the happiness to reside.

At first, I had only the two front rooms. At present I have the whole house to myself, and the use of a cultivated plot of ground in the rear, where a select circle of cabbages, a few sprigs of parsley, a score of onions, and a stone of potatoes, with a thistle or two, get on very well together, and have no one to touch them.

My landlady is a devout Wesleyan, an amiable female of stupendous proportions, and proportionate loquacity—her husband is a Wesleyan too, a shoe-maker by trade, and a spectre in appearance ; so much so, indeed, that the wife may be styled, with the strictest geometrical propriety, his " better half" and three-quarters. Upon coming to terms with them in the first instance—that is, when I had the two front rooms, and they the two back ones—an agreeable dialogue took place, of which the following may be considered a fair report :—

" Sir," said Mrs. Anderson, sticking a pin into the sleeve of her gown, and spreading down her apron before her.

" Well, ma'am," said I.

" Why, sir," says she. " You see as how it is, me and my husband be Wesleyans, and we don't like a-cooking on Sundays, and so if it don't matter to you, sir, we'd a soon not dress you any meat a that day, for we're commanded to rest and do no work upon the Sabbath, and that you see, sir, is just how it is."

" As to that," I replied, " I don't much mind having a cold dinner upon Sundays, but then, there are the potatoes ! Potatoes, you know, Mrs. Anderson, are very insipid when cold."

This was a difficulty of great magnitude. Mrs. Anderson paused, and swelled up immensely. When the swelling subsided a little, she cast an inquiring glance at her husband, as if to implore him for a text, a note or a comment, to help her out of a difficulty, in which, like a sudden deluge, the conflicting ideas of a boiled potato and the day of rest had involved her.

The glance had the desired effect. Mr. Anderson

took off his spectacles, held them with crossed hands, reverently before him ; threw back his head ; threw up his eyes, and fixing them intently upon a remarkable constellation of flies, close to a bacon hook above him, seemed to inquire from it, in the absence of the stars, a solution of the difficulty.

A moment's consultation sufficed—a new light descended upon Mr. Anderson, and yielding to the inspiration of the moment, he pronounced it to be his opinion, that a boiled potato would not break the Sabbath, and " in that, or any other way, he'd be happy to serve the gen'l'm'n."

Well, in this little cottage I manage to get through my solitary days cheerfully enough. It costs me an effort, however, to do so ; for, I am sure, nature never intended me for an anchorite, and often and often, I am as companionless and desolate here as Simon Stylites on the top of his pillar. Only one human being, for instance, has passed by my window to-day ; he was a pedlar, with fish and vegetables, from Launceston, and wished to know as he was passing, if I wanted any fresh flounders for dinner.

On the whole, I must say, the Government have acted towards us, ever since our conviction, in a fair, mild, honourable spirit. Sending us out so many thousand miles away from our homes and friends, to this cheerless penal settlement, was, to be sure, a measure of great severity ; yet, it would be hard to say they could have done less. As a Government, holding themselves to a very large extent responsible to the people of England, and, for the most part, shaping their councils and acting in accordance with the known opinion of that people, it would have been difficult for them to adjudge a lesser punishment to those, against whom, in England, the public sentiment ran so high and so determinedly. For my part, though I feel sorely, I conceive it would be unmanly and unjust to complain of it with bitterness. We played for a high stake—the highest that could be played for ; we lost the game by a wretched throw, and with a willing heart and a ready hand, we ought, like honourable men, to pay the forfeit, and say no more about it.

I write thus frankly to you, my dear Duffy, upon the subject, for it often pained me to observe the querulousness and spite with which the Government were abused in Ireland, whenever they adopted measures to repress the spirit which aimed and struck at their existence. A fairer and a nobler feeling would more gratefully befit a nation whose soul is in arms against a RULE which humbles her attitude before the world, and proscribes her flag. Calmly to foresee, and, with patient generous courage, to accept the sacrifices which defeat imposes— to bear the Cross with the same loftiness of soul as she would wear the Laurel Crown—this should be the study and ambition of our country ; and if it were so, believe me, her struggle would assume a grander aspect, and excite, through the world at large, deeper and more enduring sympathies than those which have hitherto— in our time, at all events—attended her.

So far then, you see, I have no complaint to make with regard to our present fate—dull and bleak, and wearisome as it is. But, I do complain, that, having separated us by so many thousand miles of sea, from all that was dear, consoling, and inspiring to our hearts, they should have increased the severity of this punishment by distributing us over a strange land in which the most gratifying friendships we could form would compensate so poorly for the loss of the warm familiar companionship we so long enjoyed. There is M'Manus away in New Norfolk, O'Donoghue in Hobart Town,

O'Doherty in Oatlands, Martin in Bothwell, Meagher in Campbell Town, O'Brien off there in Maria Island! Each has a separate district, and out of that district there is no redemption.

Now, generally speaking, a " district " is about the size of a respectable country parish at home. Mine, for instance, extends from thirty to thirty-five miles in length, and varies from ten to fifteen in breadth. At the end of a fortnight I came to the conclusion, that between a prison and a " district " there was just about the same difference as exists between a stable and a paddock. In the one you are tied up by a halter —in the other you have the swing of a tether.

Within the last five weeks, however, Martin, O'Doherty, and I have discovered a point, common to our three respective districts, at which, without a breach of the regulation prohibiting any two or more of us from residing together, we can meet from time to time.

This fortunate point is on the edge of a noble lake, twenty-four miles from Ross, up in a range of mountains, known as the " Western Tier." O'Doherty has to ride twenty miles to it, and Martin five-and-twenty. Monday is usually our day of meeting, and eleven, or thereabouts, the hour at which we emerge from three different quarters of the Bush, and come upon the ground.

The point itself is a small cozy, smoky bit of a log-hut, inhabited by a solitary gentleman named Cooper.[1] The hut is fifteen feet by ten, and high enough to admit in an upright position, of any reasonable extension of legs, spine, hat and shirt-collar. The furniture consists of a something to sleep on—I don't know what to call it ; a table, very weak in the extremities ; two stools ; a block for splitting chops upon ; a shelf, three feet in

[1] See Mitchel's " Jail Journal."

length, and furnished with a couple of pewter plates ;
a gunpowder flask, full of pepper ; three breakfast cups ;
a carving knife ; a breakfast knife ; forks to match ;
a tract upon Foreign Missions, and two columns of a
Sunday Observer, bearing a remote date.

Here we dine, and spend the evening up to half-past
five o'clock, when we descend the " Tier," and betake
ourselves to our respective homes. Whilst the preparations for the dinner are going on—whilst Mr. Cooper
is splitting chops, shelling peas, washing onions, and
melting himself away in a variety of labours by the
log-wood fire—we are rambling along the shores of
the lake, talking of old times, singing the old songs,
weaving fresh hopes among the old ones that have
ceased to bloom.

You cannot picture to yourself the happiness which
the days we have spent by that lonely, glorious lake
have brought us. They have been summer days, all
of them ; and through the sunshine have floated the
many-coloured memories, the red griefs, the golden
hopes of our sad, beautiful old country.

Oh ! should hearts grow faint at home, and, in the
cold, dark current of despair, or grief, fling down the
hope they once waved, like a sacred torch, on high ;
tell them that here, in this strange land, and in the
loneliest haunts and pathways of it—here, by the
shores of a lake, where as yet no sail has sparkled, and
few sounds of human life as yet have scared the wild
swan or startled the black snake from its nest—tell
them that here, upon a lone, lone spot in the far Southern
Seas, there are prayers, full of confidence, and faith,
and love, offered up for Ireland's cause ; and that the
belief in her redemption and her glory has accompanied her sons to their place of exile, and there, like
some beautiful and holy charm, abides with them ;

filling the days of their humble solitude with calm light and joyous melodies and visions of serene and radiant loveliness.

Previous to the discovery of this celebrated point—a point, by-the-bye, which would have done credit to the ingenuity of Sir Colman O'Loghlen—O'Doherty and I used to meet at another place.

His district adjoins mine, about seven miles from Ross, at a convict station called Tunbridge. A river, known by the name of the " Blackman's," forms the boundary of the two districts at this point, and over it, close to the convict station, a pretty bridge has been lately built.

One half of the Blackman's being in the Campbell Town district, and the other half belonging to that of Oatlands, the middle pier of the bridge in question was, of course, our point of contact ; and here, consequently, we " hung out " four or five Mondays successively, and spent a few hours with the utmost hilarity. At our second interview, we christened the point of junction. The ceremony, as you may well suppose, was divested of all solemnity ; but, in a very copious libation, we toasted " The Irish Pier ! " enthusiastically receiving from each other the highly constitutional sentiment that the Peerage of the Blackman's might long continue to resist the current which opposed it, and, standing erect amid the worst of storms, guarantee to us, for many days to come, the right of public meeting !

A few hundred yards above the bridge, on O'Doherty's side of the river, there happens to be an inn. This inn is built of timber, and washed over with a pale salmon colour. It is a very, very old establishment indeed ; and with all the scars and bruises left by a long life-struggle exhibits, likewise, all the cranki-

Ormonde Castle, Kilkenny, 1848

ness and extreme debility of age. When the slightest
breeze comes by it, whines, and groans, and growls,
in the most dismal manner ; and rattling the windows,
as if they were so many teeth set loosely in its aching
head, shakes from head to foot, and threatens to wind-
up and settle its last account at once.

Old, weak, infirm as it is—spite of all its ailments—a
portion of sound life remains within it still ; and with
that residue of life, many good qualities to recommend
it to the public favour. On our several days of meeting
it furnished us, for instance, with first-rate dinners.
To be sure, the passage through the air, for upwards of
five hundred yards or so, condensed the steam of the
potatoes, and solidified the gravy somewhat ; but the
old salmon-coloured inn was not to blame for that. In
all these cases, the Home Office spoiled the cooking.

One very hot day—the bed of the river being almost
quite dry—we dined under the bridge ; having, first
of all, erected something like a Druid's altar, on the
top of which we laid the cloth. The seats were con-
structed much after the same fashion ; and, the hamper
which brought the ale, the plates, and cheese, being
emptied, kicked over, and turned up-side-down, served
in the capacity of a very respectable dumb waiter.

So much then, for O'Doherty and Martin, both of
whom are in excellent health. Now for the rest.

M'Manus, as I have already mentioned, is in New
Norfolk, and, in consequence of his not having been
able to start any business there, employs himself from
morning till night, shooting, fishing, and riding. You
will be delighted to hear he is as stout as ever, and
though he has little or no society, his spirits appear to
have lost not a particle of their vivacity and heartiness.

O'Donoghue was permitted to remain in Hobart
Town in consequence of his having represented to Sir

17

William Denison that unless he was permitted to stay there he would find it impossible to support himself—his livelihood being dependent upon his professional labours exclusively.

At first he had hopes of getting into some barrister's or solicitor's office, but there was no opening for him ; and so, as a last resource, and with the view of realising an honest maintenance, he started a weekly newspaper, a few weeks ago. It is called the *Irish Exile,* and, from all I hear, appears to be succeeding extremely well.

When he first thought of it, Martin and I tried to dissuade him from the project. Martin urged several objections to it, I believe ; and I gave it as my opinion that whilst we were in such a colony as Van Diemen's Land, we ought not to mix in politics. Standing aloof from them in such a place I conceived would be the most dignified line of conduct we could pursue ; and if it would not promote, would at all events protect from mockery and slander the cause of our Native Land.

There are no sympathies here to which one could appeal in behalf of the Irish nation. I do not mean to say there are no kind, generous, gallant hearts to be found in this colony. Far from it. Of such hearts—and they are English, too—I have felt the warm throb. But these are few, indeed ; and in a community, three-fourths of which consist of convicts and officials, their influence would be completely lost. Before the leering eyes of such a community I would rather die than unveil the bleeding figure of our poor country, and for her wounds and agonies beseech a single tear.

Strongly influenced by this feeling, I urged O'Donoghue not to go on with the *Exile.* In replying to my letter —as also in replying to Martin's—he admitted, almost fully, the justness and propriety of our objections, but still maintained that since there was only this one channel open to him for the realisation of an honourable livelihood, he was bound to avail himself of it, regardless of all other considerations. Well, this was a view of the matter which could not be effectually opposed, which could not certainly be opposed with any degree of delicacy or kindness. I therefore wish O'Donoghue the best success, and will use my utmost influence to procure him subscribers.

Further than this, however, I feel the deepest repugnance to act in support of his paper. I cannot bring myself to write a word for a public amongst whom, if it were in my power to leave this evening, I would not remain another day. And most painfully does this repugnance act upon my heart, for it would delight me to assist O'Donoghue, and, by ever so slight an effort, conduce to the success of his fair and manly enterprise. Martin, however, is contributing a series of papers upon the Repeal movement.

Having written thus far upon the subject of our engaging in colonial politics, it is unnecessary for me to contradict the report which appeared in one of the South Australasian papers—the absurd report, that I had assumed the management of one of the Catholic colonial journals! I did not trouble myself to contradict it here, being perfectly indifferent what became of it at this side of the Equator, whether it sank or floated, having made up my mind to be quite composed, and, in either case, to repress the slightest emotion.

But I did feel uneasy lest it might be believed in Ireland. Not that I consider it would be in any degree discreditable to assume the management of such a paper ; but I feel it would be somewhat unworthy of me. Unworthy, for in this case I should have to turn my thoughts from Ireland, and devote them to a subject, or rather, to a number of subjects, none of which could interest me like the former ; and in dealing with which, I could work, I am sure, with no greater heart than a dull, plodding, fagged mechanic. Be assured of it, I shall never tie myself down to such a tame, insipid business.

For Ireland alone—for the liberty she has prayed, and struck, and bled for, year after year—for the glory which in many a bright creation of her genius she has seen, and sung, and prophesied—for this alone will I write, and speak, and act. In the morning of my life, whatever gifts of mind and heart Heaven had blest me with I dedicated to this beautiful, righteous, noble service ; and in this service, until death leads me to another world, they shall faithfully abide.

In consequence of O'Brien refusing to pledge his word not to escape, the " ticket-of-leave," as I have already mentioned, was withheld from him ; and he was conveyed to Maria Island, there to remain in close confinement during the pleasure of his Excellency, Sir William Denison. The restrictions imposed upon him were most stringent and severe. More than this—they were cruel to an excess.

He was confined to a little cottage, and suffered to take no exercise beyond that which a miserable plot of ground attached to this cottage, would permit. He was denied the use of a servant, had to light his own fire, make his own bed, and perform every other menial duty that was necessary. He was denied all intercourse, forbidden to exchange a word with any person on the island, save and except the Protestant chaplain. He was dogged, night and day by constables, who had to report his presence, every four hours, to the Superintendent of the Station. He was denied permission to receive a few little luxuries, in the way of sugar, rice, and raisins, which he had requested a gentleman in Hobart Town to forward to him. In a word, he was detained under these and other restrictions, he was obliged to submit to these and other privations, until, at last, his health gave way, and the medical officer of the station pronounced it no longer safe to enforce the discipline to which he had been subjected.

On January 16th, I received from our dear and noble friend, a letter, from which I give you the following extract :—

" A new phase has occurred in the arrangements adopted with respect to me. The doctor of the Station (Doctor Smart) having reported that my health was giving way under the system prescribed by Dr. Hampton, I was allowed yesterday to take a little exercise, attended by a keeper. Until I had an opportunity of testing my powers, I had no idea how much my strength had been reduced. I am now convinced that, had no change taken place, Sir William Denison would have had very little trouble with his prisoner at the expiration of another fortnight. Hereafter these proceedings may become a subject of inquiry, and, in case I should be prematurely extinguished, it will be right to inquire, whether Dr. Dawson, the principal medical officer of the colony, did, or did not, after his visit to this island, represent to the Governor and to Dr. Hampton, the Comptroller-General, that the course of treatment adopted towards me would most probably be injurious to my health."

Upon receipt of this I felt bound to bring the statement it contained under the notice of the local government; and if that did not produce any desirable result, to lay the matter before the public, through the colonial papers.

Fortunately, the very day I received it, I met

O'Doherty and Martin at the lakes, and had the advantage of their advice. It was agreed, then, I should write a respectful remonstrance to Sir William Denison, stating the facts I had heard with regard to O'Brien's health, and praying for such alterations in the treatment adopted towards him as would avert the fatal consequences it was bringing on. In case no alteration took place, it was further agreed upon, we should throw up our " tickets-of-leave," and no longer bind ourselves, by any honourable engagement, to a Government that could act in so unmanly and cruel a manner.

In consequence of this arrangement, I wrote the following letter :—

" Hope's Hotel, Ross, Jan. 17, 1850.

" May it please Your Excellency.

" Sir,—I feel called upon to inform you respectfully, that I have received a letter, dated January 11th, from Mr. Smith O'Brien ; who, as your Excellency must be aware, is at present under close confinement in the probation station of Maria Island.

" In this letter Mr. O'Brien mentions, that, in consequence of the restrictions which have been imposed upon him, and the privations to which he is subjected, his strength has been greatly weakened, and his health in general very seriously impaired.

" From what I know of Mr. O'Brien—and I have the honour and the happiness to know him well—I feel convinced that the treatment in force against him must have produced very injurious effects, indeed, to induce the avowal he has made, and which—whatever be his wishes to the contrary—I conceive it my duty to lay before your Excellency.

" I write without having ascertained the feelings of Mr. O'Brien with regard to the step I now take ; I write, indeed, with the conviction, that, had he been apprised of my intention in this respect, he would have condemned it strongly, and have urged me to renounce it. There are times, however, when friendship is best evinced in disobedience to the wishes of those for whose health and happiness one has been led to cherish an anxious and a deep desire.

" For my part, I could have no peace, no enjoyment, no repose—a thorn would rankle in my heart, and excite within me the most painful emotions—were I to be silent in this matter.

" With these sentiments, I respectfully, but urgently entreat, that your Excellency will be pleased to institute an inquiry into the treatment pursued towards Mr. Smith O'Brien, and the state to which, in consequence of this treatment, his health has been reduced.

" I am assured that, upon ascertaining the truth of the statement I have now put forth, your Excellency, influenced by a sense of common justice and humanity, will direct such relaxations to be made in the discipline to which he is subject as will restore the health, and guarantee the life of my pure-hearted and noble-minded friend.

" I have the honour to be,

" Your Excellency's obedient servant,

" THOMAS FRANCIS MEAGHER.

" To his Excellency, Sir W. Denison, Knt.,
Lieut.-Governor of Van Diemen's Land,
etc., etc., etc."

To this communication I received the following note from the Office of the Convict Department :—

" The Comptroller-General has been directed to acknowledge the receipt of the communication addressed to the Lieutenant-Governor, by Thomas Francis Meagher, dated the 17th ult."

The envelope of this note measured eight inches in length, and on the back exhibited a plaster of red wax, pretty nearly as broad as the seal on the mouth of a bottle of anchovies. This elegant adhesion bears some elaborate device, which, as yet, I have not had sufficient leisure to examine.

On the other side, I found the subjoined inscription :

" *On Public Service only.*

" *Thomas Francis Meagher,*

" *Hope's Hotel,*

" *Ross.*

" *Convict Department, 22nd January, 1850.*"

The information it contained, you will admit, was not very satisfactory ; limited, as it was, to the simple announcement that my letter had arrived safe. The morning it arrived, however, I received a letter from a friend of mine, assuring me that the treatment I had complained of had been considerably modified. Four or five days subsequently, I received one from O'Brien himself, from which I make an extract or two ; for, I am sure, they will afford you greater satisfaction than any statement, borrowed from them, of my own :—

" I am happy to be able to relieve your anxiety with respect to my health, by assuring you that I have felt better to-day than upon any day for several weeks, and that I have every reason to believe I shall soon be in a condition to undergo another of Dr. Hampton's experiments upon the strength of my constitution.

" My letter to you of the 11th was written under the impulse of vehement indignation, excited by the discovery that I had been very much enfeebled by confinement and solitude. When first I was shut up in solitary confinement, after Dr. Hampton's visit to this island, I could not help feeling that, in the case of nineteen men out of twenty, a strict enforcement of his regulations would destroy reason or life ; but still I was in hopes that I should be able to bear it without injury, as my constitution is naturally a very strong one. I found, however, that after I had been in confinement for a few weeks, I became constantly.oppressed by a palpitation of the heart—a sensation I never before experienced, not even at Clonmel—and it is my firm conviction, that if the restrictions had not been somewhat relaxed, I would have fallen a victim to what certainly has worn all the appearance of a deliberate design to shorten my life.

    *   *   *   *   *

" Since the 11th, I have been allowed as much opportunity of exercise as I could reasonably expect. I ramble about in the neighbourhood of the station, attended by a keeper, so upon this head, there is no longer, at present, any ground for complaint.

    *   *   *   *   *

" With regard to the request which I made, that you would not mention anything about my health in your letters home, the reasons for such an admonition no longer exist, as I have thought it right to let my own friends know, both that my confinement has been relaxed in consequence of its having proved injurious to my health, and also, at the same time, that there is no longer any reason for alarm."

So far, then, so good. But, is it not sickening to think that the treatment which brought on his illness was enforced for no other reason than this—that he declines to give his word not to escape, and, forthwith, he is subjected to the most harassing privations and indignities ; is shut out from all society ; is gagged, and cramped, and half-stifled in a hut ; is buried alive, in fact, upon a scrap of an island ; and from all this, knows no exemption until his life is perilled !

Ah ! the race of Hudson Lowes is not extinct ; and there are other rocks in the ocean besides that famous one of St. Helena—sweet, secluded spots—remote, snug nooks—just large enough for gaolers to test their skill and venom on, in foul experiments upon a noble life.

I have now said everything—everything that could be said, I believe, about ourselves, our voyage, and the circumstances in which we are placed. A few words, in conclusion, about the Colony.

With regard, then, to the Colony: It is a beautiful, noble island. In most, if not all, those features which constitute the strength, the wealth, and grandeur of a country, it has been endowed. The seas which encompass it, the lakes and rivers which refresh and fertilise, the woods which shadow, and the genial sky which arches it—all bear testimony to the excellence of the Divine Hand, and with sounds of the finest harmony, with signs of the brightest colouring, proclaim the goodness and munificence of heaven in its behalf.

The climate is more than healthful. It is invigorating and inspiring. Breathing it, manhood preserves its bloom, vivacity, and vigour, long after the period at which, in other countries, those precious gifts depart, and the first cold touch of age is felt. Breathing it, age itself puts on a glorious look of health, serenity, and gladness, and, even when the grey hairs have thinned, seems able to fight a way through the snows, and storms, and falling leaves of many years to come. Breathing it, many a frail form which the Indian sun had wasted acquires fresh life ; the dim eye lights up anew ; to the ashy paleness of the sunken cheek succeeds the sparkling blush of health ; the heart resumes its youthful action, and drives the blood once more in clear and glowing currents through the frame ; whilst the mind that was sinking into gloom and forgetfulness, touched, as it were, by a miraculous hand, starts into light and playfulness, and breaking far away from the shadows of death that were closing round it, exults in the consciousness of a new existence.

Oh ! to think that a land so blest—so rich in all that makes life pleasant, bountiful, and great—so formed to be a refuge and a sweet abiding-place, in these latter times, for the younger children of the old, decrepid, worn-out world at home—to think that such a land is doomed to be the prison, the workhouse, and the grave, of the Empire's outcast poverty, ignorance, and guilt ! This is a sad, revolting thought : and the reflections which spring from it cast a gloom here over the purest and happiest minds. Whilst so black a curse is on it, no heart, howsoever pious, generous, and benignant, could love this land, and speak of it with pride.

The Boyhood of Meagher

CLONGOWES COLLEGE

The dear old college stood very nearly in the centre of a circle of ancient towns. There was Clane, something like two miles off ; Kilcock, between five and six, Celbridge, pretty much the same ; Naas, not a perch further ; Prosperous, within four ; Maynooth, in the opposite quarter, about the same distance. Very old and ragged, with very little life stirring in them, they seemed to have gone asleep many years ago, and to have at last waked, half suffocated, shivering, and robbed of the best of their clothes. In the brightest day of the summer, they impressed one with this notion. In the drenching black rain of December, their miserable appearance chilled the blood of the fattest stranger who chanced to pass through them, and to the imaginative mind suggested the ruins of Baelbec. In short, there wasn't a decent town in Kildare, nor on the Kildare borders of Dublin.

Clane was one street. The street numbered a hundred houses, more or less. Every second one was a shebeen, or tavern, dedicated, as the sign-board intimated, to the entertainment of Man and Beast. I recollect that on one sign-board, next to the post office, the Cat and Bagpipes rampantly figured ; whilst on another, a red coffin, with three long clay pipes crossed upon the lid, and a foaming pot of porter pressing down the pipes at the point of intersection, gave the public to understand that the wakes of the neighbourhood would be

" convaniently " supplied. There was a police-barrack, of course, with a policeman perpetually chewing a straw outside on the doorstep, rubbing his shoulder against the white-wash of the door post, and winking and spitting all the day long. There was a Protestant church—and that, too, of course, right opposite the police barrack—with its gaunt angular dimensions, fat tower in front, sheet iron spire, and gilt weathercock on top. There was a low-sized, most modest, low-roofed, little Catholic chapel, back from the street a few yards, with a convent, sheltering three Sisters of Mercy, on the right hand side coming down from Dublin, and on towards the South.

At the southern end of the street, a quarter of a mile from the houses, drooped off the beautiful brown Liffey, deepening into gurgling pools, spreading thinly and sparklingly over beds of sand and pebbles, threw itself under the arches of the quaintest, queerest, crookedest, most broken-backed bridge that ever flung shadows on the flashing path of the speckled trout and red salmon, rushing away, with many a round of caprice and turmoil, through green rushes, sandbanks alive with martins, sedges rustling with otters, into the copper-hued darkness of Irishtown Wood.

Oh ! what a river is that exquisite wild Liffey ! How it tumbles ; glides away ; buries itself darkly in pools of fabulous depths ; leaps over rocks ; deepens, as it were, thoughtfully, under ruins and raths ; plunges down into valleys ; ripples and whispers under willows, the close leaves of the strawberry, and the purple-ivied basements of church-tower, country-mansion, and castle ; running the wildest, most ruinous, and grandest frolic imaginable, until it frowns and grows sulky a little above the King's Bridge, of Dublin, and in a turbid thick stream washes the granite walls of the quays, over which the Four Courts and Custom House rear their stately porticoes and domes.

In a yellowish, dry, worm-eaten manuscript, in the Krundelian Library of Stonyhurst, I glanced one day on a passage glowingly eulogistic of Clane. The manuscript contains an account of the Synods held, at different periods, in Ireland. This poor dribbling village of Clane was the favoured scene of one of them, six hundred years back; and, *apropos* to it, the chronicler, whoever he was, styled it the *hortus angelorum*—the Garden of Angels. It is now a paradise in ruins. The broken walls of an abbey, matted with ivy, shadowing a confused crowd of tombstones and tablets, the inscriptions of which no casual eye can decipher, alone remain to bear out the panegyric put on parchment recording its saintliness and glory.

One tomb especially, within those broken grey walls, ever attracted me, bringing me close to it, and urging me with a silent impulse back into the dim paths of the past. It was that of a Crusader. So I thought. So every one who visited it thought. So the whole neighbourhood, for miles round, and for generations, decided. Within the last week, I have been looking over one of the beautiful Tracts of the Celtic Union, entitled " The Traces of the Crusaders in Ireland," and whilst I find in its bright pages vestiges of this chivalrous Knighthood near Clonegall, in Carlow, and on the Mourne, three miles south of Mallow, and at Toomavara, near the ruins of Knockbane, and in the parish of Temple-Michael, in the barony of Clashmore and Clashbride, and at Ballyhack, close to the estuary of the Suir, I am cast adrift from Clane, where the chain-clothed legs and turtle-breasted body of a Templar, burst out, as if with an incompressible leprosy, from the dockweeds, the nettles, the rank grass, the daffodils, the nightshade, and blackberry bushes with which it is hemmed in, overshadowed, and dismally margined.

That's the fault I find with Clongowes. They talked to us about Mount Olympus and the Vale of Tempe ; they birched us into a flippant acquaintance with the disreputable gods and goddesses of the golden and heroic ages ; they entangled us in Euclid ; turned our brains with the terrestrial globe ; chilled our blood in dizzy excursions through the Milky Way ; paralysed our Lilliputian loins with the shaggy spoils of Hercules, bewildered us with the Battle of the Frogs and Mice, pitched us precipitately into England, amongst the impetuous Normans and stupid Saxons ; gave us a look, through an interminable telescope, at what was doing in the New World ; but, as far as Ireland was concerned, they left us, like blind and crippled children, in the dark.

They never spoke of Ireland. Never gave us, even what is left of it, her history to read. Never quickened the young bright life they controlled, into lofty conceptions and prayers by a reference to the martyrdoms, the wrongs, the soldiership, the statesmanship, the magnificent memories, and illuminating hopes of the poor old land.

All this was then to me a cloud. Now I look back to it, shake my hand against it, and say it was a curse.

The last, I have stated. The reason of it—at least what appears to me to be the reason of it—I may, in a little time, explain.

What true scholars and patriots they might have made, those old Jesuits of Clongowes, had they taken their pupils to the battle-fields of William Aylmer's army—skirting the Bog of Allen—or to the Geraldine ruins of Maynooth, or the grave of Wolfe Tone in Bodenstown churchyard, or to the town of Prosperous, where Dr. Esmonde buried the Red Cross under the hot ashes of his insurgent torch, or to the woods and mansion of Rath-Coffey, where Hamilton Rowan once lived, where the bay of his famous bloodhounds still echoed in my time, and where an old man—lean, shrivelled, skinny, with wiry, thin locks—still mumbled and shuffled along the decayed avenue, showing the worn pike at the end of his staff, which he had charged with against the North Cork in Maynooth—what true scholars and patriots, Irishmen in nerve and soul, might they have made us had they taken us to these sites, instead of keeping us within the pillars of the Parthenon, or the forum and shambles of the Tiber ?

I write this, not that they kept us aloof from these places of national interest ; not that they actually imprisoned us within the routine range of the classics, and shut the gates on us, as if there were no chastity or illumination without ; but that we wandered with them, day after day, miles upon miles, over these fields and localities, without a finger to mark them on our memories, or a syllable to mingle them with our joyousness, our poetry, and rhetoric. Ireland was the last nation we were taught to think of, to respect, to love and remember.

It is an odd fiction which represents the Irish Jesuits as conspirators against the stability of the English empire in Ireland. With two or three exceptions, they were not O'Connellites even. In that beautiful, grand castle of theirs, circled by their fruitful gardens and grain-fields, walled in by their stately dense woods of beech trees, walnut, and firs, they lived and taught —so it seems to me now—rather as hostages and aliens, than freemen and citizens.

But, I can't bear to say anything against Clongowes, It is to me a dear old spot. Long may that old tree,

Meagher as a boy
(From a pencil-sketch)

on which I've carved my name, put forth its fragrant blossoms, multiply its fruit, lift its aged head to Heaven, and receive thereon the dews which fertilise, and the golden beams that propagate !

Midway between Clane and Maynooth—just off the road skirting the domain of the College—lived one Father Kearney, the parish priest of the united parishes of Clane and Rath-Coffey. He was a great friend of the College ; was always on hand there, whatever ceremony or pastime, high mass or funeral, academical exercise or collegiate symposium, was to take place. With short black trousers, tight black gaiters, skimpy black dress coat, rumpled white cravat, sandy scant hair—at the tail of the plough, in the pulpit, abreast of the altar, in the chair of the study hall, examining the boys, or mixing his punch—he was ever the same, grotesque, unique, and attractive.

He had nothing to do with the college, but somehow or other, the old gentleman was constantly there. The Jesuits had a gala day once a month. The boys had football or handball, fishing or skating. They had an extra allowance of meat, whatever it was, and tart varying from apple to rhubarb, and from rhubarb to gooseberry, as the season permitted. The Jesuits had a choice banquet in one of those frescoed halls I have already described.

To this banquet came all the neighbours. The Aylmers, Gerald and William, nephews of the noble old rebel I have mentioned, were never missed from this monthly feast, during my time, and for fifteen or twenty years before it. They did right. Were I living near old Clongowes—close to it as they were—I'd dine there, not only every month, as they did, but every day, if possible.

From this monthly table, too, Father Kearney was

never absent. The boys used to say—though his
cottage was two miles off—he smelt the dinner, and,
in dressing himself, timed his toilet by the perfume,
which came to him from the chimney-top of the college
kitchen, across the woods, the fields, and the marshy
bottoms. For upwards of thirty years, Father Kearney,
in his short breeches, tight black gaiters, clumsy
rumpled cravat, and carroty scant hair, was at that
feast. On the Academical or Commencement day,
year after year, he examined a certain class in the
Third Book of Cæsar, asked the same questions, and
found the same faults. In Christmas week he visited
the theatre, sat alongside of the President, snuffed
himself plenteously, hemmed and hawed mightily,
perpetually pulled his nose and his waistcoat, brushed
his breeches over his knees, and sat there, snuffing and
puffing, the venerable Sphinx of the scene.

His cottage was known by the name of Snipe Lodge.
It was a thatched cottage, with a clay floor, naked
rafters, and four panes of green glass—each of them
with an enormous bull's eye—to let the light through.
He had a housekeeper named Biddy, and a butler
named Jim. Between Biddy and Jim, it was hard to
keep the place clean. The calf was for ever opening
his Reverence's door, upsetting the chairs, and the
turf in the corner. There was a blackguard parcel of
dogs incessantly scampering about, biting the legs of
the poor who came with their sores and their crutches
for alms, and frightened the hens from their roost.

As for the hens, they had, at last, to take refuge on
the smoked rafters, under the roof. Elsewhere, they
had neither immunity nor peace. There, night and
day, they used to crowd up, shake their wings, shut and
open their eyes, and make themselves comfortable.
Below was the hard floor of black clay, mixed with

lime. All round, on four sides, were the walls, built thickly of mud, and whitewashed within. Overhead were black rafters, crowded with hens, flapping their wings, pecking their leggings and breasts, and making themselves indecently at home.

A few weeks after the consecration of the Right Rev. Dr. Nolan, Bishop of Kildare and Leighlin, Father Kearney gave a grand dinner in the one room of Snipe Lodge. It was the great event of Biddy's existence. She had never anything but a few eggs and a cut of bacon to fry, before this. Now she had a pair of chickens to roast and another pair to boil, and a beautiful ham to dress and serve up with young cabbage, besides having the biggest potful of potatoes (pink eyes) to look after, and a cupful of fresh mustard to mix. It was a great day with Jim, by the same token. He had to lay a clean cloth, scrub the year's rust out of the knives and forks, borrow three or four chairs from the neighbours all round, and keep the hens off the rafters, and the table immediately under them. This was the worst trouble of all. For though Jim, now and then, took the sweeping brush to them, and occasionally his Reverence's blue cotton umbrella—opening and shutting it suddenly, to frighten the birds from their roost— and though in these efforts he was assisted by Biddy, who took the basting-spoon to help the umbrella, it was all to no purpose. The hens would keep to the rafters, flapping their wings, dropping their spare feathers, and, whenever Jim turned his back, and Biddy was bent over the pot on the fire, popping down straight on his reverence's clean table-cloth, to have a crumb or two from the loaf which lay there, on a blue-rimmed dinner-plate, waiting for the chicken, potatoes and bacon to come on. Father Kearney himself used sometimes to look in, and whisk his yellow silk pocket handkerchief at the obstinate fowls which overlooked the scene of his feast. But the fowls didn't mind him. As Biddy observed, they didn't care a straw for his reverence, and she wouldn't be surprised if they misbehaved before the bishop himself !

" You might as well," Biddy used to say to her master, turning round from giving the roasting chickens a turn, her face and hands pouring over with gravy, " you might as well lave them alone, for the devil's in them to-day."

The company arrived. Father O'Connor, the Procurator of Clongowes, was the first on the ground. Next came the Aylmers, William and Bob, the latter the best horseman that ever crossed a ditch from the Boyne to the Barrow. Then came Father Kearney's curate from Clane, and Father Dignan, of Clongowes, and Dr. Walsh, all the way from Naas, and the parish priest of Prosperous, and two Professors from Maynooth, and Dr. O'Flannigan, the comfortably-fed druggist and doctor from Celbridge.

O'Flannigan, by-the-by, was the physician in ordinary to the College of Clongowes. He visited it once a week —every Tuesday, if I recollect rightly—walked through the Infirmary, felt pulses, knocked against chests, fixed his castor-oil eyes upon tongues, muttered monosyllabically to Judy, the head nurse and matron of the Infirmary, wrote something in a book which Judy kept in her cupboard, along with her tea, sugar, prayer-books, and two or three withered, inflexible lemons.

His invariable prescription was senna and salts. The boys called it " black draught." It made no difference what ailed you, that dose was prescribed. Toothache, neuralgia, constipation, scarlatina, pleurisy, lumbago, ringworm, lockjaw, or softening of the brain—for everything, the most trivial or most desperate, that " black draught " was Dr. O'Flannigan's corrective. It was with him that same " sweet oblivious antidote which cleansed the stuff'd bosom of that perilous stuff which weighs upon the heart," and purged it to a " sound and pristine health."

His assistant was a lay brother of the College, one Philip O'Reilly, of whom I propose to write more fully in the course of these grateful recollections. Judy always administered the dose. She mixed it, stirred it with a teaspoon, forced it inexorably on the patient, piously ejaculating : " Take it now, for the poor souls in Purgatory ! " When it was swallowed, she gave the patient the quarter of a dry apple, recommending him just to take the taste off his mouth, and not to eat it all.

Close upon the heels of Surgeon O'Flannigan, Major Rind, a Protestant neighbour, came in. Then somebody from near Bishop's Court, Lord Ponsonby's place, where O'Connell tumbled D'Esterre. The bishop came last.

The dinner was laid. The roast chickens were put at the foot, and the boiled at the head, and the ham at the side, right under Bob Aylmer's magnificent scimitar-shaped nose, and the potatoes everywhere around. Father Kearney carved the boiled chickens, with the Bishop on his right, and Major Rind on his left. Jim bustled about with a new apron, and a clean napkin under his arm, doing everything wrong, with Biddy, as red as the poppy and as hot as a hob, standing at the kitchen door—it opened into the parlour—and ordering him to do this, and do that, and bewildering him wholly.

" Sure, I can't, if you tell me," he used to cry out, turning upon Biddy, with a plate full of fowl, or a cut of the loaf on the top of a knife.

By-the-by, Jim had an idea that, for everything, the plates should be warm. If Dr. O'Flannigan asked for a little bread, Jim ran into the kitchen, snatched a plate from the plate-warmer, cut a slice of the loaf, and handed it on the hot plate to the doctor. If Father O'Connor, the huge Procurator, asked for the mustard, Jim pushed Biddy aside, snatched up another blazing hot plate, and planting the mustard pot on it, ran it in to the Procurator. Old Bob Aylmer asked him one time for a corkscrew. Jim brought it to him on a hot plate. The hot plate was his absorbing idea.

The dinner was pleasant—indeed, it was jovial. The company forgot the clay floor they were sitting on, and the black rafters overhead, where the harpies were roosting. The sherry had gone round half a dozen times at least. The port, too, had more than once circled the board.

" Let's have the champagne," said Father Kearney. " Jim, hand round the champagne."

Jim made a dart for the kitchen for a hot plate. Biddy stopped him, however, spreading her check apron before him, and so bringing him quick to a halt, like the Roman race-horses pulling up in a sheet on the Corso.

" You omadhawn," says she, " what do you want ? "

" A warm plate, Biddy," says he.

" The divil warm ye," says she, " can't ye have betther manners before his blessed lordship the bishop ? "

With this reproof, Jim came to his senses, and twisted the wire off a silver-crowned bottle. Then he drew a carving knife across the veins of the throat, and up went the crowned head—neck and all—with a flash. At the same instant, frightened out of their wits by the report, and one of them being hit by the cork in the wing, down came the harpies with a rush, and a flap, and a spatter—three of them straight on the table—one of them into the potato-dish—another on Dr. O'Flannigan's wig—another into the good bishop's lap—whilst the cock made for the one pane of glass behind his lordship, and darting through it, went fluttering and splashing, all fuss and feathers down the dirty boreen which led from Snipe Lodge to the high road. It was some time before order was restored. It was some time before Biddy and Jim succeeded in dislodging the harpies. It was a very long time before Dr. O'Flannigan of Celbridge composed his offended feelings, and straightened out his wig.

" Gerald," Father Kearney calls out to Bob Aylmer's brother, " stick your hat through the window, and keep the cold from the back of the bishop."

Father Kearney of Snipe Lodge never entertained after that day. Biddy, I believe, died of a rush of blood to the head. Jim, disgusted with the world, went to Mount Melleray, and was there clothed with the gown and cowl of La Trappe. Poor old Bob Aylmer has shouted his last *Tally-ho*. Dr. O'Flannigan still dispenses senna and salts, though Judy, his beautiful Ganymede, has returned to dust. The guest of the feast sleeps beneath the pavement of Carlow Cathedral, and the host is troubled no more with obstreperous fowl, and the affairs of Snipe Lodge.

He put together a large sum of money. His will broke it up and distributed it amongst the sweetest and noblest charities of the country. Two months after his death, it was all found in a tin box, under the thatch, over the front door of Snipe Lodge.

Recollections of Waterford

On board the old steamer *William Penn* I came up the Suir, the second morning of Easter week in 1843. I had wished good-bye to Stonyhurst. My College days were over, my life in the world had begun. It was a stormy year. O'Connell had opened it with a shout for a Repeal. The Repeal debate in the Dublin Corporation had taken place. It was a splendid controversy. Vivid eloquence on both sides of the house ; a manly spirit of fair play ; a chivalrous love of Ireland ; intelligence, courtesy and patriotism characterised the event. The interest of the people was awakened—their enthusiasm excited. They had been inert, sluggish, listless. No people could have been more so. But the true chord once struck, everything was restored. Hope, delight, ecstasy, defiance—a tumultuous life leaped to the summons. The great meeting at Navan had taken place. Limerick, too, had poured out thousands through her ancient gates to meet the Liberator. The first waves of the vast sea coming on, had struck the beach. It was at such a moment I returned to my native city.

A bright sun was lighting up the dingy walls of Duncannon Fort as we paddled under them. There was Cheek Point on the left, towering grandly over the woods of Faithlegg. Further on, at the confluence of the Barrow and the Suir, were the ruins of Dunbrody Abbey—an old servant, with torn livery, at the gateway of the noble avenue. Further on, the grounds and stately mansion of Snow Hill, the birthplace of Richard Sheil. Then the Little Island, with its fragment of Norman castle and its broad corn fields and kingly trees. Beyond this Gaul's Rock, closing in upon and overlooking the old city. Last of all, Reginald's Tower —a massive hinge of stone connecting the two great outspread wings, the Quay and Mall, within which lay the body of the city—Broad Street, the cathedral, the barracks, the great chapel, the jail, the Ballybrlcken Hill, with its circular stone steps and bull-post.

The *William Penn* stopped her paddles, let off her steam, hauled in close to the hulk, and made fast, I was at home once more. Twelve months had passed since I bid good-bye to it. Everything was just as I had left it. The same policeman, chewing a straw, was dawdling up and down the flag-way opposite where the steamer came to anchor. The same old Tramore jingle was lazily jingling by. The good old Dean of the Protestant Cathedral, in his black knee-breeches and long black gaiters, his episcopal hat and ebony cane, was still pattering and puffing along the smooth broad side-walk, from the Mayor's office to Mrs. M'Cormac's confectionery, and back again. The same casks, the same bales of soft goods, the same baulks of timber I had seen there ten years ago, were still lying on the Quay, between the river and the iron chains and the pillars. The same rueful, wild haggard face seemed to be pressed against the rusty bars of the second window from the basement of the Ring Tower —the same I had seen as I drove past in her Majesty's mail coach on my way to Dublin the summer before. And there was the spire of the cathedral right up against me ; and there was Cromwell's Rock right behind me ; and the Abbey church ; and Grubb's steam-mills ; and White's dockyard ; and the glorious wooden bridge, built by Cox, of Boston, a mile up the river from where I stood ; and the shipping ; and the big butter market ; and the shops, and stores along the

Quay—an awkward squad of various heights and uniforms, several hundred yards in length. Waterford never appeared to me to change. For a century at least, it has not gained a wrinkle nor lost a smile. In every season, and for a thousand seasons, it has been, and will be, the same old tree. If no fresh leaf springs, no dead leaf drops from it. The Danes planted it; Strongbow put his name and that of Eva, his Irish bride, deep into its bark: and King John held court beneath its boughs; James the Second hid his crown into the crevices of its roots, and fled from it to France. It has witnessed many other events, many other familiarities have been taken with it. Many worse blows have been given it, since the Earl of Pembroke hacked it with his sword. But it has suffered nothing. The dews, and the storms, and the frost, and the summer heat come and pass away, hurting nothing; improving nothing; leaving it, at the end of ages, the same, old, dusty, quiet, hearty, bounteous, venerable tree. Heaven bless it! And may the sweet birds long fill its shady trellisses with music; and the noble stream with full breast nourish the earth where it has root!

But a great change had taken place in Waterford since I had last been in it, though appearance gave no intimation of it. The old corporation or city council had been displaced and a new one, installed in the ancient seats, had been talking and voting, and in a small way governing for the last six months. The former—an irresponsible, self-elected, self-conceited, bigotted body—closed its existence amid the jeers, and jokes, and groans of the people. The Bill of parliament under which this change took place like every other Bill of remedial tendency emanating from the same place was illiberal and grievously defective. It authorised the election of the city council by the people, but curtailed its powers. It was the enunciation of a principle—the principle of a popular government—with careful provisions annexed so that the clauses should, defeat the preamble. It was a fair skin with the cancer below it.

It looked well. Apparently worked well. It was a glorious thing, the people thought, to see some of their own sort in possession of the Town Hall ; to see the Mayor going to Mass ; to see him presiding at a public dinner given to O'Connell ; to see Larry Mullowney, the Repeal Warden from Mount Misery, an Alderman ; to see some other political friend and favourite constable of the fish market. It was a blessed thing, they thought, to have the repairing of the streets, of nuisances, and the government of the Holy Ghost and Leper hospitals, all in their own hands ; and sure they never thought they'd see Felix the basketmaker, the bitterest Orangeman of them all, carrying the white wand before his Catholic Worship, as his Worship, with the gold chain about his neck, went up to Ballybricken to preside at Petty Sessions.

All this was deeply gratifying to the masses of the people. But, in the surprise and delight it excited, the restrictions on the popular power, which accompanied the municipal honours, were altogether overlooked. Hence the reform in the city government was estimated far more highly than it should have been, and from the orators of the democracy called forth congratulations so profuse and ostentatious for the advantage conferred. In Ireland it has always been so. Generous and credulous to excess, the people give the largest credit on the smallest security, and repay the poorest favours with a prodigal measure of thanks. So it was when George the Fourth set his corpulent majesty on the granite beach of Dalkey. He wore a clump of shamrocks on his breast, shook hands with some country gentlemen in the Phoenix Park, and promised to drink their healths in whiskey punch. Whereupon there was a roar of joy, and Dublin went mad with loyalty. So it was when Catholic Emancipation was achieved. On every hill a bonfire, in every window a lamp or candle, in every chapel a thanksgiving ; throughout the country the wildest merriment, as though the land were free, as though each man had his vote, gun and acre ; as though the conquest had been repealed ! Shelley, the poet of Republicanism, wrote truly when he wrote these words :—

" Catholic disqualification affects the law. The subjection of Ireland to England affects the thousands. The one disqualifies the rich from power, the other impoverishes the peasant, adds beggary to the city, famine to the country, multiplies abjectness, whilst misery and crime play into each other's hands, under its withering auspices."

Catholic Emancipation has enabled a few Catholic gentlemen to sit in parliament, and there concur in the degradation of their country. It has brought a handful of slaves from the field, and gives them appointments in the master's house. The privileged class but wear the livery of the proprietorship which compels the obedience of an entire country, exacts its labour, and appropriates its profits. As it was with the King's visit, and with Catholic Emancipation, so it was, as I have said, a balloon handsomely painted, which carried up a boat-load of gentlemen a little higher in the world than they had been before. The people cheered as the balloon ascended : and, carried away with their enthusiasm, fancied that they themselves went with it.

In this ecstatic mood I found my fellow-townsmen on my return from college. My father was sitting in

the curule chair. Chief Magistrate of the city, he
presided at the meetings of the city council, and the
bench of borough justice. Amongst the aldermen and
town councillors, were the most conspicuous politicians
of the place. Men who had poured out their souls in
fiery streams upon the shackles of the Catholic and
the ruins of Ireland for years and years, and who
would have fallen in ashes but for the fresh fuel supplied
them constantly from Dublin—these men were now
seated at the red table in the assembly room—a senate
on the scale of a dwarf, with the limp of a cripple, and
the look of a beggar. The few faculties they possessed,
and these faculties for the most part hampered—the
fact of their not being able to borrow the smallest sum
for the improvement of the city without permission
of the Lords of the Treasury and their being allowed
to apply their own funds only to a few purposes, and
these not the most useful—circumstances such as these
justify the language of contempt in speaking not only
of the municipal government of my own city, but every
city or borough town in Ireland. Indeed, to call it a
government, is to indulge in a courtesy which borders
on a sarcasm. The sheriffs of the city were appointed
by the Lord Lieutenant. The police were under the
control of the commissionership in Dublin.

The day after I had arrived, the trades of the city
held a public meeting to petition parliament for the
Repeal of the Union. The meeting took place at the
Town Hall. There was a dense crowd. The enthusiasm was vehement—the rhetoric still more so.
The speakers rose with the occasion, and from the
loftiest clouds flung hail and lightning on the listeners.
Two of these soared far above the rest. Strikingly
different in their " physique " and speech, the one
impersonated the Iron age, the other the age of Gold.

The one was an alderman and draper ; the other was a schoolmaster, and earned his bread by dispensing the fruit of knowledge. James Delahunty was the alderman's name. James Nash was the schoolmaster's name.

James Nash.

The schoolmaster was full of humour, full of poetry, full of gentleness and goodness : he was a patriot from the heart and an orator by nature. Uncultivated, luxuriant, wild, his imagination produced in profusion the strangest metaphors, running riot in tropes, allegories analogies, and visions. Of ancient history, and books of ancient fable, he had read much, but digested little. He was a Shiel in the rough. Less pretentious than Phillips, he was equally fruitful in imagery and diction, and more condensed in expression. His appearance was in keeping with the irregularity and strangeness of his rhetoric. That he had a blind eye was a circumstance which, at first sight, forcibly struck one. The other was crooked, but evidently gifted with a wonderful ubiquity of vision. It was everywhere. In a crowd, it took in every visible point ; and, though revolving on an eccentric axis, impartially diffused its radiance all round. He had a comical face. Every conceivable emotion and mood was blended there in an amusing enigma, the exact meaning of which it was most difficult, if not impossible, to solve. Addressing an audience, his attitude excited the highest merriment, whilst his sound sentiments and capital hits called forth the loudest cheers. His usual attire was an old claret-coloured coat, buttoned to the neck. What his trousers consisted of, or looked like, I nearly forget ; but it would be no great mistake to say, they were of drab cloth, hung very voluminously about the ankles, and were deeply stained. The hat—as comical an affair as the face—was cocked on one side of his head, and suggested a devil-may care defiance of the world.

"Mr. Mayor and fellow citizens," it was thus he addressed the meeting the morning I returned to Waterford, "I came to attend this meeting, driving Irish *tandem*—that is one foot before the other." With exuberant adjectives he then went on to compliment the distinguished people who were present at the meeting. The Right Worshipful the Mayor of the city was in the chair. The Right Rev. Dr. Foran, the Catholic Bishop, was on the platform. "Patriotism," exclaimed Nash, "flashes from the mitre of the one, and burns in the civic bosom of the other." Then he proceeded, in an amazing medley of facts, and metaphors, and figures of arithmetic, to enumerate the evils which legislative union had produced. "What has been the upshot of it all?" he asked, "Why it comes to this, they haven't left us a pewter spoon to run a railroad with through a plate of stirabout." The threats of coercion uttered by the government next claimed his notice. He despised them; repelled them; haughtily flung them back. He defied the government; he defied them to come on. "Let them come on," he exclaimed, "let them come on; let them draw the sword; and then woe to the conquered!—every potato field shall be a Marathon, and every boreen a Thermopylæ."

Three summers after this, I was one morning walking out the old road to Tramore—a famous watering place, most beautifully situated, six miles from Waterford. Hearing footsteps behind me, I turned round—it was Nash. I had never spoken to him; never had an opportunity of doing so. I was resolved not to lose the present, and I wished him good morning. Rapidly turning that ubiquitous eye of his on me, and giving his hat an extra jerk on one side, he returned the salute.

He did not know who I was, and I pretended not to know him. Our conversation was, consequently, the more familiar. The secession of the Young Irelanders from the Repeal Association had very recently occurred. We reverted at once to the event. Nash was a great O'Connellite. He thought him immaculate—incapable of error. Not wholly approving of the step taken by the Young Irelanders, he was willing to admit there was much to provoke it. Whilst, on the one hand, he would have wished them to have been more ductile and subordinate to the Liberator—holding the opinion that it would have been more wise and gracious of them to have been so—he could not deny but that in the recent policy the Liberator had advised, and the general tone and management of Conciliation Hall, there was a great deal that was repulsive to the hot blood of youth and irreconcilable with the honour of a people. Nash was just to Young Ireland despite the fanaticism of his devotion to O'Connell, and very sensible in his remarks on all such topics, notwithstanding the richness and riotousness of his imagination. He spoke of *The Nation* newspaper in superlatives of praise. It was the greatest paper published! Nothing could transcend the sublimity of its teachings! The prose left the Dream of Plato in the background, and the poetry eclipsed the Iliad! "Just before I die," said Nash, "my last request shall be, to have the last number of *The Nation* stitched about me as a shroud, so that when I appear hereafter I may have something national about me." In this manner he went on for an hour or so, until we came to the bridle-road, when, shaking me by the hand, he wished me good-bye. "My school is below there," he said, "and I flog the boys every morning all round, to teach them to be Spartans."

Of a class now almost extinct in Ireland—the Irish

Thomas Francis Meagher
(As Brigadier-General of the Irish Brigade, 1861-4)

schoolmasters—he was the finest specimen I ever saw. Had Carleton seen him, he would have immortalised him in type. As it is, he is dead, buried in some Potter's Field. Like all the poor, honest, gifted men— the rude bright chivalry of the towns and fields—who thought infinitely more of their country than of themselves—he died in utter poverty, companionless, and nameless. Yet, should anyone give me a file of the *Waterford Chronicle* from 1826 to 1847, there would be in my possession the materials of an epic, of which poor Nash, with his headlong honesty and reckless genius, should be the hero. He was a conspicuous figure, in the political action of Waterford, for more than twenty years. During the days of the Catholic Rent, he was conspicuous. In Stuart's election, which broke down the prestige and power of the Beresfords, he was conspicuous. In the elections of 1830 and 1832, he was equally so. In 1843 he emerged from his classic seclusion—for a season gave over flogging his boys and making them Spartans—and appeared once more as a Demosthenes on the hill of Ballybricken, the Acropolis of Waterford.

The last time I saw Nash was the day of my father's election as representative of Waterford, in the month of July, 1847. It was about five o'clock in the evening. The polling was nearly at a close. Sir Henry Winston Barron and Mr. Wyse were sadly beaten. The excitement of the people was intense. For years they had longed for this victory; and at last, in a fuller measure and with a more precipitous speed than they expected, it had come. They hated these gentlemen, for these gentlemen were aristocrats in social life and imperialists in politics. They were not of the people, nor among them, nor for them. Both would lord it over them. The one from vulgar affectation; the other instigated

19

by the haughtiness of superior intellect. For a long time they had kept their seats, not with the assent of the people, but favoured by circumstances and a temporising policy, dictated by the leaders of the people. Circumstances were changed—radically changed—and the temporising policy, before the breath of the national spirit, was impetuously swept away. Hence the defeat of these Whigs—both of them respectable men, and one of them an eminent scholar—who had so long misrepresented in the supreme political convention of the empire the heart and mind of the chief city of the Suir.

A huge crowd was before the Town Hall The Mall was impassable. The windows on both sides of the thoroughfare were filled with eager and excited gazers. The doorsteps, the lamp-posts, the leads and skylights of every house within sight or hearing of the Town Hall, were densely thronged. A troop of dragoon guards, coming down Beresford Street in double file, pushed their way through the enormous crowd, and suddenly facing about formed line in front of the Town Hall, in the centre of the Mall, thereby cutting the crowd in two. At this moment Nash made his appearance in one of the front windows of the Town Hall immediately facing and looking down on the dragoons. His queer eye played through the multitude for a moment. Then giving his hat, as was usual with him on all such occasions, a jerk on one side, he turned up the cuffs of his coat, unbuttoned his shirt sleeves, took a bite of an orange, and commenced his harangue.

" Men of Waterford !—The day is ours. Barron is beaten. Wyse is beaten. The boys are with us. The girls are with us. The soldiers are with us—aren't ye, boys ?

There was a tremendous cheer at this. Many of the

dragoons seemed pleased. Their captain, however, became highly incensed. Banners and green boughs, and
scarfs, and handkerchiefs, and hats, and bonnets, were
flung out and shaken to and fro, up and down, in
tumultuous delight. The horses of the dragoons became restless. They champed their bits impatiently,
flinging flakes of froth here and there upon the crowd.
They pranced a little, and shied a little, and backed a
little. The cheering still went on. In the midst of
all, at that window in the Town Hall, with his crooked
eye in full play, and his hat still on one side, stood
Nash, with the most comical complacency, waiting for
the excitement to subside. It did subside a little, and
he went on to say that he loved a soldier's life, and would
be a dragoon before long. The only objection he had
to the service was the red jacket. Why shouldn't it
be green ?

" Why shouldn't it, boys ? " he exclaimed, addressing
himself to the dragoons, " why shouldn't it be green—
our own immortal green ? "

There was another tremendous cheer when this was
asked, and the dragoons gave way to the good nature
and enthusiasm of the crowd. They laughed out loud,
and some of them cheered, and not a few of them waved
their swords.

" Do you see that ? " cried Nash, and he dashed his
hat about, and tore his coat wide open, and hurrahed
with all his might. But the captain, a handsome young
snob, with sleepy eyelashes, and the daintiest mustachios,
looking down the line, gave his men the order to move
off, which they did amidst the loudest cheers—poor
Nash all the time twisting his eye, and shouting as
before with all his might. That was the last time I
saw him. His object was to remove the dragoons ;
and the speediest way to do so was to appeal to their

patriotism. He thought so, and his calculations were right. The dragoons were ordered off ; and Nash and his audience had it all to themselves. The day was their own.

THE STUART ELECTION.

My recollections of Waterford for the most part refer to political events and personages. The earliest I retain is that of Stuart's election, when the pride of the house of Curraghmore was humbled to the dust. In one huge mass the country rose against the Beresfords, and drove them from the haughty domination they had so long and with so much terror and prestige maintained. To the sagacity of the Right Rev. Dr. Kelly, the Roman Catholic Bishop of Waterford, this triumph of Democracy must be ascribed. At a public dinner given in the Trinitarian Orphan House, by the managers of that institute, the Bishop had statistically exposed the relative strength of the Catholics and Protestants of that county. A preponderance so very decided appeared in favour of the former that a trial of their strength with the champions of the Protestant Ascendancy was enthusiastically resolved. A parliamentary election coming on shortly after, the trial took place, William Villiers Stuart—now Lord Stuart de Decies, Lord Lieutenant of the county, and Colonel of the Waterford Militia Artillery—was put forward by the Catholics. Lord George Beresford at the head of the Tory landlords and the Orange squireens and parsons, a vast and ruthless army in which all the police, tax gatherers, bailiffs, sheriffs' deputies, gaugers, and all the garbage of the foreign government were included— entered the field, his crest dripping with the blood of '98, the stalwart Front-de-Bœuf of the Established Church and garrison. Stuart was a Protestant, but a chivalrous friend of the Catholics. Young, wealthy, accomplished, handsome, he was endowed with almost all the gifts which attract the multitude, securing popularity for their possessor, and imparting *eclat* to the cause he personates. Nor was he wanting in eloquence. He could speak fluently, though with a subdued grace, which had the appearance of timidity, Backed, however, by a crowd of dauntless orators—all of them experienced and famous in their art—his defects made no impression. Whatever they were, they were lost sight of in the blaze and tumult which burst around him from the pedestals on which those inexhaustible apostles of the people stood.

There was Dr. Peter Kenny, whose tongue was like a sabre—bright and flexible, and strong—flashing whilst it wounded, and wounding whilst it had a foe to strike. The Doctor had been a volunteer in the Venezuelan expedition under Devereux. He had worn the green and gold in the Republican cause of Bolivar, and into the political campaigns of a cooler climate infused the impetuosity and fire, the brilliant abandon and recklessness of his tropical adventures. Shiel writes glowingly of him in his sketch of the Clare election. Shiel himself, if I recollect rightly, was in Waterford the time I speak of. O'Connell certainly was. Wyse in his History of the Catholic Association, describes his appearance in the city during the election, and quotes a memorable joke of his. A steamboat had been sent up the Blackwater to bring down a large body of the Beresford tenantry to the poll. O'Connell heard of it—went out in great haste on the balcony of Shannon's hotel—announced the circumstance with a burst of alarm, and wanted to know " if the wives would let their husbands trust their lives to an old kettle of boiling water ? " The steamboat was then a mysterious novelty to the country people. They did not understand it, and their fears respecting it were easily excited. The question put to them with so much anxiety and alarm, and in language which most forcibly conveyed their own notion of the danger, had the desired effect. The steamboat returned without a voter.

But of the local celebrities in that contest, the most prominent and powerful was the Rev. John Sheehan, the parish priest of St. Patrick's. I speak of him as " a local celebrity." To his fame the phrase is a great injustice. He was known to the country. He was known far beyond it. He was one of the few whose strong voices reached the highest places where a stupid royalty secluded itself from the people, the wrongs they felt, and the truth they spoke. "Father John's speeches," a distinguished member of the Munster bar said to me one day, " shook St. James's." An expert controversialist, an eloquent preacher, an experienced divine, he was a light of the sanctuary and a pillar of the Church. Pious as he was, his social tastes were genial. He was fond of fashionable society. He cultivated the acquaintance of the titled and persons of distinguished birth. There were few families of any eminence in the social scale in England or Ireland with whose history he was not acquainted. On heraldry he was a copious authority. No one could better trace a genealogical tree through all its roots and branches. The older the tree the more clearly and nimbly he swept through it ; but if he paid court to fashionable people, to people of high birth, to people of distinction—if he was glad to be asked to their tables and thought it an honour to be seen in their carriages, he seldom disguised and never compromised his political opinions to gratify them. Privately and publicly he boasted he was a Democrat.

On the repeal question, however, he was precarious. In 1843 he attended repeal meetings, and made repeal speeches. In 1847 he voted against the repeal candidates. His inconsistency was susceptible of one excuse, and he did not fail to urge it with effect. The repeal movement in Waterford was in the hands of the illiterate and vulgar demagogues. The Alderman I have mentioned was the chief of them. Educated men grew intolerant of such coarse dictatorship, and asserting their freedom, unconsciously compromised their integrity. This was the case with the Rev. John Sheehan. In the days of Catholic agitation, however, he had no offensive dictation to repel, and every step he took was consistent with his convictions and his words.

Stuart's election, of course, is to me a misty scene. It is a phantom rather than one of the distinct realities of memory. I was a child, and not exceeding three years old—when it took place. The incidents and figures of the scene have left upon my mind no visible impression. The men who conspicuously figure in it, and most of whom I have mentioned, were introduced to me at a much later day. They were old men, and dying men, the day I first appeared in public life. But the sound of the hot strife is buzzing in my ears, and my eyes grew dim in the glare which burst from it, amid the swaying to and fro of gaudy banners, and the discharge of cannon.

The result of the election was the defeat of the Beresfords. It was a sweeping defeat. It was the annihilation of their political consequence. They never recovered it. The enormous expense it entailed so thoroughly disgusted the present Marquis of Waterford —gave him so fearful an intimation of the penalties of public life—that nothing could ever induce him to set his foot within its frontiers. He has scrupulously kept aloof from politics. Not even the Mastership of the Buckhounds would he accept, though offered to him at the cordial suggestion of Prince Albert. What was the gain to the people ? What power accrued to them in the overthrow of the house of Curraghmore ? The power to return fat noodles and rich stupidities in the name of religious freedom and Tenant Right to parliament. Pusillanimity succeeds to bigotry, and bloated inactivity to aristocratic domination. There's the victory, and then there's the gain. One acre of land, good against all claims, ensured to him for ever, were better to the Irishman by a thousand times than a thousand of such triumphs. It would make him richer, freer, happier, nobler. That one acre, would have more wealth and virtue in it, than a catacomb stuffed with Emancipation Acts. With that one acre to take his stand on, a legion of Beresfords would be no more to him than a pyramid of mummies.

SOCIAL LIFE AND SNOBBERY.

I have said that my recollections of Waterford refer, for the most part, to political events and personages. Of other events and personages there was a dearth. Social life was at an ebb in the old city. There were very few gaieties. A ball in the Assembly room, two or three dinner parties, a picnic in summer—these were the only events that enlivened the sobriety of the twelve months. The fashionable circle was very small. Composed principally of these who had enjoyed municipal honours and emoluments under the old Tory reign, it had no affinity with the people. It was stiff with illiterate conceit. Socially selected from, it was politically hostile to, the great body of the citizens. The Conservative candidate for parliamentary honours always had its sympathies. If the Whig, or pseudo-Liberal, was sometimes favoured with them, it was owing to the aristocratic acquaintances and tastes he cultivated. Mr. Wyse was esteemed by this dainty society of noodles less for his eloquence and scholarship, than for his being a favourite guest in London at the tables of distinguished Whig noblemen. One evening discussing the chances of Mr. Wyse's defeat in the parliamentary contest of 1847, an amiable authority of this select circle I speak of—a kind old soul, who no doubt imagines there are velvet cushions and lounges in heaven for all those who have been " respectable " on earth, and bare benches only for those who have sat in the " lower classes " below—this kind old soul, his mouth running over with excitement, and black rapee, told me of a visit he had recently paid Mr. Wyse, at his residence, Walton Terrace, London. " The table," he said, " was literally covered with invitations from the highest nobility in England. There was an invitation from the Marquis of Lansdowne to supper. There was another from the Earl of Shrewsbury to lunch. Another from the Earl of Ellesmere. Another from Baron Brunow, the Prussian ambassador. A dozen or two from such men as Lord Morpeth, Viscount Mahon and the Duke of Cleveland. And is it such a man—a man who receives such invitations as those—is it him you are going to turn out of parliament ? " This was the logic, the philosophy, the patriotism of the municipal nobility, the genteel, broken-down old fogyism of Waterford. With the loss of the city treasury and town hall, they lost their importance, and the consciousness of the deprivation was visible in the penitential sobriety of their features. In this condition the people seemed to regard them with a pity slightly adulterated with contempt.

The first thing which struck me, and that which roused my imagination most on returning to my native city, was to find a number of admirable men—men in various departments of business, and building up their fortunes with skill and honour—occupying socially an obscure position. These men never had their dinner parties, their balls, their festive gatherings. The city fathers, seated in the town hall, alone indulged in such plays. So haughtily did they indulge in them, no other people, not even their betters, presumed to be convivial. A worthy tobacconist of Patrick Street, though eminently entitled to do so by his good presence, courtesies, and fair circumstances, would as soon have thought of committing sacrilege as of making his appearance in the same room, though it were a public one, where Alderman Babcock and his daughters, or Sheriff Gillott and his showy wife, or Captain Yellow-wig and his enchanting niece, were figuring on the floor. A strong disdain for men in business was active in these gentlemen. The feeling was not confined to Waterford. It prevailed all over the country. The lower classes, as they called them, were diseased with it as well as the higher. The bitterest thing that could be said against a public man, was that his father made boots, was successful as a tailor, or tanned the best leather. No young fellow, sure of an income of £200 a year, or less, ever thought of going into business. They entered their names, perhaps, at the Queen's Inns, and ate the prescribed number of dinners, to qualify them for admission to the bar. It was considered genteel to be a member of the bar, the celebrities of the profession constituting, with the officers of the army, and the retinue of the Castle and other public establishments, the only aristocracy of the Irish metropolis. Besides, it was the main road to political preferment. A barrister of six years' standing, whether he practised or not, was eligible to a colonial salary, or some berth at home, and was sure to receive the one or the other, provided he was valuable enough to be bribed.

The Waterford Club.

Yet with all their conceit and pretensions, there were good souls amongst the old Tory fashionables of Waterford. I was a member of the County and City Club, and had many opportunities afforded me of learning their worth, and conceiving a genial fondness for them. The Marquis of Waterford, the Earl of Huntingdon, Lord Carew, Sir Joshua Paul, Sir Henry Barron, Sir Nugent Humble, were members of it. Purely a social club—a club for pleasant intercourse and merry meetings—politics were rigorously excluded from its walls. No one entered with his Repeal button or Orange sash. Both were left in the umbrella stand at the outside door. Whatever they were without—however widely they differed in the streets, within all were Irish gentlemen, cordial, generous and jovial. Very nearly three-fourths of the club were Conservatives or Tories. Only two or three were Repealers. I had the honour to be one of the latter. Politically considered, it was a desolate minority. But so true were the members to the fundamental principle of the Club, that they might all have been Repealers for anything offensive ever heard to the contrary. The majority were loyalists to the marrow, and never lost an opportunity to assert the fact. They were sincerely so. Truthful, high-toned, gallant, their loyalty won my respect, though it failed to invite my concurrence. Loyal as they were, however, they were friendly and affectionate to the Rebel. Inwardly condemning his insubordination to the Queen, they openly loved him for his fidelity to the Club. A staunch friend of the pleasant institution they knew me to be. Of the principle on which it was established they knew I warmly approved. They knew that in public, over and over again, I had prayed for that tolerant, genial, generous brotherhood amongst Irishmen, of the feasibility and beauty of which, in a little sphere, they themselves had furnished such delightful evidence, and, to the last moment, for these reasons, I believe I continued to be their favourite. Well do I remember how cordially they used to drink my health and cheer my stammering speeches at their dinners. Well do I remember the jovial welcome and the shuffling of chairs round the fireplace, every night I came in. Early or late—the later the better—they always had a chair and a cheer for me.

Well, too, do I remember the kind importunity with which many of them endeavoured, as the fatal time drew near, to dissuade me from the enterprise, the failure of which, they predicted, would remove me from the old house on the Adelphi for ever and a day. Some of them a few days before my arrest in July, 1848, met me at dinner at a friend's of mine, close to the Lunatic Asylum on John's Hill, and urged me to withdraw from the movement.

" There's no use—you'll fail—you'll lose everything."

" Must stand my ground," I said.

" Oh, nonsense ! " they replied, " quit it, and come with us."

" Where to ? " I asked.

" To Italy—to Greece—to Egypt ! " they exclaimed. The invitation was a tempting one. A party of honest, cheerful, spirited fellows, full of life, intelligence, and the best good nature, to ramble with from the Suir, through the Mediterranean, to the Nile, was a prospect almost too enchanting to resist. Struck with it I felt my patriotism relax. Had it not been of iron, it would have melted in the warmth of such friendship and the seductions which it breathed. The iron may have rusted but it is iron still.

Of this club and all belonging to it I cherish the liveliest remembrance. Many a time do the old faces I so often saw there re-appear to me, sparkling and laughing, grinning or frowning, darkening into horror at some catastrophe, or bursting into boundless mirth at some rich joke, as they used to do, night after night, in that magic circle round the fireplace in the smoking room. Many a time, as I sat on deck on my way to the world's end in her Gracious Majesty's sloop-of-war, the *Swift*, have I travelled back through the waves, the sea birds and the clouds, through boisterous and dismal scenes of all sorts to that big weather-slated house, looking out over the Adelphi across the Suir to the Abbey Church and Cromwell's Rock, and there forgetting everything else but the club house, though the trade winds were in our sails and the southern stars were shining clear and full and fresh above us, and the albatross swept down and wheeled about us, in his majestic plenitude of wing—have I read the papers and eaten my anchovy toast and smoked till midnight, gossiping and joking over the occurrences of the day with my old friends in that snug and dusky room, right opposite the timber yard of Jacob Penrose, one of the most sedate and estimable quakers of the *Urbs Intacta*.

It was, indeed, a pleasant thing to drop in there about nine or ten o'clock at night. A little while after you opened the door, you could discern nothing plainly. The smoke was dense, filling the four corners. The group about the fireplace was but a darker cloud. As you

approached, it resolved itself into several distinct fragments. Each fragment was a gentleman. The gentleman had his cigar, his short clay pipe, his manilla, or
his chibouque. Night after night, for the twelvemonth,
it was the same. For the last twenty or thirty years it
had been the same. The *habitues* of that cozy and
capacious fireplace formed a stock company of the
pleasantest performers on the provincial stage of life.
An unctuous laziness kept them at home. Had they
moved abroad, their good qualities and wit would
have shone as brightly in a broader sphere. Neither
the Kildare Street Club, in Dublin, nor the Carlton nor
the Athenæum, in London, would have been too ambitious a theatre for many of them to have figured in.
Endowed by nature and improved by art—by travel,
reading, constant intercourse with endless varieties of
people—they were well qualified to shine, draw down
applause, and be the favourites wherever they chose
to stay.

One was an attorney—a wild-looking, big-boned, disorderly dressed gentleman—whose ideas and language
partook strongly of the excitement of his appearance.
His anecdotes were voluminous, and his speculations
interminable. Profuse and incongruous, his descrip-
tions of scenery bewildered himself as well as his hearers.
I was present one night he described a storm at Killarney.
His hair flew about in every direction from the top and
back of his head. His waistcoat unbuttoned—his
neckerchief wriggled and danced, like an eel, about his
neck. With hands wide open, and the fingers standing
violently apart, his arms swept the air, up and down,
right and left, to and fro, here and there, and everywhere—a pair of condor's wings in the ecstasies of
plunder.

Mangerton was hid in one enormous cloud ; the Reeks

and the Toomies had disappeared ; the waves were
leaping up and pouring over Ross Castle—the thousands
of bones and skulls in Muckross Abbey were tumbling
and dashing about and splitting each other to splinters
with the wind ; " And," he exclaimed, his eyes ready
to burst, and his hair tearing itself out from the roots,
and his long wild arms jumping away from their sockets,
" and the wind and the water, and the woods and the
mountains, were all, my dear Keating, on fire ! "

Immediately after such an effort as this, the poetic
attorney struck by the aspect of incredulity all round,
would compose himself a little, and put the question,
" Don't you think it was so ? " It matters not whether
he was answered in the affirmative or otherwise.
Having put the question he concluded he was perfectly
understood, and subsided for a time into less riotous
enjoyment. He filled his pipe. If I remember rightly,
it was an old black pipe—very short and very dirty—
the ugliest dwarf of an old dudeen. Crossing his legs,
he lit his pipe, buttoned a button of his waistcoat, and
silenced himself in smoke. Still, however, the big
brown eye glared upon the company, flashing back the
red coal which filled the grate. From his momentary
trance he was sure to wake up with a jerk, to inflict a
rhapsody of science on the survivors of his original
audience. He was better than the Riot Act for dispers-
ing a crowd. No crowd could withstand his delirious
vocabulary an hour.

A convivial soul, unconsciously pouring over with the
strangest fun, he was a bewildered theorist and a precarious politician. In his profession alone could one
depend on him. There he was steady, intelligible,
reliable, decidedly successful. At one time he was proprietor of the *Waterford Chronicle,* and vehemently
insisted on Repeal. His editor was an eccentric and

fruitful genius, used a copious pen, and used it boldly. Though he died very dismally, and few followed him to the grave, poor Quarry Barron will not be forgotten in and around Waterford for many a year to come. His speeches, less startling in their imagery than those of Nash, were more solid in their matter and subtle in their wit. He died a Repealer. His employer, the incongruous attorney, the proprietor of the *Chronicle*, lives happily as a Whig in improved business as Queen's prosecutor at Quarter Sessions. Unworthy of an epitaph commemorative of patriotism, I trust he shall have one reminding the readers of his tombstone, that with all his vagaries in public life his good-fellowship in private was consistent, whilst the sobriety of the attorney made ample amends for the madness of the poet.

Another member of the Club of whom I preserve a durable impression, was old Bell of the Manor. He had served in the Waterford militia long before the peace of 1815, and in civilian dress ever after kept up the consequence of the periodical profession. I forget whether he was Captain Bell, or Major Bell, or Colonel Bell. It is of little importance. Whatever his military distinction may have been, he was a great old Bell, with a hard, old-soldier face, bushy black whiskers, a white cravat, having a comical tie ; always a big dinner coat of a very dark shade ; big, baggy trousers, a little top short ; white stockings, loose shoes, a purple wig, an overshadowing hat, a pair of brown worsted or leather gloves, and a stupendous umbrella of brown cotton. It was refreshing to see the old soldier, shoulder-ing his inseparable umbrella, with his shoes freshly blackened. turning out of his house, opposite to Harry Downes' extinct distillery, and calmly moving through the tumult and perils of the Tramore car-stand, into Beresford Street, along the footpath under the

Meagher's Irish Brigade Flag of the 69th Regiment

Bishop's wall, of a morning to the Club. Calmly, silently, solidly, he moved along, disturbed by nothing under heaven, on his way to read the papers. Having got through the papers, he returned as he set out, complacently and slowly, with an unruffled countenance, a rigid face, and a fearless gait. What became of him the rest of the day, the public never knew. About eight o'clock in the evening, however, he was down again to the Club. As before, he came along by the Tramore car stand, through Beresford Street, under the wall of the Bishop's garden, with his heavy umbrella across his shoulder, with a steady conscience and a measured step, without a word, without a quiver of the lip. Silent, erect, large, old-fashioned, sombre somewhat, and almost grim, Bell carefully stacked his umbrella in some safe nook, and, without a syllable, took his accustomed seat amongst the smokers. His seat was on the left hand side of the fireplace. There was a handy little shelf, midway up close to the chimney-piece, projecting from the wall. It was fitted with a brass hinge, and could be let up or down like the leaf of a table. The first thing old Bell did at the fireplace, was to take a chair. It was usually an armchair. The second thing he did, was to call for a glass of grog—brandy and cold water. The third thing he did, was to set this glass of grog upon the old shelf beside him at his elbow. The fourth, to draw out his pipe from the breast pocket of his dinner-coat. The pipe, invariably, was a clean, white pipe, with a pretty long shank, and a thin, smooth coating of red sealing-wax at the top. Obviously, pipes were his only expense. The fifth thing Mr. Bell did was to cut a pipe-full of tobacco. The sixth, to fill his pipe. The seventh, to light it well. The eighth and last, to smoke it to the bottom of the bowl. All this was done in deep silence. The veteran

20

hardly raised his eyes once during the deliberate proceeding. If spoken to, he lifted one eye-lid and eye-brow a little, smiled perhaps, and then relapsed. Forced to speak, he spoke economically, with a small expenditure of breath, using the shortest syllables. Bell was an Orangeman, a staunch, bluff, inveterate worshipper of William of pious memory. More hateful to him than Beelzebub, the Pope was his perpetual dread. With all the kindness of his nature, he was ever more or less suspicious of his Catholic acquaintances, and looked upon them as people rather to be tolerated than trusted. He would not hang, but would keep a keen watch on them. He would not, perhaps, deprive them of a vote, but would never give them a gun. He could never forgive them the Gunpowder Plot or the Spanish Armada. When the statue of King William was blown up in College Green, he flourished his umbrella, swore the militia must be called out, and the Emancipation Act instantly repealed. As for Daniel O'Connell—no fate was too bad for that monstrous disturber of the peace.

I know not if the big cotton umbrella is at rest. I know not if the last white pipe, in the cozy corner I have spoken of, has been smoked. But if the worst has come, if the bells have tolled for Bell—if Bell sleeps in the same sweet earth with those he feared in life—then peace and happiness and glory be to him ! He was a true and gentle soul, unobtrusive, yet uncompromising. Slow but sure. A Cromwell in his way, but a Cromwell with more heart than brains.

That the evenings at the club to which such men resorted were pleasant in the extreme need not be said. In my native city—in that old city of the Suir—social unity was sadly wanting. In Ireland—all through Ireland—it was wanting, too. This social unity is a ground-work of a unity yet more stable, yet more con-

spicuous and fruitful in great events and blessings.
The unity which the army of Lord Charlemont, despite
of the weakness of its leadership, and the defectiveness
of its enterprise, with ineffable brilliancy portrayed.
The unity for which Wolfe Tone—the clearest, boldest
spirit sprung from Irish soil—studied, toiled, travelled,
begged, organised, moved the military genius of a
colossal empire, manned a noble fleet, fought, bled, was
manacled, and in his dungeon died. The unity, to
accomplish which the young scholar, historian, poet,
orator—known to us as Thomas Davis—sprang to light,
struck the harp, burned the midnight oil, thought, and
sang, and rambled ; thought like a grey-haired saint of
old ; sang, like a feudal bard of old, 'mid lifted spears,
and flowing horn cups, and clashing swords and spurs ;
rambled for, like the hunted outlaw, over moor and
river, through bog and glen, by rath and cairn, and
chapel, plucking flowers, and golden relics, and laurels
bathed in blood, and offerings from every race settled
by conquest or misfortune in the land, all for the crowning
of the future nation, rising from the dead, and with
liberty to be made immortal ; and so thinking, singing,
rambling, toiling—wasting brain and heart—was struck
to earth with the splendour of the vision—died delirious
with the destiny in the full blaze of which, with lion
heart and eagle-wing, he soared.

With all their childishness, with all their folly, with
all their indolence, with all their incentives to driftless
gaiety and frolic, with all their loyalty to England and
her King or Queen—the darkest turpitude of all—may
the social institutions flourish which bring Irishmen
together, make them know each other, trust each other,
love each other, and, in convivial circles, teach them
they are brothers all ! This done, there is a family.
From a family comes a camp. From a camp a Nation.

The Galway Election

The Connemara pony galloped us into Loughrea in less than no time, the boy on the box shouting the whole of the way, at the top of his voice, for O'Flaherty, Repeal and ould Ireland. The streets were crowded as if it were a fair day. Detachments of the 8th hussars, slowly riding up and down in front of Kilroy's Hotel, up and down before the Courthouse, and round and round Eyre Square, threw a variety of brilliant touches into what would otherwise have been a very sombre picture. The day was dull. A thaw had set in. The ground, covered with a soft crust, was inclined to be muddy. An ashy sky arched the old Spanish houses, the quaint, solemn look of which deepened the gloominess of the scene. Everyone, except the hussars appeared to me to have been out all night on Lough Corrib, and to have come into town in wet clothes. The hussars themselves, with all the swinging finery about them, and the fire and beauty of their horses, were not wholly free from the damp and mouldiness which seemed to prevail. The fur on their jackets looked moist—looked like a brown rabbit would after being dragged out from under a heap of wet leaves. The mulberry nose of a sinewy, broad-shouldered sergeant sitting calmly in his saddle, close to the back door of the Courthouse, was covered with something resembling a very cold dew. The white sheets of calico, with O'Flaherty's name and patriotic sentiments in lamp-black upon them, shared the general depression. Tacked to the dreariest bare poles, they dangled from the window-sills of houses that looked as if they never knew what a good fire or a laugh was. The banners were on the outer walls, but were all the worse for being so. Lifeless, colourless, and clammy, they were calculated rather to depress than to excite the enthusiasm of the City of the Tribes. Patriotic sentiments were never before so destitute of drapery. The undertaker must have been the painter, costumier, upholsterer, and decorator to the Repealers of Galway on this slovenly and dismal day.

The dulness, however, was all outside. It was superficial gloom and stupidity. There was life enough, a little way out of sight, behind those dead banners. Galway was piled up, and crushed within four walls that day. They were the walls of the Courthouse. Every man who had a heart, an arm, or a kick in him, was there. Every man with a shirt on his back was there. Every man who could shout for Repeal was there. Every man who could boast of a roof over his head, a penny in his pocket, or a crust for his breakfast was there. Landlords of every description were there. The tyrant of the field, the swindling sportsman, the beggar in fine linen and broadcloth, the sneaking supplicant for Government favours, the political traitor making a joke of his perfidy, the vulgar toady of the great house whose owner he knew would have a coronet on his coffin when carried to the toads and leeches—all were there, jumbled up together, flushed, disordered, sweltering, tossing hats and handkerchiefs about, now and then fiercely shaking fists, shouting, crushing one upon another, many of them foaming at the mouth, all heightening the turbulent and stormy scene with the wildest excess of words, threats, cheers, oaths and gestures.

Mitchel and I looked down from the grand jury gallery upon the tumult. Stunned by the terrific

shouts, our eyes swam in the hot, suffocating haze
through which thousands of arms and legs and heads
—most of them in rags, many of them bleeding, all of
them coated with dust, whitewash, and dishevelled—
flung themselves frantically to and fro, aloft and everywhere.   Under a canopy of red maroon, in the middle
seat of the judge's bench, sat the high sheriff of the
borough, Michael B. Browne, Esq.   A thin white wand,
which he nervously held fast to, denoted his official
rank.   Had it been a magic wand he might have stilled
the tumultuous wave of the black sea beating at his
feet.   As it was, he sat like Canute rebuking the flood,
but incompetent to compose its fury, or resist its en-
croachments.   Mr. Browne was a genteel spectacle of
powerless dignity, exciting a polite pity, which his
smile of resignation and urbanity deepened.   In the
corner on his right, in a compact pillar of shining white
teeth, aristocratic noses, proud flesh, and superfine
cloth, were bundled the supporters of the Government
nominee, James Monahan, the Solicitor-General.   The
Lynches were there ; so were the Blakes ; so were the
Burkes, Martins, Gregories, St. Georges, and every
other silken and scented slave of the neighbourhood
in the interest of England.   In front of them stood
Monahan.   In front of them—but with head stooped
and eyes steadily spying about him, exhibiting in-
stinctively all the cowardly caution and cunning of a
practitioner in the lowest grade of his profession, and
the humility of the unpolished parvenu in the presence
of his patrons.   The parvenu in this boisterous scene
seemed deeply conscious of the debt of gratitude,
deference and homage he owed to his patrons.   The
patrons glowed with the vain thought of the mischief
and noise they were making with so plebeian a client.
Shabbily dressed, with a sallow skin, mottled with the

blue refuse of his coarsely shaved beard, with inches of crumpled, soiled linen lapping over his necktie and puffing out from under his cuffs, he stood there, in gait, costume, and look, the veriest varlet and hack which the worst Government, or the meanest aristocracy subject to the worst Government, could hire to do their jobs within Parliament, under the blind eyes of Justice, in the outhouses and at the back-door of the Castle. A large, wide-drawn, heavy mouth, perpetually twitching and hardening between the firmness due to his office and the trepidation which men of coarse natures and sudden success experience, he shuffled, twisted, and shrugged himself before the crowd which hooted and cursed him in that Courthouse, the very image of the night-bird to which Devin Reilly, with his picturesque power and truthfulness, likened him. Of the humblest origin, the Irish people, who have a proud reverence for the princely old stock, spurned him as a mushroom, the spongy growth of a night. Sullen in his features, awkward in his gait, stinted in blood and muscle, having nothing whatever grand, or gallant, or gentlemanly even, in his aspect or address, he failed to exercise the influence which handsome features and a chivalrous air in many instances command, where morals are suspicious, or birth is dubious, or genius is deficient. The driest pedagogue in the school of law—with a mind originally rude and barren, rendered still more sterile by the dead knowledge he heaped upon it, and which he disposed of as a phrenologist does his skull, shoulder blades, and hip joints—without a flower of poetry to beautify, or a solitary pyre-gleam of philosophy to illuminate his studies, social conversation, or professional discourse—selfish, calculating, crafty, mean in heart as he was in look—ungrammatical, illiterate, inarticulate for the most part, slovenly and insipid—he had none of those radiant gifts, none of that intellectual fire which melts down prejudices and fuses the speaker and the audience into one glowing mass, and which, beating down with a sword fashioned of sunbeams, as it were, the conceits which frown upon the cradle of the poor, wins from Plantagenet and Tudor—from the lordliest brat who struts the stage of life in the wardrobe of some dead plunderer—the Cross of Honour, and in the majestic cathedral of history wears it till the sun grows cold.

On the left of the sheriff were many of the sturdy honest merchants of the town, the Irelands, MacLoghlans, Mangans ; representative men of the trades, such as Mahon and Barnacle ; young, spirited, professional men ; some few of the landed proprietary, such as Cummins, French, and Foster ; several of the Catholic priests, amongst the latter the Rev. Messrs. Roche and Daly. In the body of the hall, blocking up every avenue leading to it, hanging on the pillars of the gallery, clinging to window-sills, swinging out of iron brackets in the walls, thrust upon each other's backs, surging and struggling, gaping with the heat and violent pressure, yet flinging up their brawny arms with an enthusiasm almost delirious, and cheering with all their might—cheering until their eyes started, grew red and flashed, and the veins in their foreheads filled with burning blood—were the " rabble," as the dainty, sleek aristocrats on the right of the High Sheriff called the poor, the ragged, the unpurchasable honesty, the impetuous patriotism which, living on crusts, were content still to live, so that they could see the Green Flag flying and their country free.

With considerable difficulty we made our way past that calm, mulberry-nosed sergeant of hussars, on guard at the back door, up the stone steps of the Courthouse to the lobby of the grand jury room, and from the lobby to the gallery. At the entrance of the gallery, Michael Joseph Barry met us.

" We'll have to fight," he said.

" Fight ! " exclaimed Mitchel.

" Fight ! " I re-echoed.

" Yes," said Barry, somewhat hurriedly, but distinctly, " Monahan's party will drive us to it—O'Gorman goes out in half an hour."

This was agreeable news to hear the moment we got into Galway. What a hurry we were in to be shot ! Mitchel and I looked earnestly at Barry, then at each other, and then back at the steps up which we had rushed. Mitchel steadied his countenance, smiled for a moment, twisted a lock of his hair, jerked himself back, stood straight before Barry, and burst into laughter.

It was a fierce contest. Night and day the combatants were at work. For more than a week they fought. From dawn to sundown, the battle surged and thundered within the courthouse. From sundown to dawn the theatre, the lanes, the streets, some of the oldest houses in the city, the suburbs, the roads all round, were scenes of furious action.

The theatre was a ridiculous old building. The walls inside were salmon-coloured. The paint, here and there and everywhere, had been rubbed off. Occasionally some gashes appeared. The white underground shone through these. Monstrous noses, boldly delineated with burnt stick, revealed themselves in swelling curves upon the walls. Cobwebs were plentiful. They were there by the yard, the perch, the mile. They were there in pocket-book editions and the folio size. They were there as small as a snuff-box and as huge as a bale. It was a warehouse of cobwebs.

Two or three of the side scenes were standing. One was a stricken oak. Another a dingy pilaster with an Ionic volute. A third represented an abutment of sandstone, with an iron ring hanging out of it—a large black pudding describing a circle on the door of a kitchen. The gas footlights seemed very little better off than the rest of the furniture. They were dismally out of repair. Most of them were no better than rush-lights. A few of them did too much. Extravagant beyond control, they went literally to blazes. The rest of them, choked with dust, and otherwise incapacitated, were not a spark of use.

Nothing more favourable can be said of the stage. Full of holes ; with a trap-door now and then giving way ; with a scene-roller at intervals breaking loose from the ropes, or the ropes snapping ; with the scantiest allowance of light bare wall on either side, and a bare wall in the rear ; it was the most disreputable platform any patriot could have the infatuation to stand on. For years no tragic step had made it creak. For years no ghost had risen through the shifting apertures from the musty regions underneath. For years no death by bowl or dagger had provoked the approving thunders of the soapless gods.

Seven o'clock, every evening of the contest, saw that paintless, lustreless, dishevelled temple of the drama in possession of the stormiest crowd. Pit, boxes, galleries, every seat, every standing place, from floor to ceiling, were black with people. The orchestra didn't escape. The first into the theatre, the moment the front door opened, had that. Instead of trombones and fiddles, bassoons and kettle-drums, we had devoted Repealers who beat time with their heels, and, previously to the chair being taken, enthusiastically whistled " Garryowen " with variations. One of these per-

formers was a man of huge limbs, upwards of six feet
in height. His shoulders were broad enough to carry
a dray, whilst the girth and shape of his arm realised
what has been told us of the colossal pugilist of Crotona.
This famous Italian carried a young bullock over forty
yards, and then killed it with one blow of his fist. Our
friend in the orchestra might easily have accomplished
a similar feat. He was the image of Hugh in the story
of " Barnaby Rudge." Every inch as sinewy and
large, he was as wild and shaggy in appearance, and
almost as desperate in his onslaughts. During the
election his exploits were terrific. In the courthouse,
the day of the nomination, he seized four men round the
neck with his right arm, and crushed them together as
if they were walnuts and he himself was a nutcracker.
Another time he pulled a big sergeant of hussars clean
off his horse—saddle, saddle-cloth, and all—with one
jerk at the spurred heel of the trooper.

About twelve o'clock one night he called on one of
the Confederates. Creeping inch by inch softly into
the room on tiptoe, he stood—with his broken hat in
his hand, his brown mass of hair strewed about his
face and shoulders, and his coarse shirt, spattered with
mud, torn open from the throat—the very picture of a
Rapparee outlaw.

" I'm done for," says Mullin.

" How so—what's the matter now ? "

" Done for," says Mullin.

" Let us know how."

" It's up with me entirely," says he.

" But what's the matter ? " asks his friend the Confederate.

Mullin straightens himself up, twirls his hat twice,
throws back with his left hand a dozen brown flakes
off his face, and leaning over towards the table where

his confidential adviser was sitting, in a dismal whisper informs him that he's had no less than eleven petty sessions notices served on him for assault and battery since morning.

" Now what's to be done ? " said he.

" Make them a dozen," was the prompt reply of his counsel.

Mullin, without saying a word, but with a comical shrug of one shoulder, walked out. Slowly and heavily he descended the stairs, plaintively whistling as he went, but making up his mind to make it the dozen. He did so.

Mullin was the terror of Monahan. He was the terror of every man of the Government party. The latter would have been beaten to rags were it not for the sabres of the hussars and the bayonets of the police. Mullin would have done it. Alone he'd have fluttered the Volsces in Corioli.

A little after seven the chair in the theatre was usually taken. The chair was a picturesque piece of stage furniture. Made entirely of the plainest wood, with a high arched back, and no opening between the legs, it was painted to harmonise with the colour of the walls. It had been the judgment-seat of the Doge in the " Merchant of Venice," had also supported in their dying moments several dynasties of kings and queens, and, with its back to the audience, and the help of a little black and white canvas, had served for the rostrum from which Mark Antony, more than once, poured out his eloquent sorrows over the senseless body of Cæsar. It was all that was left of the gorgeous palaces, temples, villas, banquet halls, and solemn courts of justice, which had collapsed and withered into cobwebs.

One evening the orators and committee were half

an hour late. The people, grown utterly impatient, and despairing of the usual performance, resolved on having something by way of a change.

It was very near eight o'clock, when a few of us entered the green-room. From the door opening on to the stage, we beheld the chair planted close to the foot-lights, and a number of legs and arms, with a head and a pretty big stick, flashing from it on all sides. They were evidently keeping time to a rollicking song :—

" I'm a ranting roving blade,
Of never a thing was a ever afraid ;
I'm a gentleman born, I scorn a trade,
And I'd be a rich man if my debts were paid.
Right fal lal de lal lal."

This was the sentiment of the singer, and in this sentiment, in ranting roving chorus, the tumultuous theatre seemed to concur. They had voted some frolicsome vagabond into the chair, and this bright lad, with his hat tipped on three hairs, and the wrists of his coat turned up, was flourishing a beautiful knobby bit of blackthorn in the handsomest style, striking out with his elbows and fists and handling his legs with bewildering ease and rapidity. Now and then, when he chanced to do something perfectly marvellous—when the blackthorn gave an extra twist or twirl, or his elbows and toes seemed to strike one another and knock fresh music out of his throat—there was a roar of applause, during which the shillelagh and legs worked away as if the boy were possessed.

The committee having arrived, we moved towards the vocalist. A shout, lusty enough to sweep every cobweb, the toughest and blackest, from the walls, greeted our entrance on the stage. Again and again and again it broke out. The ranting roving blade, carried away with the enthusiasm of his art, infatuated with the belief that it was all meant for him, redoubled his efforts and continued his song. We came closer. The shouts grew louder. The blackthorn frantically swept the air, the elbows shot out right and left, the legs fairly flew asunder. Closer still. Up to the chair. Deafening shouts! The roving blade was one blaze of musical and gymnastic insanity!

In the midst of the next chorus he saw it all. One sudden glance to the left disclosed to him the committee and Dublin deputations, Tom Steele at their head. The stick fell from his grasp. His head fell back. His hat fell off. His legs shot out, and quivered at full length. 'Twas all over with him. The thought stunned him. Recovering a little, he leaped headlong from the salmon-coloured chair into the densely packed orchestra, and disappeared for the rest of the contest. I never saw him after that night. I never heard that anyone else did. Indeed, I never heard that he was seen in Galway again. His hat and favourite blackthorn, left behind on the surface as he vanished with a plunge, were charitably fished up by the treasurer of the committee, carried away as trophies, and deposited in the library of that gentleman.

The speeches in the theatre can be easily imagined. They were philippics against the Whigs. They were panegyrics on Repeal. The servility of the landlords—the Marquis of Clanricarde especially—swelled many an indignant period. From the graves with which the famine had crowded the land, flowers of the darkest hue sprang up. With the hard, stern facts which years of vicious government had set one upon another these flowers were woven. It was the ruin and the ivy. Both had their roots in the soil strewed with wreck and consecrated to the dead. The history of the Whigs, in connexion with the popular party in Ireland, was laid open with the boldest hand. Tom Steele denounced them as the deadliest enemies of Repeal. The Rev. Mr. Roche spoke with a thrilling emphasis of the " cruel and criminal policy of the Whig Government." That the people were reduced to starvation ; that all the corn and Indian meal stored in Galway was permitted to rot ; that the gain of the English merchants was preferred to the very lives of the people ; that coroner's inquests daily and hourly took place, whilst the storehouses and granaries were overflowing ; these, he said, and many other evils, were the rank fruit of the policy maintained by that heartless Government. Richard O'Gorman, Michael Joseph Barry, and Michael Doheny, shook that old building with an eloquence which would have saved Galway the disgrace of being beaten by the public prosecutor of the British Government, if eloquence could have prevailed against the power of a corrupt Government, backed by a servile aristocracy, and hundreds of tenants reduced to serfdom.

APPENDICES

I

THE NIGHT OF THE CONVICTION

[From " The Nation."]

There were heavy hearts in Clonmel Gaol, on Saturday evening, October 22nd, 1848. Thomas Meagher was in the dock, awaiting the verdict of the jury who had tried him. The large cell, at the top of the building, which was the sleeping apartment of M'Manus, O'Donoghue, and Leyne, and the common saloon, during the day, of some twenty others, was silent and cheerless. The central table was covered with a miscellaneous equipage of carousal—glasses of all shapes and sizes, cups, mugs, jugs, and contraband black bottles, containing specimens of Irish Resources, proscribed by the Board, but seditiously introduced for the comfort and jollification of a very boisterous gang of Irish rebels. Ordinarily, at the hour, Meagher presided at our evening festivity. And such a capital president as he made! He was the life of our circle—so frank, gifted, and beloved. His humour, his eloquence, which stirred us even there, and his intrepidity, were the sunshine that made the old walls seem brighter than a palace. Oh! around that board I have had as glorious visions, and felt as riotously happy, as if no cloud were resting upon Ireland—as if no chain were clanking at my feet. Many a grand old Irish song was sung there ; many a gallant sentiment was uttered ; many an inspiring ballad recited ; many a broken-voiced lament whispered for the failure ; and many a prophecy of future success rapturously applauded. Within the four seas, there was not, at times, so disorderly a body of criminals, mad with merriment ; and, when the fit had passed, oh ! but there were deep and earnest communings on the past, and conjectures of the future, of our dear Ireland. On one night we listened to fiery speeches, full of the old spirit and burning eloquence that had roused the heart of the nation, the words falling like the fiery tongues on the Apostles. On another, we masqueraded at a concert, Meagher leading the band on his clarionet, accompanied by twenty manly voices, and every variety of sound that could be extracted from accordions, kettles, tins, and tongs. On the next, we fought at the barricades. A heavy table used to be placed in the centre of the room, and taken possession of by half the detachment ; the other moiety stormed the garrison. We fought with pillows—very formidable and destructive weapons, if properly handled. Such charges, such shouts, such blows, such defences, such drubbings ! I think I should be invaluable as a barricade-man, after that warm practice and invigorating discipline. I would engage to tumble the most stalwart member of the " B " detachment, if I had choice of my weapon—a short, hard-crammed pillow, or symmetrical bolster, that would swing like Boadicea's flail. The contest lasted till we could fight no more.

To a spectator, the meetings round that mess table would have worn the appearance of the festive gathering of an insurgent camp, not the poor prison revels of conquered rebels. Lord ! how we frighted the gaol from its propriety. And then, as the approach of one of the prison officers was heard, all the evidences of seditious enjoyment used to disappear with miraculous celerity, and on the entrance of the grave governor (who was a good fellow at heart), one-half of us would be found buried in books, the other devoted to the innocent and improving combinations of the profound science of backgammon. The remonstrance of the governor, or his noble-souled, generous deputy, would be listened to in affected respect and hypocritical silence. On his disappearance, good zealous man, convinced that he had converted us to " peace, law, and order," the revolutionary mania would break forth again, and Clonmel Gaol be changed into a " Model Prison " according to our contumacious notions of " physical " enjoyment. Ah, these hours of prison life had their own joys ! They bore flowers that for some of us shall ever bloom. They ripened friendships which the cold artificial world of intrigue and fashion knows not, with all its rigid formalities and genteel stupidities.

This Saturday night there are no revels. Meagher's place is vacant. But he is in all our thoughts. We canvass the chances of his escape ; and every now and then one of us approaches a window, which overlooks the street, and communicates with a secret sentinel, who brings news from the Courthouse. How eagerly we speculate on every report that reaches us—on the character, position, and, alas ! religion, of each jury-man—on the delay in the finding of the verdict. The table and its stores are deserted. O'Donoghue, who, with O'Brien and M'Manus, had been already convicted, lies on his bed, in an agony of suspense for the issue of the night. He idolised—he absolutely lived but to think of him. M'Manus, erect as a rifleman on parade, strides vehemently up and down the apartment, mutter-ing now and again some impetuous aspiration, or trying to inspire others with the confidence he feigns to feel. Anthony O'Ryan and Leyne sit with folded arms, side by side, in a remote corner, speaking not a word. The others are variously disposed. Some read-ing Madden's " United Irishmen " ; others transcribing ballads from the " Library of Ireland ; others sketching portraits of Meagher, Mitchel, O'Brien, and Duffy ; and one or two drawing pikes of formidable proportions on the whitened walls, with the original crayon, a charred stick.

It was a solemn hour. The fate of the most beloved

of brothers trembled in the scale ; the fate of him, for whose restoration we would have died with bounding joy. Suddenly the preconcerted signal is given from below ; and the message delivered to us that " the jury had disagreed." Not a sound for a moment, and then such a thrilling uproarious shout of joy arose as never issued from mortal voices, since the angels sung the world's birth-hymn. Alas ! our delirium was but short-lived. Another signal below, and this the message of doom : " The report was false. He is convicted. They are bringing him from the Court ! " I shall not seek to paint the change that fell like the announcement of eternal woe to us poor disenchanted mourners. Then came bursts of sorrow and imprecations of rage. We had borne up against every reverse and discomfiture. We had seen three others torn from us, and doomed by the law. But while Meagher remained, we scarcely knew a regret, certainly had not utterly despaired. But, now—now !

They did bring him from the Court. We received him at the end of the corridor, and through the iron gateway grasped his hand. We had not the usual welcome for him this night. He laughed gaily when he met us ; " Good night, boys ! Here I am, and found guilty ; and glad, too, that they did convict me, for if I had been acquitted, the people might say I had not *done my duty*. I am guilty, and condemned for the old country. . . . Come in, come in to the cell, and let me have my dinner." We accompanied him to the cell. Some of us could not remain. Leyne stood on the corridor, weeping bitterly. O'Donoghue was spell-bound, at the doorway. M'Manus, shaking with agitation, held Meagher in his arms. The young convict was deeply affected by these evidences of grief and affection. But he soon recovered composure, and coming into the passage drew into the room—" Come in—come in—I'm starved. Let us have one hour's fun." His spirit infected us as by magic. We sat around him, and heard the details of his trial given with inimitable humour and mimicry. He had us all laughing at his drollery in a few minutes. I shall never forget the merriment M'Manus evoked by asking in his fiercest tone, when Meagher had finished his recital: " I say, Meagher, did you say anything to the d—— scoundrels when the verdict was read?" Meagher shrieked with delight.

We *had* an hour's fun. As Davis has sung of another gathering :—

> " With bumpers and cheers we did as he bade,
>   For Tom Meagher was loved by the Irish Brigade!"

We drank to O'Brien and Butt. We toasted " the Convicted Traitors "; " Gavan Duffy and the Prisoners in Newgate and Kilmainham "; and we pledged a brimming glass to " The Irish Republic." Meagher, O'Donoghue, and Leyne, spoke speech after speech. And the last sang Duffy's noble song: " Watch and Wait!" to a chorus that made the old walls reel again. How rapturously we thundered the concluding key-verse :—

> " Brother, if this day should set,
>   Another yet must crown our freedom ;
> *That* will come with roll of drum,
>   And tramping files, with MEN to lead them.
>   Who can save
>   Renegade or slave ?
> Fortune only twines her garlands
>   For the Brave!"

" Gintlemin," observes an intrusive turnkey, poking his head inside the door—" the governor has heard the shoutin', an' he's comin' up, flamin' mad."

" Oh, the D——l take all governors to-night! Hurra, boys, hurra !—

> " Who can save
>   Renegade or slave ?
> Fortune only twines her garlands
>   For the Brave!"

" Hurra, again!" Poor turnkey stands aghast. Enter governor, looking " bolts and bars." " Gentlemen, to your cells. This is most improper conduct. I shall report to the Board, and have you separately confined." Meagher intercedes. "The fault is his. He is the head and cause of the irregularity. But as he is going to be hanged, he hopes the Board will not sentence him to solitary confinement, *in addition* to that decisive discipline." Loud laughter from governor, corps of turnkeys, and rebels. *Exeunt omnes,* in good humour, shaking hands fiercely.

This was the celebration of the Conviction. There was no shrinking within the gaol. Three days before, the prison officers had been seen, by some of our comrades, examining " the drop," preparing the scaffold for the sacrifice of the genius, the hope, the forsaken chivalry of the trembling country. The appointed victims knew this. And still the love of Ireland, which had been their pure and glorious incentive, made them rejoice to mount the bloody platform of execution, carpetted with the torn banners of Ireland.

Oh ! often in loneliest solitude, in that old cell, when I alone remained of the gang of Rebels in Clonmel Gaol, have I thought of the heroism and intrepidity of the Traitors. When hope was wild in their hearts, in the first days of the revolt ; when they seemed within a bound of success and glory ; when, a short week after, they were hunted outlaws, stealing through the country by night, hiding by the day in woods and on hill-sides, crouching in the sanctuary of the village chapel, concealed in the rude shieling of the peasant, or nursed by the warm hospitality of the gentleman-farmer ; flying from the police patrols, and the recreants from Dublin, who dogged their steps as the sleuth-hounds of the Castle ; captured, hopeless, convicted, condemned— never did one ignoble fear soil their purpose, nor one dastard regret violate its vows pledged to Ireland.

And I say to you, poor, cringing slaves of Ireland, that beyond his glory in the tribune, beyond the fame which diademed his brow, beyond all the triumphs of his eloquence, beyond the dominion of your passions, beyond the witching homage of fair women, and the affection of bold men, was the grandeur of the intrepid bearing of the young orator of revolution, when he stood, rejoicing, defiant, and inspired, in the shadow of the gibbet, content " to bear the cross with the same loftiness of soul with which he had worn the laurel crown."

Seven days later, and it was whispered that the humane Government of her Most Gracious Majesty, Queen of England and various other countries, whether through remorse or policy, I know not, had delicately recommended that the hungry hangman should be robbed of the prey allotted to him by the law. A grace purchased by no "selfish penitence," by no apologies from the "condemned cells." There was no loyal jubilee for this exertion of the apocryphal prerogative. Neither " God Save the Queen,' nor " Rule Britannia," echoed in the prison. The Marseillaise and " The Wearing of the Green," were our vesper-hymns.

II

The Felons

[This poem, by Dr. Campion, is founded on an incident in the wanderings of Meagher, Leyne, and O'Donoghue, after the failure at Ballingarry.]

" Good peasant, we are strangers here,
　　And night is gathering fast ;
The stars scarce glimmer in the sky,
　　And moans the mountain blast ;
Can'st tell us of a place to rest ?
　　We're wearied with the road ;
No churl the peasant used to be
　　With homely couch and food."

" I cannot help myself, nor know
　　Where ye may rest or stay ;
A few more hours the moon will shine,
　　And light you on your way."

" But, peasant, can you let a man
　　Appeal to you in vain,
Here, at your very cabin door,
　　And 'mid the pelting rain—
Here, in the dark, and in the night,
　　Where one scarce sees a span ?
What ! close your heart ! and close your door !
　　And be an Irishman ! "

" No, no—go on—the moon will rise
　　In a short hour or two ;
What can a peaceful labourer say,
　　Or a poor toiler do ? "

" You're poor ?　Well, here's a golden chance
　　To make you rich and great !
Five hundred pounds are on our heads !
　　The gibbet is our fate !

Fly, raise the cry, and win the gold,
  Or some may cheat you soon ;
And we'll abide by the roadside
  And wait the rising moon."

What ails the peasant ?   Does he flush
  At the wild greed of gold ?
Why seizes he the wanderers' hands ?
  Hark to his accents bold :

" Ho ! I *have* a heart for you, neighbours—
  Ay, and a hearth and a home—
Ay, and a help for you, neighbours :
  God bless ye, and prosper ye—come !

" Come—out of the light of the soldiers ;
  Come in 'mongst the children and all ;
And I'll guard ye for sake of old Ireland
  Till Connall himself gets a fall.

" To the devil with all their gold guineas ;
  Come in—everything is your own ;
And I'll kneel at your feet, friends of Ireland !
  What I wouldn't for king on his throne.

" God bless ye that stood in the danger,
  In the midst of the country's mishap,
That stood up to meet the big famine—
  Och ! ye are the men in the gap !

" Come in—with a ' Cead mile failte ' ;
  Sit down, and don't make any noise,
Till I come with more comforts to crown ye—
  Till I gladden the hearts of the boys.

" Arrah ! shake hands again—noble fellows
  That left your own homes for the poor !
Not a man in the land could betray you,
  Or shut up his heart or his door."

III

TWO POEMS BY MEAGHER

Prison Thoughts

Written in Clonmel Gaol, October, 1848

I love, I love these grey old walls!
Although a chilling shadow falls
Along the iron-gated halls,
    And in the silent, narrow cells,
    Brooding darkly, ever dwells.

Oh! still I love them—for the hours
Within them spent are set with flow'rs
That blossom, spite of wind and show'rs,
    And through that shadow, dull and cold,
    Emit their sparks of blue and gold.

Bright flowers of mirth!—that widely spring
From fresh, young hearts, and o'er them fling,
Like Indian birds with sparkling wing,
    Seeds of sweetness, grains all glowing,
    Sun-gilt leaves, with dew-drops flowing.

And hopes as bright, that softly gleam,
Like stars which o'er the churchyard stream
A beauty on each faded dream—
    Mingling the light they purely shed
    With other hopes, whose light was fled.

Fond mem'ries, too, undimmed with sighs,
Whose fragrant sunshine never dies,
Whose summer song-bird never flies—
    These, too, are chasing, hour by hour,
    The clouds which round this prison low'r.

And thus, from hour to hour, I've grown
To love these walls, though dark and lone,
And fondly prize each grey old stone,
   Which flings the shadow, deep and chill,
. Across my fettered footsteps still.

Yet let these mem'ries fall and flow
Within my heart, like waves that glow
Unseen in spangled caves below
   The foam which frets, the mists which sweep,
   The changeful surface of the deep.

Not so the many hopes that bloom
Amid this voiceless waste and gloom,
Strewing my path-way to the tomb,
   As though it were a bridal-bed,
   And not the prison of the dead.

I would those hopes were traced in fire,
Beyond these walls—above that spire—
Amid yon blue and starry choir,
   Whose sounds played round us with the streams
   Which glitter in the white moon's beams.

I'd twine those hopes above our Isle,
Above the rath and ruined pile,
Above each glen and rough defile,
   The holy well—the Druid's shrine—
   Above them all those hopes I'd twine.

So should I triumph o'er my fate,
And teach this poor desponding State,
In signs of tenderness, not hate,
   Still to think of her old story,
   Still to hope for future glory.

Within these walls, those hopes have been
The music sweet, the light serene,
Which softly o'er this silent scene,
   Have like the autumn streamlets flowed,
   And like the autumn sunshine glowed.

And thus, from hour to hour, I've grown
To love these walls, though dark and lone,
And fondly prize each grey old stone,
  That flings the shadow deep and chill,
  Across my fettered footsteps still.

———

THE YOUNG ENTHUSIAST

Though young that heart, though free each thought,
  Though free and wild each feeling ;
And though with fire each dream be fraught
  Across those bright eyes stealing—

That heart is true, those thoughts are bold :
  And bold each feeling sweepeth ;
There lies not there a bosom cold,
  A pulse that faintly sleepeth.

His dreams are idiot-dreams, ye say,
  The dreams of fairy story :
Those dreams will burn in might one day
  And flood his path with glory !

Thou old dull vassal ! fling thy sneer
  Upon that young heart coldly,
And laugh at deeds *thy* heart may fear,
  Yet *he* will venture boldly.

Ay, fling thy sneer, while dull and slow
  Thy withered blood is creeping,
That heart will beat, *that* spirit glow,
  When thy tame pulse is sleeping.

Ay, laugh when o'er his country's ills
  With manly eye he weepeth ;
Laugh, when his brave heart throbs and thrills,
  And thy cold bosom sleepeth.

Laugh, when he vows in heaven's sight,
  Never to flinch or falter ;
To toil and fight for a nation's right,
  And guard old Freedom's altar.

Ay, laugh when on the fiery wing
  Of hero thought ascending,
To fame's bold cliff, with eagle spring,
  That young bright mind is tending.

He'll gain that cliff, he'll reach that throne,
  The throne where genius shineth,
When round and through thy nameless stone.
  The green weed thickly twineth.

IV

THE PETITION OF THE CONFEDERATION

During the earlier career of the Irish Confederation a sub-committee was appointed to draft resolutions and a petition to the English Parliament claiming Repeal of the Union. The members of the sub-committee vainly tried to draft a petition satisfactory to themselves and they appealed to Mitchel to get them out of the difficulty. He consented and furnished them with the following petition drafted by himself :—

" TO THE HONOURABLE THE COMMONS OF ENGLAND IN PARLIAMENT ASSEMBLED :

" *The Petition of the undersigned Irishmen*

" Humbly Sheweth—That every people should mind their own business, and are best fitted to mind their own business ; and that the people of Ireland, of whom your petitioners are a few, are quite willing and well fitted to mind theirs.

" That since the 1st of January, 1801, Ireland, the native land of your petitioners, has been, to its sorrow, degradation, and misery, ' incorporated ' with the British Empire.

" That this incorporation was legally effected by a certain grievous act of your honourable house, called ' An Act for the Union of Great Britain and Ireland ' ; and in reality by the systems of assassinage, incendiarism, and subornation, which your honourable house has always sanctioned as fit means for the extension of English dominion.

" That since the incorporation aforesaid, in the name of the act aforesaid, and by means of armed troops, regular, and of police, spies, placemen, and others (the means which your honourable house has always approved for the sustentation of English dominion), divers persons, calling themselves successively, the ' Imperial Government,' have, to the utmost of their ability, and under the sanction of your honourable house, abused the native land of your petitioners for the sole benefit of the English, and the complete misery of the Irish people.

" That the accumulated evil-doing of those persons aforesaid has at length necessarily inflicted upon the native land of your petitioners famine and pestilence unprecedented in the world.

" That your petitioners are ignorant of, and indifferent about, the intentions of these divers persons aforesaid, forasmuch as they are all of necessity incompetent to govern the native land of your petitioners, which really needs to be governed ; and forasmuch as those of them whose intentions were said to be worst did least ill to your petitioners' country, fearing to interfere in the affairs of your petitioners' fellow-countrymen where they could avoid such interference, and being opposed tooth and nail by the majority of your petitioners' fellow-countrymen, on account of their reported intentions, whether their acts were bad or worse ; and those of them whose intentions were said to be best did most harm, inasmuch as, at various times, saying they would ' lay the foundation of most just systems in,' ' better the condition,' ' improve the lot,' ' extend the happiness,' and the like, of your petitioners' native country, they were permitted by your petitioners' simple fellow-countrymen to make divers cruel experiments for such purposes.

" That the incorporation aforesaid of your petitioners' native country into the British Empire has been necessarily followed by the incorporation of Irish labour into the English capitalist, the incorporation of Irish wealth into the English treasury, the incorporation of Irish blood into the English armies, the incorporation of the Irish flag into the English Jack, and the incorporation of Irish food into the English stomachs ; all or any of which incorporations would not be submitted to by any other people in the world, and are so cruel and humiliating to your petitioners that your honourable house may well be, since you can safely be, surprised at our inhuman patience and our unchristian resignation.

"That, however, self-preservation is a severe necessity. That of the natives of your petitioners' country not more than one million are yet starved. And that, whereas, one John Russell, a grave member of your honourable house, having rashly said to the remainder of your petitioners' fellow-countrymen (they being now in a state of direst famine, caused by the English having devoured their food), 'Help yourselves, and God will help you,' your petitioners are grievously afraid their fellow-countrymen will hearken to the advice of the Honourable John Russell aforesaid, and help themselves, whether your honourable house will it or no, to their own food, and their own country, in future.

"Wherefore your petitioners, being peaceable men, anxious to save the lives of millions of their fellow-countrymen by obtaining for them the eating of their own produce, 'peaceably, legally, morally, and constitutionally,' do beseech your honourable house to repeal the aforesaid act of 'incorporation,' called an 'Act for the Union of Great Britain and Ireland,' in order that, without offence to your honourable house, your petitioners' fellow-countrymen may be enabled to drive the armies of your honourable house, the laws, and other grievous impositions of your honourable house, the police, English accent, Manchester clothes, 'felon flag,' and all things English, off the face of their own country into the sea—an event, for which the judgment of Heaven, the incompetency and the crimes of men, are daily preparing the nations of Europe.

"And your petitioners will ever pray."

This petition increased the troubles of the sub-committee. "It should be written with red ink," said Meagher, "and presented on the point of a sword." Finally the subjoined petition, reluctantly drafted by Meagher, was agreed upon :—

" To the Honourable the Commons of England in Parliament Assembled :—

" *The Petition of the undersigned Irishmen*

" Humbly Sheweth—That this island was once ruled by the king, lords and commons of Ireland.

" That under this government the island advanced in arts, in commerce, and in character.

" That such is the destiny of every country that preserves the faculty of self-government, whether the form of that government be democratic, mixed, or monarchical.

" That in the year 1800 this island ceased to be governed by the king, lords, and commons of Ireland, and has since been governed, nominally, by the king, lords, and commons of Great Britain and Ireland—virtually by the power, and for the benefit, of England alone.

" That under this new form of government this island has lost its character, its commerce, and its food. That such is the fate of every country that does not possess the right to govern itself. That, deprived of this right, this island must ever depend upon the charity of other people—be an idler and a bankrupt—ruined in fortune, in spirit, and in health. That, deprived of this right, the island has not the power to act for itself, and will have no guarantee for its freedom.

" That the country which does not possess this power is uniformly a beggar, and, if sometimes in wealth, it is always a slave.

" Therefore, your petitioners pray your honourable house to restore the ancient form of government to this kingdom, and enact that it may be for the future governed by no body of men save the king, lords, and commons of Ireland.

" And your petitioners will ever pray."

22

CONTEMPORARIES

BARRON, SIR HENRY WINSTON (1795–1872).—M.P. for Waterford, 1832–41, and again, 1848–52 and 1865–1868. A steady backer of English Government, from which he received numerous posts for his relatives and a baronetcy in 1841.

BARRY, MICHAEL JOSEPH (1817–89).—Writer of the Prize Repeal Essay, editor of " The Songs of Ireland " and author of " The Green Flag " and other martial verses. A successful barrister, he abandoned the national cause as hopeless after 1848.

BERESFORD, LORD GEORGE (1773–1862).—Second son of the first Marquis of Waterford. Subsequent to the famous Waterford Election he became Archbishop of Armagh, where he restored the Cathedral.

BLACKBURNE, FRANCIS (1782–1867).—A Tory lawyer of the bitterest type. Administered the infamous Insurrection Act in Limerick and was subsequently appointed Lord Chief Justice and finally Lord Chancellor of Ireland.

BRIGHT, JOHN (1811–89).—English politician, associated with Cobden in the leadership of the " Free Trade " movement. Professed friendship for Ireland, but opposed Home Rule and voted for Coercion.

BRENAN, JOSEPH (1828–57).—The youngest of the Young Ireland leaders. He attempted to revive the insurrection in Waterford and Tipperary in 1849 and, failing, made his way to America, where he died.

BURDETT, SIR FRANCIS (1770–1844).—English Radical leader. Converted himself to Toryism after the passing of the Reform Bill.

BUSHE, CHARLES KENDAL (1767–1843).—A leading

opponent of the Act of Union in the Irish Parliament, where he represented Callan. Afterwards Chief Justice of the King's Bench.

BUTT, ISAAC (1813–79).—The intellectual leader of the Irish Unionists in the Young Ireland period. Afterwards founder of the Home Rule movement as a compromise between Repeal and Unionism.

CARLETON, WM. (1794–1869).—Author of " Traits and Stories of the Irish Peasantry." Son of a Tyrone cottier.

CAVAIGNAC, LOUIS EUGENE, GENERAL (1802–57).—Minister for War in the French Republican Government. He was prepared to advocate French intervention with England if the Young Irelanders were successful in the beginning of the insurrection.

CLARENDON, EARL OF (1804–70).—English Viceroy in Ireland, 1846–50. He hired James Birch, an ex-convict who edited the Dublin *World* newspaper, to publish libels upon the personal characters and public motives of Mitchel, Meagher and the other prominent Young Irelanders. Birch, who received £3,400 from the Secret Service Fund for his assistance, brought an action in the Law Courts to recover a balance of £7,000 he alleged to be due. He was subsequently convicted of criminal libel on a lady and returned to prison.

CLONEY, THOMAS (1775–1850).—Popularly known as General Cloney. Son of a gentleman-farmer near Enniscorthy. He took a leading part in the insurrection. On its conclusion he was arrested, courtmartialled and condemned to death, but reprieved through the influence of several Wexford political enemies whom he had protected from violence when they were in the hands of the insurgents. He was kept in prison for a considerable period and again arrested and imprisoned after Emmet's insurrection.

COBDEN, RICHARD (1804–65).—Leader of the English " Free Trade " movement under which the English mercantile interest successfully wrested political power from the English landed interest.

DAVIS, FRANCIS (1810–85).—Author of a considerable amount of verse, published under the pseudonym of " The Belfastman," some of which appeared in the *Nation*. Davis was by birth a Cork man, but he carried on his trade as a working weaver in Belfast, where he passed most of his life.

DAVIS, THOMAS (1814–45).—Founder of the Young Ireland movement, and chief writer of the *Nation* newspaper from its inception until his death.

DELAHUNTY, JAMES (1808–80 ?).—An Alderman of Waterford and some time Coroner and City Treasurer. Leader of the baser section of the local O'Connellites. Afterwards for a period Whig M.P. for Waterford City, and later for Waterford County.

DENISON, SIR WM. (1804–71).—Brother of Evelyn Denison, Speaker of the English House of Commons. Denison was sent from Australasia to India, where he opposed all vestige of self-government for the Indians.

DEVEREUX, JOHN.—General of the Irish Legion in Bolivar's Army of Independence. Devereux was styled by Paez the Lafayette of South America.

DILLON, JOHN BLAKE (1816–66).—A barrister from the West of Ireland, associated with Davis and Duffy in starting the *Nation* newspaper. On his return from exile he fell under the influence of John Bright and his school, and unsuccessfully attempted to found an Irish Parliamentary Party to co-operate with the English Radicals.

DISRAELI, BENJAMIN (1804–81).—English Radical, Young Englander and Tory politician. Twice Premier of England.

DOHENY, MICHAEL (1805–61).—Solicitor and Law Adviser to the borough of Cashel. He escaped after the insurrection to France and thence to the United States, where he joined O'Mahony and Stephens in founding the Fenian movement.

DOHERTY, JOHN (1783–1850).—Chief Justice of the Common Pleas ; a Dublin barrister of mediocre legal knowledge but remarkable powers of debate, elected to the British Parliament in 1824 and created Solicitor-General through the influence of his relative, George Canning. Doherty gambled in railway shares and losing heavily, died of depression.

DUNCOMBE, THOMAS (1796–1861).—English Radical politician. He presented the Chartist petition in 1842, and assisted in Louis Napoleon's escape from Ham.

DUFFY, CHARLES GAVAN (1816–1903).—One of the founders of the *Nation*, and its editor from 1842 to 1854, when he went to Australia, where he became Prime Minister of Victoria and was afterwards knighted.

EBRINGTON, LORD (1783–1861).—English Lord Lieutenant of Ireland, 1839–41.

GREY, EARL (1802–94).—Colonial Secretary in the British Government of 1846–52.

GREY, SIR GEORGE (1792–1882).—English Home Secretary under Russell and Palmerston, He unsuccessfully attempted to turn the Cape into an English penal colony.

GROGAN, EDWARD.—Unionist M.P. for Dublin for a quarter of a century ; first elected in 1841. He was created a baronet for his services.

HALPIN, THOMAS M.—A Dublin artisan who acted as Secretary of the Confederation. Halpin denied receiving the instructions for the Dublin Confederates, which Meagher asserts in his Narrative of 1848 he gave him. Investigation acquits Halpin of either treachery or cowardice and points to a misunderstanding between Meagher and himself. He appears, however, to have been lacking in the energy and initiative necessary in the crisis. After the insurrection he made his way to the United States.

HAUGHTON, JAMES (1795–1873).—A Carlow Quaker and Humanitarian politician. He was a member of the Repeal Association, and to an extent in sympathy with the Young Irelanders. Attempting to force

Mitchel and Meagher after their arrival in America to " declare themselves against African slavery," he evoked the controversy between Mitchel and Henry Ward Beecher in which Mitchel upheld the case of the Southern States.

HOGAN, JOHN (1800–58).—One of the five great sculptors of the nineteenth century. The Repeal Cap worn by O'Connell was modelled by Hogan and Henry MacManus, the painter, from the Irish crown.

HOLLYWOOD, EDWARD (1814-73.—A leader of the Dublin artisans. He escaped after the failure of the insurrection to France, where he worked as a silk-weaver for some years. Subsequently he returned to Dublin, where he died.

HOLMES, ROBERT (1765-1859).—Brother-in-law of Robert Emmet. He refused to accept promotion at the Bar while the Act of Union between Great Britain and Ireland was upheld as legal.

KENYON, FATHER JOHN (18— –69).—Curate and subsequently Parish Priest of Templederry in Tipperary. A vigorous writer and a strong and bitter opponent of Daniel O'Connell, whose policy he regarded as cowardly and corrupt. He was, with the exception of John Martin, the most intimate of Mitchel's friends.

LALOR, JAMES FINTAN (1810–49).—Son of Patrick Lalor, M.P., of Leix, one of the little handful of Irish M.P.'s who did not sell their Repeal principles for place or patronage. Lalor's agrarian doctrine, first enunciated in the *Nation*, exerted a strong influence on the subsequent history of the Irish Land War. In 1849 Lalor was concerned with Brenan, Savage and others in an attempt to rekindle the insurrection.

LAMARTINE, ALPHONSE DE (1790-1869).—Minister for Foreign Affairs in the French Republican Government of 1848.

LAWLESS, HON. CECIL.—Son of Lord Cloncurry and a strong O'Connellite opponent of the Young Irelanders.

LEDRU-ROLLIN, ALEXANDRE DE (1808–74).—Minister of the Interior in the French Republican Government of 1848. He was a strong sympathiser with Ireland, to which he was connected by marriage, and favoured French intervention against England.

LOUIS PHILIPPE (1773–1850).—Son of Philippe Egalité and half-brother of Pamela, wife of Lord Edward Fitzgerald. King of the French from 1830 to 1848.

LOUIS NAPOLEON (1808–73).—Nephew of the great Napoleon and subsequently Napoleon III. In 1848 he was inclined to French intervention on Ireland's behalf if the insurrection won initial engagements against the English army in Ireland.

MACAULAY, LORD (1800–59).—The most brilliant and superficial of the English Whig writers of the nineteenth century. Except Froude, he is the most unreliable of modern English historians.

MARTIN, JOHN (1812–75).—Brother-in-law of John Mitchel. Sentenced to ten years' transportation in 1848 for treason-felony. After his return to Ireland he took part in the foundation of the Home Rule movement.

MAUNSELL, DR.—One of the Dublin Conservative leaders, and a member of the Dublin Corporation. He advocated a Rotatory Parliament—*i.e.*, the sitting of the British Parliament alternately in London, Dublin and Edinburgh.

M'GEE, THOMAS D'ARCY (1825–68).—The son of a Louth Coastguard, he emigrated to the United States as a boy, where before he was twenty years of age he won a high reputation as a journalist. On his return to Ireland he joined the *Freeman* staff and later that of the *Nation*. He escaped disguised as a priest to the United States, after the failure of the insurrection, and subsequently quarrelled with most of his former colleagues in the Young Ireland movement and considerably altered his views on the relations of Ireland and England. Going to Canada, he entered politics there and became a member of the Canadian Government. He was assas-

sinated in 1868 and his bitter denunciations of the
Fenian movement led to the crime being charged
against the Fenian Brotherhood.   Although the assassin
was alleged to be a Fenian, local political hatred of M'Gee
seems to have been the active motive of the deed.

MACHALE, DR. JOHN (1791–1881).—Archbishop of
Tuam, and the greatest of the Irish Bishops of the
nineteenth century.

MACMANUS, TERENCE BELLEW (1823–60).—A
prosperous Irish merchant in Liverpool, who left his
business and crossed over to Ireland to join the
insurrection.   He escaped from the English penal colonies
to San Francisco, where he died in poor circumstances.

MELBOURNE, VISCOUNT (1779–1848).—English Chief
Secretary for Ireland, 1827–28, and subsequently
Premier of England.

MITCHEL, JOHN (1815–75).—Chief writer of the
Nation newspaper from the death of Davis until the end
of 1847, when he left it to establish the *United Irishman*,
in which he preached passive and active resistance to
the English Government in Ireland.   To crush him that
institution rushed through its Parliament the " Treason
Felony Act," under which certain political offences were
made felonious.   Mitchel was put on trial before a jury
composed of Englishmen, Castle tradesmen and members
of the Orange Lodge, convicted and sentenced to fourteen years' transportation.   At the end of five years he
escaped to America, and continued the unrelenting
enemy of Irish compromise with England until his
death.

MONAHAN, JAMES HENRY (1804–78).—A man of poor
origin and indifferent legal talents, appointed Attorney-
General for Ireland in 1848, and subsequently Chief
Justice of the Common Pleas.   He arranged the packing
of John Mitchel's jury.

MONTEAGLE, LORD (1790–1866).—Thomas Spring-
Rice, first Baron.   Whig M.P. for Limerick, and later
for Cambridge.   He was chosen by the English Government to reply to O'Connell's Motion for Repeal of the

Union. After being Chancellor of the Exchequer in Melbourne's second English administration, he sought and lost the Speakership of the English Commons but was consoled with a peerage.

MURPHY, SERJEANT (1810–60).—One of the Fraserians or writers for "Frazer's Magazine." M.P. for Cork, 1837–53, in which year he was appointed a Commissioner of Bankruptcy by the English Government.

NORMANBY, MARQUIS OF (1797–1863).—Lord Lieutenant of Ireland, 1835–39. Distributed soft words amongst the O'Connellites in return for their support of his Government, and intrigued in France in 1848 to prevent assistance being given to Ireland.

O'BRIEN, WM. SMITH (1803–64).—Second son of Sir Edward O'Brien. He entered the British Parliament as an Irish Unionist, but after some years joined the Repealers, and sided with Young Ireland in its opposition to placehunting which led to the split with O'Connell. After his release from transportation he visited Greece and America.

O'CONNELL, DANIEL (1775–1847).—Successor to John Keogh in the leadership of the movement for Catholic Emancipation. After the passing of the Catholic Relief Act he started a movement for Repeal of the Union, but shortly afterwards abandoned it and co-operated for a period with the English Whigs. On the return of the Tories to power he resuscitated the Repeal Movement ; but when the Whigs regained office he agreed to put the demand for Repeal in abeyance and secure the support of Ireland for the English Liberal Government in return for promised remedial legislation and patronage. This led to the revolt of the Young Irelanders against his leadership.

O'CONNELL, JOHN (1810–58).—The chief political assistant to his father, Daniel O'Connell, and the bitterest of the Irish political enemies of the Young Irelanders. After the final collapse of the Repeal Association, he received a place from the English Government.

O'CONNELL, DANIEL, JUNIOR (1815–97).—O'Connell's youngest son. He received two lucrative appointments from the English Government.

O'CONOR DON, THE (1794–1847).—An O'Connellite Repeal M.P. for Roscommon. He deserted to the English Government and was made a Lord of the Treasury.

O'DOHERTY, KEVIN IZOD (1823–95).—A Dublin medical student who helped to found, and contributed to, the *Irish Tribune* newspaper, which took the place of Mitchel's *United Irishman* in 1848. Transported under the Treason Felony Act he subsequently settled in Australia where he became prominent in science and politics.

O'DONOGHUE, PATRICK (18——-54).—A Dublin Law-Clerk and one of the most active of the leaders of the Dublin Confederates. He died in New York.

O'FLAHERTY, ANTHONY.—Defeated by four votes in the exciting Galway election of 1847, O'Flaherty was returned some months later and sat in the English Parliament until 1857, when, although again elected, he was unseated on petition. O'Flaherty for some years acted the part of an honest representative, but he eventually became associated with the infamous " Brass Band," led by Sadlier and Keogh.

O'GORMAN, RICHARD, JUN. (1826–95).—Son of a wealthy Dublin woollen merchant and stockbroker, who had been one of the leaders of the fight for Catholic Emancipation. O'Gorman, after the failure of 1848, escaped to the Continent and thence, later, went to the United States, where he became a Judge of the Superior Court of New York.

O'LOGHLEN, SIR COLMAN (1819–77).—Son of the Master of the Rolls, and afterwards M.P. for Clare.

O'MAHONY, JOHN (1816–77).—A Tipperary gentle-man-farmer of ancient lineage and high scholarship. In the United States he founded, with Michael Doheny and James Stephens, the Fenian movement.

O'NEILL, JOHN AUGUSTUS.—Of Bunowen Castle. One of O'Connell's henchmen in Conciliation Hall.

O'REILLY, EUGENE (18— –74).—A Meath Young Ireland leader who planned to seize Navan with the aid of the Dublin Confederates and raise an insurrection in Meath and Westmeath. After the miscarriage of his plan he abandoned hope of Irish independence, went to the Continent, entered the Turkish service, fought with distinction through the Crimean War and died at Fez O'Reilly Pasha.

PEEL, SIR ROBERT (1788–1850).—Chief Secretary for Ireland and subsequently Premier of England. He organised the Governmental police force in Ireland—hence known by the people as " peelers." ›

PHILLIPS, CHARLES (1787–1859).—Author of " Curran and his Contemporaries." An ornate orator. He was appointed Commissioner of the Insolvent Debtors' Court of London in 1846.

PALMERSTON, LORD (1784–1865).—Foreign Secretary in Lord John Russell's Government, 1846–51, and afterwards Prime Minister.

PLUNKET, LORD (1764–1854).—M.P. for Charlemont in the Irish Parliament and one of the Anti-Unionist leaders. Afterwards Lord Chancellor of Ireland.

PORTER, GREY.—Unionist High Sheriff of Fermanagh. Indignant at the neglect of Irish interests and the continued invasion of Irish rights by the English Government, he proposed the formation of an Irish Militia to defend the National position. Davis's " Song for the Irish Militia " was inspired by Porter's proposal.

RAY, THOMAS MATTHEW (1801–81).—Secretary to O'Connell's Repeal Association. Subsequently received a place from the English Government.

REILLY, THOMAS DEVIN (1823–54).—A member of he *Nation* staff and afterwards chief assistant to Mitchel as editor of the *United Irishman*. After the failure of the insurrection, he escaped to America where he died.

RUSSELL, LORD JOHN (1792–1878).—Premier of England, 1846–52, and again in 1865. He was responsible for the Famine legislation and successfully opposed Lord George Bentinck's proposal to employ those threatened by famine on the construction of Irish railroads.

SHIEL, RICHARD LALOR (1791–1852).—One of the leaders of the Catholic Emancipation movement, and for a time of the early Repeal movement, which he abandoned, describing it as " a splendid phantom," for place under the English Government.

SMYTH, P. J. (1826–85).—The most intimate of Meagher's colleagues in the Young Ireland movement. Smyth was the son of a prosperous Dublin manufacturer. He escaped to the United States after the collapse of the insurrection and afterwards successfully carried out the rescue of John Mitchel from Van Diemen's Land. In after years he sat in the British Parliament for Westmeath and subsequently for Tipperary.

STAUNTON, MICHAEL.—A Dublin Alderman and one time Lord Mayor, Proprietor of the *Morning Register* newspaper, a Whiggish organ in which Davis's first political writings appeared.

STEELE, TOM (1788–1848).—" Head Pacificator " of Conciliation Hall. A Protestant gentleman of Clare who supported O'Connell in the famous Clare election and became devotedly attached to him. For many years before his death Steele suffered from weakening intellect. After the death of O'Connell he attempted to drown himself.

STEPHENS, JAMES (1825–1901).—One of the Kilkenny Confederates. After the failure of the insurrection he escaped to the Continent and subsequently founded, with Doheny and O'Mahony, the Fenian Brotherhood.

STUART, VILLIERS (1803–74).—Henry Villiers Stuart, grandson of the Earl of Bute, afterwards created Lord Stuart de Decies.

STOCK, SERJEANT.—John Stock, M.P. for Cashel, 1838–46, when he was appointed Judge of the Admiralty Court.

WATERFORD, MARQUIS OF (1811–59).—Meagher's references are intended for the third, not the second Marquis, who died in 1826. The third Marquis, who devoted himself to sport, was killed by a fall from his horse in 1859.

WHITESIDE, JAMES (1804–76).—Leading counsel for many of the State prisoners in 1848. Afterwards Lord Chief Justice in succession to Lefroy.

WILLIAMS, RICHARD DALTON (1822–62).—One of the poets of the *Nation* and a chief contributor of its squibs and humorous verse. The Government failed to secure his conviction for treason-felony. After 1848 he went to the United States, where he became Professor of Belles Lettres at the University of Mobile.

WYSE, SIR THOMAS (1791–1892).—One of the leaders of the Catholic Association, of which he wrote a history. He afterwards took office from the English Government and acted for many years as British Minister to Greece.

INDEX HOMINUM

ImTheStory.com

Personalized Classic Books in many genre's

Unique gift for kids, partners, friends, colleagues

Customize:

- Character Names
- Upload your own front/back cover images (optional)
- Inscribe a personal message/dedication on the

  inside page (optional)

Customize many titles Including
- Alice in Wonderland
- Romeo and Juliet
- The Wizard of Oz
- A Christmas Carol
- Dracula
- Dr. Jekyll & Mr. Hyde
- And more...

CPSIA information can be obtained at www.ICGtesting.com
Printed in the USA
LVOW01s2351040114

368094LV00024B/2170/P